Managing Strategy Implementatic

'Every manager, academic or participant in a strategic implementation process will find in this book invaluable advice as to how to deal with issues that will be all too familiar. It provides a comprehensive menu from a series of experts who really understand their topic and it is an attractive read – as a reference book or cover to cover – because it is mercifully free of jargon.

In an era when environmental change – often driven by the Internet or other technological factors – can change the horizon for many businesses at an astonishing fast rate, the book will be most timely in helping managers and/or academics considering strategic change issues.'

Kieran McGowan,
formerly chief executive IDA Ireland

'This book comes at the right time. The field of strategy is moving fast, and the key issue today is more effective implementation. The book represents an important contribution in this respect. I am particularly impressed by the fact that strategy implementation is addressed from several important, complementary angles: the behavioural, the managerial, and the critical success factor angle. Taken together, these viewpoints provide an excellent road map to strategic implementation from the practitioner/manager's point of view. It is also wonderful inspiration for researchers regarding further work that will be necessary within the strategy implementation arena.'

Dr Peter Lorange
President, IMD

'Many books have been written setting out in detail the steps required to successfully implement strategic change. This being the case, why has Strategic Implementation been so difficult to carry out? The reason is that while the broad principles may follow a clear path, the detailed and real issues that decide success or failure are different in every organisation.

This is one of the first books that accepts this and it attempts to develop an understanding of the dynamics of the complex issues that are involved in the implementation process. This it does and by increasing the level of understanding of what is going on it can contribute to the development of more successful implementations of Strategic Change.'

Terry Hinds
General Manager
Flair International Ireland

We wish to dedicate this book to our wives and children for their ongoing love and support during the many stolen hours while the writing project was underway.

– Donna, Alissa, Chris, Andrew Stephen Kinney, and Andersen Taylor Carroll
– Brenda, Zoë and Jane Dromgoole
– Patricia, Christopher and Patrick Ellis Flood
– Breda, Cliona, Roisin and Colm Gorman

Managing Strategy Implementation

An Organizational Behaviour Perspective

Edited by

Patrick Flood
University of Limerick & London Business School

Tony Dromgoole
Irish Management Institute

Stephen J. Carroll
Robert H. Smith School of Business, University of Maryland

Liam Gorman
Irish Management Institute

BLACKWELL
Business

Copyright © Blackwell Publishers Ltd 2000

Editorial apparatus and arrangement copyright © Patrick Flood, Tony Dromgoole, Stephen J. Carroll, Liam Gorman 2000

First published 2000

2 4 6 8 10 9 7 5 3 1

Blackwell Publishers Ltd
108 Cowley Road
Oxford OX4 1JF
UK

Blackwell Publishers Inc.
350 Main Street
Malden, Massachusetts 02148
USA

British Library Cataloguing in Publication Data

A CIP catalogue record for this book is available from the British Library.

Library of Congress Cataloging-in-Publication Data has been applied for

ISBN 0-631-21766-5 (hbk)
ISBN 0-631-21767-3 (pbk)

Typeset in 10 on 12 pt Sabon
by Kolam Information Services Pvt. Ltd, Pondicherry, India
Printed in Great Britain by MPG Books Ltd, Bodmin, Cornwall

This book is printed on acid-free paper.

Contents

Preface   vii

Foreword   viii

Acknowledgements   xi

Introduction
STEPHEN CARROLL AND PATRICK FLOOD   1

Part 1   New Perspectives on the Strategy Implementation Process   13

1. Strategic Management in a World Turned Upside Down: the Role
    of Cognition, Intuition and Emotional Intelligence
    PAUL SPARROW   15

2. Implementing Strategic Plans through Formalized Goal Setting
    STEPHEN CARROLL   31

3. Analysing Strategic Activity through Narrative Analysis
    SARAH MOORE   44

4. Strategy Implementation and Polarity Management
    TONY DROMGOOLE AND DAVID MULLINS   57

Part 2   Behavioural Barriers and Problems in Strategy Implementation 69

5. The Emotional World of Strategy Implementation
    DAVID O'DONNELL   71

6. Change Management and Stress
    CAROL BORRILL AND SHARON PARKER   80

7. Strategy Implementation in Public Sector Organizations
    DAVID MCKEVITT   96

8. Leading and Managing the Uncertainty of Strategic Change
    JEAN HARTLEY   109

Part 3   Key Roles in Strategy Implementation   123

9. From Advice to Execution: Consulting Firms and the
    Implementation of Strategic Decisions
    TIMOTHY MORRIS   125

10. The Leadership of Learning: the Core Process of Strategy
    Implementation
    DENNIS GILLEN   138

11. Middle Management Resistance to Strategic Change Initiatives:
    Saboteurs or Scapegoats?
    MARK FENTON-O'CREEVY   152

12. Constraints on Strategy Implementation: the 'Problem' of Middle
    Managers
    PHILIP STILES   168

Part 4   Barriers and Enablers to Strategy Implementation   181

13. The Primacy of Imagination
    CHARLES CARROLL   183

14. Developing and Implementing Strategy through Learning
    Networks
    TONY DROMGOOLE AND LIAM GORMAN   196

15. Implementing Turnaround Strategies in Strongly Unionized
    Environments
    NIALL SAUL   210

16. Teams in Strategy Implementation: Some Case Examples
    KEN SMITH AND HENRY SIMS JR   224

Editors' Conclusion   236

Biographical Notes   246

Index   251

Preface

Management literature contains dozens of books and articles on strategic planning. The same applies in the case of organizational development. There is almost no solid literature or applied research on the connection between the two, and how 'strategy implementation' makes the connection.

The editors of this volume have done those of us who study, teach or consult on management a great service. They have brought together in one book some of the best thinking of leading academic, practitioners and organization leaders. The very organization of the contributions makes an excellent teaching resource or set of insights for consultants and managers.

The Irish Management Institute is to be congratulated for funding this project. It is very consistent with its almost unique programme of a 'dialogue between academics and managers', in optimizing the application of leading edge management knowledge to the 'real work' challenges and opportunities – an approach I've found in use there in my twenty-five years as visiting faculty.

For anyone interested in digging deeper than the 'how to' of many books and articles, this book is a 'must'.

Richard Beckhard
Richard Beckhard and Associates
Professor of Management, Emeritus
Sloan School of Management, MIT

_____ Foreword _____

This book has its origins in a joint research programme set up between the Irish Management Institute (IMI) and the College of Business, University of Limerick in 1997 under the joint leadership of Tony Dromgoole and Patrick Flood.

The IMI has a national role, and has been working with individual managers and with organizations since the 1950s, with a mission to develop the practice of management to world-class standards. The Institute has helped to shape the new generation of skilled, confident, and outward-looking managers who are driving Irish economic progress. IMI activities are mission driven, and the Institute has a long history and experience with the action learning approach to management development. Our research activities are therefore highly practical, and focused on issues that are very relevant to practising managers.

We work with many forms of organization – business, not for profit, political, administrative, educational, representational, and service delivery, including health services. Strategy is usually seen as the organizing principle, the source of energy combating entropy and holding the organization together to ensure survival and development in the face of the chaotic forces unleashed by the gales of creative destruction during the modern industrial revolution.

Much has been written about the formal processes of planning and developing strategy, the tools and techniques of rational analysis, the disciplines needed to satisfy markets, and the project planning approaches used to manage implementation.

At the same time, many strategic plans become obsolete as they are overtaken by events, or are isolated to the upper levels of corporate hierarchies, and never penetrate organizations to become part of the pattern in action, the way things actually get done, on the ground.

Patrick Flood, together with Tony Dromgoole and Liam Gorman of the IMI and Stephen Carroll of the University of Maryland, set up a research colloquium to discuss and debate these problematic issues in September 1998. They assembled an eclectic group of academics, consultants and managers from different backgrounds, disciplines and cultures, all of whom shared an interest in the problems of implementing strategy. The colloquium generated intense discussion, with a sense of intellectual excitement, and new ground being broken and cultivated.

This book was written to capture the insights shared at that seminar. It should be of interest to theoreticians concerned with pushing forward the boundaries of knowledge. It should also be of interest and use to practising managers searching for new ways to develop and manage their organizations, for there is nothing as practical as good theory.

The Irish Management Institute is pleased to have been able to provide the funding to allow some very talented people to contribute to this book, and thus make some small advance in adding to the body of knowledge on the process of implementing strategic change.

Barry Kenny
IMI Chief Executive

_____ Acknowledgements _____

As Editors we wish to express our thanks to Barry Kenny, Chief Executive, Irish Management Institute, and Dr Noel Whelan, Dean, College of Business, and Vice President, University of Limerick, for their support for the establishment of the joint IMI–University of Limerick Research Programme under whose auspices this book was developed.

We also wish to thank the President and Council of the IMI for their support of this research initiative.

We would also like to thank the following people for their contributions to the book and attendance at the Book Research Colloquium on _Managing Strategic Implementation_ held at the Irish Management Institute on 21–22 September 1998.

Carol Borrill, University of Sheffield; David Cannon, London Business School; Stephen Carroll, University of Maryland; Charles Carroll, Irish Management Institute; Tony Dromgoole, Irish Management Institute; Laura Empson, University of Oxford; Mark Fenton O'Creevy, Open University (Milton Keynes); Dennis Gillen, Syracuse University; Liam Gorman, Irish Management Institute; Jean Hartley, Warwick Business School; Terry Hinds, Flair International; Niall Kelly, Lane Kelly Associates; David McKevitt, University of Limerick; Sarah Moore and Sarah McCurtain, University of Limerick; Timothy Morris, London Business School; David Mullins, AIB Group plc; David O'Donnell, University of Limerick; Niall Saul, Irish Life Assurance plc, Henry P. Sims, University of Maryland; Ken A. Smith, University of Maryland; Paul Sparrow, University of Sheffield; Philip Stiles, University of Cambridge; Liam Bannon, University of Limerick; Frank Byrne, Irish Management Institute; John Fahy, University of Limerick; Mike Fizser, Irish Management Institute; Michael Keogh, Irish Management Institute; Tom McConalogue, Irish Management Institute, Stephen McCormick; John McInerney, and Des McDermott, Irish Management Institute; Teresa O'Hara, Royal College of Surgeons, Gerald Smyth, Irish Management Institute International; Donal Wills, Irish Management Institute.

In addition we wish to thank Siobhán O'Toole, IMI, for her tremendous work in word processing the entire book and for her extremely efficient administrative skills. Others who contributed to this process included Emer Doyle and also Margaret Heffernan and David O'Donnell, University of Limerick.

_____ Introduction _____

Understanding the Process of Strategy Implementation

Social organizations are complex and adaptive systems, properties that they share with their physical and biological counterparts. As systems, they contain a large number of human, technical and managerial subsystems. These subsystems perform distinctive and interdependent roles necessary for the survival of the whole. Maintenance of a dynamic equilibrium within the larger system demands continuous attention to the integration and harmonization of each separate subsystem and slight changes in any of the components can cause ripple effects throughout the entire system. The incredible number of interactions among organizational subsystems is just one element in their complexity along with the many contradictory elements that must, somehow, be managed and controlled. This is compounded by the typical problems created by unclear means–ends relationships which are omnipresent in the strategy process where strategy creation and implementation frequently blurs as emergent strategies are developed. Today's hypercompetitive world, with its emphasis on rapid response to competitive forces, requires significantly more specific knowledge and skill on the part of business units and individuals than previously. The need to integrate business and management processes within the firm has also increased as organizations attempt to eliminate functionally based silos within the boundaries of the firm. This compounds the problems of integration at both the vertical and the horizontal levels. As if this complexity were not enough, private and public organizations also have complex relationships with countless other organizations and institutions throughout the world. Given all of this, the statement made by the president of the Academy of Management a few years ago, that management was the most difficult and challenging job in the world today, does not seem out of place.

While management in any era has been difficult, many organizations are currently attempting to implement third-generation strategies using what Ghoshal and Bartlett (1998) have described as second-generation organization structures and processes and first-generation managers. This recipe is guaranteed to generate massive problems in the strategic change process. Clearly, strategy implementation – the successful implementation of strategic decisions – demands compatibility between technologies, managerial processes and practices, and matching management talents to environmental imperatives. Gaps or deficiencies with respect to such a compatibility process can be identified not only through benchmarking against the best organizations, but also through capability assessments of organizations against models of organizational excellence developed through organizational research which identifies the key factors involved in organizational success. The renowned Baldridge total quality management (TQM) system is just one such system that has had a pervasive impact in this area. Benchmarking assessments based on Baldridge type criteria examine leadership, people management, process analysis, resource use, and other assessments in addition to policy and strategy assessments. In this system, however, there are presently many more guides to strategy creation than to strategy implementation. Part of the problem lies in the uncertainty about which of the key factors are most significant in an effective strategy implementation effort. Hopefully the information presented in this book will help to contribute to the development of such a model of strategy implementation excellence.

Fuelled by the obvious adaptability problems associated with unrelenting and fast-paced environmental changes, strategic management as an academic discipline, as a field of consulting, and as a differentiated activity within organizations of all types has grown at an exponential rate in the past two decades. With this growth, new academic and practitioner journals, hundreds of books and thousands of papers have been published on the subject of strategic management, and many of these have been discussed in countless new management development and executive education programmes devoted to this topic. There is now a growing recognition that the most important problems in this field are not in strategy creation but in strategy implementation. Percy Barnevik, chairman of Asea Brown Boveri and an experienced business leader, has consistently stated that successful strategy consists of 5 to 10 per cent vision and around 90 per cent execution. Research studies on organizational success seem to bear this out. For this reason, recent books on strategic management often contain one or more chapters on strategy implementation but the amount of information on this subject seems quite insufficient given its importance and relevance to organizational success and survival. Also, there appears to be some recognition that what is published on this topic appears to be somewhat inadequate in terms of its scope and depth. The successful implementation of strategic decisions involves such a multitude of factors and complex relationships that the all too common prescriptions of better leadership and better reward contingencies are, at best, often extremely misleading.

Today, emphasis is increasingly being given to competing more effectively on the basis of knowledge and intellectual capital. This requires high levels of tacit knowledge and adroitness in converging, co-ordinating and applying specialized expertise and skill. Moreover, it requires the willingness to exchange and pool knowledge in a common endeavour to advance the interests of the organization. Issues of trust and integrity are at the heart of this willingness to combine and exchange information. Resource-based perspectives on organizational advantage (Flood and Olian, 1996) highlight the fact that sources of unique competence are very few indeed. Given the obvious complexity of strategic change, knowledge and skill in the area of strategy implementation can provide an obvious distinctive competence, which can be extremely useful in achieving high levels of organizational performance.

All the contributors to this book are experienced in the managerial/executive education field. We all felt the need to develop an integrated set of readings on the topic of strategy implementation with a strong organizational emphasis for the very good reason that few such up-to-date readings exist and very few advance an organizational behaviour perspective. As one of the authors wryly commented on the recent integration of organizational behaviour concepts into the strategic management literature: 'Strategy has invaded the pitch and there is a need to fight back!' A leading provider of executive education, the Irish Management Institute, recognized the validity of this felt need and kindly agreed to sponsor a research colloquium on this topic under the auspices of the recently initiated joint research programme developed with the College of Business at the University of Limerick. A research colloquium with an explicit focus on Strategy Implementation was held at the Irish Management Institute in September 1998. This conference was attended by an invited group of international academics and practitioners who had worked as theorists, researchers, or change-agent practitioners in the strategy implementation area. The Irish Management Institute, which is actively involved in management education, change management consulting, and management research not only in Ireland, but in Europe and internationally, has a strong interest in this topic and was willing for these reasons to sponsor this programme. This book represents an outgrowth of this conference and consists of extensive revisions of many of the papers presented at the colloquium. These papers highlight new theoretical perspectives as well as research findings and case studies on the subject of strategy implementation. We feel that this book also represents in a small way a growing integration of the world-wide community of management scholars and practitioners.

We note that a significant degree of restructuring and other organizational changes in response to environmental changes are taking place in public as well as private organizations. Virtually every recent management innovation, or fad, depending on your viewpoint, such as rightsizing, process-oriented re-engineering, self-managed teams, horizontal customer-oriented structures, and so on have been attempted in public as well as private organizations. These change programmes are typically initiated for a strategic purpose although obviously political reasons are also frequently the drivers. Resistance to such change initiatives can be as great in public organizations as in private firms or even more so. For this reason a number of cases from public organizations as well as private companies have been included in this book.

Contents and Structure of the Book

In terms of content and structure, we decided to organize the chapters into four parts. The chapters in each part appear to have some common focus or theme, which are: some perspectives on the strategy creation and implementation process; some behavioural problems and issues in strategy implementation; some key managerial roles in strategy implementation; and some factors related to strategy implementation success in companies. Of course, in reality, many of the chapters have information or ideas that are relevant to all four themes.

We would now like to identify some of the ideas in the various chapters that we think should not be overlooked. Of course, readers will have their own ideas of which issues in a chapter are most important to them, given their own interests, values, and cognitive or behavioural experiences. In our concluding chapter, we will attempt to provide some integration of the material in the various chapters and present what we see as, perhaps, some of the less obvious but important major insights and lessons for strategy implementation.

Part 1: New Perspectives on the Strategy Implementation Process

In this part we have four chapters that describe various approaches and perspectives on the strategic management process with an emphasis on implementation as it has evolved over time. Of course, as we gain knowledge about how humans, especially managers, think and behave we can more realistically develop management processes and practices that work. There must be some congruence between what we do as managers and the actual thinking and behaviour propensities of organizational members instead of using more simplistic and perhaps idealized models of human behaviour.

The first chapter, by Paul Sparrow, is a good example of aligning the facts of human behaviour with the tasks and roles they must perform. In presenting a useful history of the strategic management perspective, Sparrow points out that at one time strategic management was perceived to involve primarily a choice from among a list of limited strategies. The goal was to choose the one which best matched various contingencies in the firm, such as product life cycle, type of technology, experience base of human assets and so on. Rather simplistic strategy implementation processes were recommended and, in general, there was neglect of the emotional reactions of organizational members to proposed changes and little awareness of the cognitive limitations and biases of organizational members, including the strategy creators. In addition, there was little understanding of the cognitive process itself and of planning and decision making and rather simple linear rationalistic modes of thought were assumed. Since those times, a great deal of research has been carried out on human cognition, and a much more realistic assessment can be made of the ability of organizational members at all levels to understand and process information. This research illuminates many factors deemed to have hindered the strategy creation–implementation process. Sparrow, however, goes beyond these insights to explore in some depth the new cognitive competences, emotional maturities, as well as skill and knowledge imperatives of the managerial role. One of his most interesting discussions focuses on what is referred to as the 'intelligent unconscious' which explores the importance of intuition and creativity in complex decision making, where information is almost always incomplete. Certainly in the strategic decision-making area we have situations in which we require individuals who can complete a puzzle without all of the requisite pieces or steps being present.

The second chapter, by Stephen Carroll, describes how the strategic management process has evolved over time in some successful large companies from a top-down management by objectives (MBO) centred approach to a new persuasion management approach. This is accompanied by goal-setting and performance management processes that ensure compliance with strategic decisions. He points out that the strategy-making process requires that, at some point, visions or projected future states necessitate the completion of perhaps thousands of sequenced and co-ordinated acts or events by many individuals and groups. This in turn requires a means of directing, evaluating and perhaps rewarding such acts. Thus goal setting, with its emphasis on accountability, is always a requirement in strategy implementation. MBO was, in fact, initially created as a means of implementing strategic goals, although the term 'performance management' or some other such term is now often used to describe this process. Carroll documents the use of this evolved MBO approach in some leading companies. He reminds the reader of the validity of the research on the goal-setting process as demonstrated in hundreds of studies to which he makes reference that continue to be relevant to managerial practice. He also identifies how the goal-setting and performance management processes must alter their emphases in order to be congruent with some of the new human and organizational realities. Carroll's chapter also provides some support for chapter 3 by Sarah Moore. Her emphasis on narrative as a useful strategy implementation perspective is supported by Carroll's discussion on the use of the metaphors used by General Electric CEO, Jack Welch.

The third chapter, by Sarah Moore, explores the advantages and disadvantages of the new visioning and emergent strategy formation process as compared to the old rational planning models. She performs a very useful function in identifying the limitations of the newer visioning model as well as the older rational planning model. While visioning and rational planning are not contending opposites, the distinction is none the less useful. She introduces a newer model which, although it has recently received some attention among academics, has yet to be understood and utilized by practitioners to any significant degree. It would appear that this interactive narrative approach presented does indeed have considerable potential for more effectively influencing organizational members to accept and carry out new strategic directions. Stories have always had a very powerful appeal to human beings all over the world. They attract attention perhaps because they provide lessons for life in all its aspects. They help to meet the aspirations of individuals who need to know how to live and are attracted to stories or narratives about the people or institutions with whom they identify in an emotional way. Stories score high in interest and perceived relevance to most human beings. Of course, every organization and the people in them have stories and the symbolic value of myths and fables has a rich tradition in anthropological accounts of organizational culture. Most employees will feel an organizational story is, at least in part, their story even if the plot in the story has not always been to their liking. Visions and strategic plans cast in the form of stories or tied to existing organizational stories are likely to be not only noticed but accepted by organizational members. In chapter 2 by Carroll it can be seen that Jack Welch may have evolved to this narrative approach as a means of improving upon the weaknesses of the vision approach described by Moore. Many aspects of the narrative approach are implicit in his discussion of persuasive management behaviours.

Tony Dromgoole and David Mullins, in the final chapter in this part, describe an all-too-familiar change situation in which significant amounts of uncertainty exist not only about what is happening and why, but also about what the success criteria should be as well as the means that should be employed to achieve success. In addition there may be many other significant negative factors and problems to deal with which are unclear and difficult to solve. This lack of clarity is so profound that entirely different models of strategic change are now required. It is necessary, they argue, to view the attainment of interdependent opposites as the typical situation, and this will require significantly different mindsets and ways of thinking than those used in the past. One recommended mindset is the use of a dialectic of constructive conflict in which different sets of assumptions about a situation held by different individuals and groups are brought to light and allowed to conflict with each other until the realism of various assumptions can be decided. They suggest that the old problem-solving modes of thinking are not appropriate to the new realities and instead the effective management of polarities or interdependent alternatives is required. They develop a model of a process of polarity management – referred to as a polarity map – which can guide thinking in the 'messy' situations that they describe.

Part 2: Behavioural Barriers and Problems in Strategy Implementation

Of course, there are countless behavioural problems in implementing strategic decisions. Thousands of articles and books have been written about typical communication and resistance to change difficulties over the past seventy-five years or so. There is no need to describe all of these here but in this part several observers remind us of factors that can, and often do, influence the success of a strategy implementation effort. For example, David O'Donnell reminds us that many organizational scholars over the years have indicated that we ignore the emotional side of human behaviour at our peril. Organizations as well as individuals are emotional entities and they react emotionally to communications and behaviours before reacting to them on a rational basis. There is always an emotional reaction to events even if third-brain rational reasons are given as *ex-post* explanations for behaviours. Rationality and emotionality interpenetrate and complement each other. Of course, the degrees of emotion experienced are due to the way events or communications are perceived which, in turn, may depend on how they are framed by the initiator and on aspects of the situational context. Thus the emotional world of the organization must be considered in all implementation efforts. O'Donnell describes alternative change strategies that are used by organizations to elicit a commitment on the part of organizational members to the acts desired by the change initiator. He points out that there is no universal change model that is always effective and different approaches are appropriate, depending upon various contingencies such as the amount of change needed, the readiness of the organizational members for change, and the time available to obtain the needed degree of change acceptance. Some of these factors, such as the readiness of the participants, are in turn influenced by other factors such as the perceived need for the change. This is an important point and there is a good deal of research support for the concept of a contingency approach to change implementation.

The chapter by Carol Borrill and Sharon Parker identifies stress as a major problem in strategy implementation. Change in itself produces stress and this stress can create certain dysfunctional consequences which, in turn, can hinder the achievement of strategic initiatives by negatively impacting performance. Of course some stress can be beneficial to performance but higher levels can be quite negative if they exceed individual tolerance levels. There is strong evidence that excessive stress can create health problems for individuals, increase absenteeism, and can negatively impact mental functioning. Furthermore, many of the strategic initiatives that are occurring today, such as the restructuring of jobs and duties and increasing work-loads through downsizing, are especially likely to induce stress and its dysfunctional effects. There is great variation by individuals in reactions to the stressors that cause stress so we could expect that if only those with high stress tolerance and psycho-logical hardiness were hired there would be fewer stress problems. However, this is probably quite impractical for most jobs given the limited numbers of those with quite high stress tolerance and the need to select individuals on the basis of job competencies. Also, some approaches to introducing changes produce less stress than others. The important thing is to consider and recognize stress as an inevitable consequence of change and to design the changes and approaches for introducing change to minimize dysfunctional stress. This is especially true for lower level personnel since they tend to experience more stress than managers at higher levels.

The third chapter, by David McKevitt, focuses on some additional variables that may impact the success of strategic initiatives in public sector organizations. His research points to the problems which may occur when the nature of certain strategic initiatives is in conflict with the professional norms and values of the occupational group that is empowered to carry them out. All professions develop a set of norms and values. Members are indoctrinated or occupationally socialized in these during the training and educational process. Thus physicians, social workers, engineers, scientists, teachers and so on may have great difficulty in accepting certain strategic initiatives if these are in conflict with their personal and professional values. There are many obvious examples of this today in the field of medicine as medical organizations are forced to cut costs and become more efficient and experi-ence the need to change or restructure diagnostic or therapeutic processes. As McKevitt points out, however, the difficulties experienced here vary because of national differences in the way such professional services are utilized. Obviously, there are also many other national differences in cultures and practices that may impact on the acceptance of various strategic initiatives in public sector organiza-tions.

The final chapter in part 2, by Jean Hartley, identifies some other potential problems in the implementation of strategic initiatives. These include issues of differential reactions to uncertainty and issues of politics and power that pervade the strategy implementation process. In her case study of a government agency, she particularly focuses on the concept of organizational uncertainty and notes how this has been growing not only in the private sector but also in the public sector. She points out that increased uncertainty in the private sector comes about not only from the actions of competitors but also from changing expectations of various stakeholders such as the community, customers, and government itself. She provides a useful summary of several different types of uncertainty identified by scholars that must be adjusted to by different organizational members. There is the uncertainty about how the environment is changing, about how the environmental changes will impact the organization, and also the responses to these changes that are possible for the organization. There are also internal uncertainties as well as external uncertainties. Thus it is clear that all levels of an organization must face different types of uncertainty and some uncertainties are created by the manner in which a higher level of management responds to the uncertainties they face. For example, in the public sector organization, because the politicians on top do not like to reach closure on strategic imperatives for which there is political opposition, the managers who must take action and wish for closure must suffer frustration and be held up in their attempts to accomplish or carry out new strategic initiatives.

Given all this, it is necessary for managers to learn to live with and manage uncertainty. Managing uncertainty involves many activities such as selecting those who are capable of living with and handling uncertainty and creating internal systems to cope with such uncertainty. Coping with uncertainty through the establishment of internal practices, structures and processes involves creating appropriate information search and processing systems as well as judgemental procedures for making sense of incomplete and ambiguous situations. It would appear that, in today's new realities, organizations must recognize that many of the new uncertainties will exist for many years and that older methods of management created under more stable conditions are no longer appropriate. It is clear, therefore, that the management of uncertainty is one of the areas most in need of research and study, and this chapter makes a contribution towards identifying some of the issues needing further investigation.

Part 3:   Key Roles in Strategy Implementation

In strategy implementation there are many players performing quite different roles. If certain of these roles are not performed adequately, successful strategy implementation may not happen even though other roles perform quite well. In strategy implementation the significant role players are probably consulting firms, top managers and middle managers. The chapters in this part discuss some issues in the performance of these different roles by these groups.

The first chapter, by Tim Morris, describes the very important role of consulting firms in both strategy creation and strategy implementation. It also describes with great understanding the internal characteristics and dynamics of consulting firms that influence how such firms perform these strategy roles. First he points out that consulting firms differ widely in their areas of specialization and their capabilities. While some firms are capable of handling large change projects and many different types of change programme, some specialize in particular types of change only. Consulting firms are sometimes hired not to suggest or direct a change effort but merely to confirm what many key company managers already want to do. Morris points out that there are problems associated with utilizing consulting firms in such strategy change situations. Many consulting firms use a particular off-the-shelf system, but this may not fit the client's needs. He also points out that consulting firms are profit-making businesses which attempt to find and sell new systems and practices that may not always be suitable for particular organizations. Research does indicate that ready-made solutions tend not to work as well as customized solutions. Also, certain individuals in a consultancy may not have the required skill or competence to solve a particular firm's problem. In addition, firms may become too dependent on consultancy firms and fail to develop their own change skills sufficiently. On the other hand, benefits can be derived from the use of consultancy firms. They often do have significant practical experience with managerial innovations having worked in many firms, and often serve as a major conduit through which valuable and helpful information flows from better performing companies to weaker performing companies.

The second chapter in this part, by Dennis Gillen, explores the key role of all managers, especially the CEO, in fostering the type of organizational learning necessary to generate acceptance of strategic initiatives. Gillen points out that all strategic initiatives involve learning new ways and incorporating this learning but this will not occur unless it is actively led. While he assigns the CEO the pivotal role in activating this learning process he argues that leaders at all levels must also accept this role. While what is to be learned must reflect each situation, Gillen identifies some especially critical roles for the leader of learning. The leader must, for example, make sure that the organization is focused on learning that is essential rather than non-essential because of the opportunity costs of learning. The leader can also facilitate the learning process by creating a vision of the organization in the future and establishing a set of necessary core values since these tend to focus and direct attention to desired ends and the behaviours that are necessary to reach those ends. Visions and core values, when internalized, also provide for a shared outlook facilitating information exchange. Gillen points out that with the development of new structural arrangements involving a movement away from bureaucracies towards more decentralized entities, there is now a greater need for the development in organizations of convergent knowledge. Convergent knowledge refers to how the more specialized knowledge of different businesses and even functions is connected. Gillen describes how an organization's orientation towards competitors also helps to focus learning. As market competitiveness increases, the learning rate must be higher, and when this is achieved, market success improves. His case study of a General Motors subsidiary is just one example of how convergent learning can be a key to success in a manufacturing operation. His case study of a widely disbursed food co-operative is another example of how highly decentralized multiple boards of directors, who accept a strong learning culture, can achieve high levels of competitive performance.

The third chapter, by Mark Fenton-O'Creevy, also describes middle managers as key players in strategy implementation. He documents the fact that in many companies middle managers have blocked change initiatives. He then explores some of the many reasons why there is such resistance on the part of middle managers and mentions such factors as perceived loss of power and control, threats to job security, and the rule rigidity induced by threats to upward mobility. Causes of resistance in the organizational systems themselves include the influence of pay, performance evaluation, and the promotion systems in shaping behaviour towards certain ends, the lack of training and development for the new skills and behaviours required, and the necessity of achieving contradictory goals. He points out that it is important to align all organizational systems in order to reinforce new strategic initiatives and points to one of his own studies to support this. Clarity in emphasizing top management support for a strategic initiative also impacts acceptance.

The fourth chapter, by Philip Stiles, further describes the key role of the middle manager in strategy implementation and discusses how they serve as enablers or constrainers of strategy implementation initiatives. His insights are based on a research study conducted in eight large companies in the United Kingdom. This was a large-scale empirical research study using employee questionnaires and interviews with many stakeholders. An important finding was that the expertise and trustworthiness of the source of the change influenced acceptance of the change, as would be expected by previous research on this topic. Change initiatives were also more likely to be accepted if they met the recipient manager's needs/rules, conformed to present practices and structures, were understandable, and were perceived to have been developed through a fair process. Problems involving resistance were more likely when the change involved threats to organizational members – such as possible job loss.

Part 4: Barriers and Enablers to Strategy Implementation

Over the years some hundreds and perhaps even thousands of case studies of public and private organizations undergoing change have been published in various outlets. Case studies may be especially useful in studying organizational change since they can document the many small details and characteristics of systems that may be especially important levers in achieving successful change. More empirical studies carried out on larger samples of companies must of necessity focus only on a limited number of possible causal factors. Since organizations are systems, important interactions among factors and subsystems may be missed. Of course cases are usually not meant to be research studies but rather illustrations and examples of approaches and practices and sources of hypotheses to be studied by more systematic means later. Case studies of successful changes are especially useful since, because of extraneous variables, failure often occurs in companies irrespective of the management actions taken. Obviously we can put more faith in cases if there is some consistency in results from one case to another and if there is also some congruence between theory and research.

In the first chapter in this part, Charles Carroll presents a very interesting case illustrating the importance and usefulness of using imaginative ways to communicate to employees the need to change in order to achieve a higher level of competitive company performance. The case illustrates that poor performance is often the result not of just one cause but of many factors, all of which have to be addressed separately in order to find improvement. It also demonstrates the desirability of using a wide variety of persuasion techniques that are dramatic enough to arouse the attention of the intended audience in addition to factual benchmarking comparisons that an audience can understand. The case also shows that incremental improvements are a useful way to obtain change as extensive experience in TQM indicates. Obviously patience in attempts to achieve significant change is a virtue. Perhaps more importantly the case illustrates Carroll's thesis that a creative imagination or a perceptive intelligence – which is the result of openness to a wide range of information and ideas from dissimilar situations – is very useful for change agents of all types. Along with this need for a creative intelligence, an excellent understanding of how human beings actually think and perceive the world is also required. Symbolic thinking is just one example of this and to what ends they are attracted, towards order, away from chaos and so on. Effective persuasion therefore requires, as the research literature would indicate, a very high level of knowledge of audience characteristics.

In the second chapter, Dromgoole and Gorman describe a rather unique network-based action-learning programme. The movement of the organizations in the direction of becoming learning organizations is the core focus here; the latter being the 'holy grail' in today's exponentially changing world. The need to propel management into action before crises loom is an essential goal of this action-learning network intervention. The starting point of their programme is detailed instrument-based self-assessment and peer company feedback in a process termed 'sympathetic confrontation'. This in turn drives action for change as the process induces felt social pressures to produce progress on their company's efforts.

A number of key differentiating features of this programme are worth mentioning. An eclectic mix of organizational development approaches are used in the course of this programme to guide, provide feedback, monitor and evaluate achievement. A second key feature is the tightness of the network developed and the intimacy that develops, promoting trust and shared learning. Thirdly, the action-learning dimension forms the backbone of all approaches used, which are firmly rooted in the real concerns of the business. The managers are making changes in real time which is realistic and they learn with and from each other in the network. Finally, the degree of control exerted by the managers over the direction of the network is distinctive. The authors cite the behavioural assumptions and psychology underpinning the technology, functioning and reported success of this action-learning network.

The next chapter, by Niall Saul, an experienced change practitioner, describes the special problems in difficult-to-change unionized environments experiencing a crisis situation. His chapter is particularly insightful as such situations are very common and difficult to deal with, considering the number of restrictive practices that change-oriented managements may face in unionized environments. As Saul indicates, increasingly particular plants find themselves in a performance crisis situation not only because of competition from other companies but now from competition with other plants of the same company. He also points out that in any large change effort, improving the level of trust between management and the workforce can be a positive outcome that will be of considerable benefit later. This is especially true because in unionized turnarounds there are often sacrifices to be made by the workforce, including layoffs and wage cuts. It is unlikely that these will be accepted, he points out, unless there is some obvious future benefit to compensate and unless the principal of equal sacrifice at all levels of the organization is adopted. The Waterford Crystal case cited illustrates a number of change tactics that may be useful in other settings. Certainly the massive and continuous communications taking place between management and the workforce created a crisis orientation and an understanding of the need for change on the part of the workforce. Allowing union representatives to participate in strategy sessions and in the restructuring programme obviously helped to build trust. The fact that small successes occurred after some changes had been made reinforced the change efforts. The company did attempt to meet worker fears by some guarantees and by some early retirement benefits. The creation of a permanent system to facilitate change when it was needed in the future was probably an important factor in the ability of the company to sustain their performance improvements.

The chapter by Smith and Sims describes the increased emphasis given to the team concept in organizations today. Of course, organizations have always been composed of groups, but groups differ from teams in that group output is the sum of individual efforts while teams represent a more truly collective or interdependent effort. Teams are often or even typically multi-disciplined and may have considerable authority to make a collective decision, or at least a set of recommendations on an issue. Top management groups (TMGs) are obviously heavily involved in the entire strategy process. We would expect that those TMGs that are *real* teams rather than just groups (as many are) would be more effective in implementing strategy for many reasons such as the ability to better resolve implementation conflict and co-ordination issues. Teams at the middle level in some organizations are significantly involved in the strategy process. These strategy teams – which often report to the executive committee of the organization and may consist of the immediate reports of members of the top management team – have the responsibility to update and revise current strategic plans, including implementation programmes for various initiatives. Self-managed teams at lower levels may collectively devise ways to implement new strategic initiatives. Teams can obviously bring to bear more social pressure on individuals to accept change than can an individual work assignment system, especially when the team members create the means of complying with change imperatives. Team-based organizations in a real sense represent an organizational strategy to cope with fact-based change requirements where strategy formation and implementation merge in a continuous emergent process.

References

Flood, P. and Olian, J. 1996: Human resource strategies for world-class competitive capability. In P. Flood, M. Gannon, and J. Paauwe (eds) *Managing without traditional methods: international innovations in human resource management*. Reading, MA: Addison-Wesley.

Ghoshal, S. and Bartlett, C.A. 1998: *The individualized corporation*. London: Heinemann.

Nicholson, N. 1997: Evolutionary psychology: toward a new view of human nature and organizational society. *Human Relations*, 50(9), 1053–78.

Nutt, P.C. 1987: Identifying and appraising how managers install strategy. *Strategic Management Journal*, 8, 1–14.

Part 1

New Perspectives on the Strategy Implementation Process

1. Strategic Management in a World Turned Upside Down: the Role of Cognition, Intuition and Emotional Intelligence
   Paul Sparrow

2. Implementing Strategic Plans through Formalized Goal Setting
   Stephen Carroll

3. Analysing Strategic Activity through Narrative Analysis
   Sarah Moore

4. Strategy Implementation and Polarity Management
   Tony Dromgoole and David Mullins

1

Strategic Management in a World Turned Upside Down: the Role of Cognition, Intuition and Emotional Intelligence

PAUL SPARROW

Introduction

The nature of our thinking about strategic management changed throughout the 1990s, drawing attention to a number of psychological issues associated with the pursuit of effective strategy (Sparrow, 1994). This chapter draws attention to new academic thinking from the fields of organizational and cognitive psychology and is intended to bring insights for the reflective practitioner. Researchers have drawn upon many disciplines in order to understand the beliefs, perceptions and decisions that organizations and their members make or hold, but why should we take stock of the lessons emerging from this type of research?

We must consider the implications for the quality of strategic implementation within organizations. Historically, strategists placed considerable emphasis on the concept of 'fit' – the need for a fit between strategy and structure, strategy and culture, and strategy and the life cycle stage of the organization. This created the illusion that strategy consists of a clearly defined position or stance – a series of either/or choices – against which various aspects of the organization and its people can be aligned. The experience of chaotic change in the 1990s put paid to such simplistic views on life. The emphasis on simple contingencies, and the attempt to create a 'fit' against them, was an illusion that did not match reality. In reality managers had to create, comprehend and manage a complex series of 'dualities' within their organizations. These were frequently counter-intuitive, such as the need to both differentiate and integrate the organization, to focus on low-cost as well as high value-added, and to enter into both competition and partnership within the same organization. Management surveys showed that few employees believed that the strategy would be implemented in line with the plan, largely felt to be due to uneven and poor management skills, poor comprehension of roles, insufficient co-ordination, unclear lines of account-ability and a lack of commitment. While strategic visions were seen to come (and go) overnight, the efforts needed to effectively implement strategic change received increasing attention. As attention in the human resource management literature shifted to the issue of *how* managers could make strategies work, the strategists too began to refocus their interests. They stressed the need to translate the strategic capabilities of the organization into an underlying set of strategic 'competences' in order to provide both the organization and its managers with some 'fixed points' around which to plan. As product life cycles shortened and skill development life cycles lengthened, it was felt that the active management of the skill base of the organization and organizational learning would become the mainstay of com-petitive strategy. At the beginning of the decade it was argued that the greatest challenge facing the field of strategic management was to comprehend the most appropriate combination of skill sets, and the cognitive processes by which managers could understand their organizational world and translate their strategies into action. Are we any nearer to this understanding? The challenge is re-examined at the millen-nium in this chapter in the light of the latest cognitive and organizational psychology research.

The chapter argues that we must think differently about what it means to be intelligent in a modern organization and what it takes to be an effective imple-menter of strategic change. It highlights the nature of 'intelligent cognition' in organizations, and the managerial mental skills and competencies that are coming to the fore. Two themes have dominated recent academic discussions of strategic management:

1. An increasingly emotional environment within which managers have to make strategic judgements.
2. An uncertain world which is turning attention to new concepts of intelligence and analytical ability – what is called the 'intelligent unconscious'.

Strategy in organizations today is a more emotive affair than of old. The world has been turned upside down for managers trying to implement change. Research on a series of deep emotional issues now takes over the academic headlines and questions managerial assumptions, including:

- breach of the 'implicit' or 'psychological contract' and the HRM consequences of this;
- an endemic lack of trust, and change in the nature of trust within organiza-tions;
- the perception of fairness and the role of organizational justice in managing accountability for events that have negative impact on material or psycholo-gical well-being;
- the need for better retrospective sense-making and an ongoing creation of reality in what is a complex and ambiguous organizational world; and
- the growing need for organizations and their managers to make the knowledge and experience of individuals and groups more explicit and understandable.

The first theme is increased emotionality at work. Processes of globalization, downsizing, and restructuring are heralding deep shifts in the pattern of work and society and are influencing fundamentally the perceptions that employees and their managers have of work. Until recently two parallel worlds were seen in the way we treated the topic of strategic management (Cassell, 1999), the action of managers, and the skills and competencies we assumed they needed. The first – and still dominating – world was rational and precise, in which '...cool strategic thinking is not to be sullied by messy feelings. Efficient thought and behaviour tame emotion and good organizations manage feelings, design them out or remove them' (Fineman, 1996: 545). This is the school of thought that says 'let's keep emotion out of this and deal with things rationally' (Cooper, 1998). The parallel (until recently, of less significance) world acknowledged emotionality by considering the role of stress, levels of satisfaction, trust and the psychological contract. Positive discussion of emotion at work notes that organizations can and must generate feelings of excitement, high personal engagement and positively influence behaviour (what psychologists refer to as 'emotional contagion') among their employees. Negative discussion notes that much organizational strategy today seems to be making people more angry, resentful, anxious or depressed. The divide in management thinking between the rational and the emotional then no longer holds. The new orthodoxy argues that emotions cannot be separated from the managerial thought process and the process of strategic change. Both the thought processes (henceforth called cognition) and the social processes that surround strategic decision making are influenced by emotion (Daniels, 1999). Specifically, the quality of the mental models that managers develop is influenced by their emotional state, which determines the attention they give to information processing, the perceived level of stress and threat in the environment, and their ability to recall appropriate information. *If managers live in a more emotional world, then the very content of their thought processes becomes more emotional.*

The second theme is that of uncertainty, the need for sense-making, and to surface managerial assumptions. In their chapter, Tony Dromgoole and David Mullins point to the need for managers to consider the 'revenge effects' of an assumed solution. Managers are faced with an environment that is increasingly complex, ambiguous and is changing discontinuously. In theory, the rules of the past rarely guide current action (as we shall see, they do in practice, and there is the rub). Managers now have to absorb, process, make sense of and disseminate a bewildering flow of information in order that the organization might make effective decisions and solve problems. They must establish rich questions which redefine the problem, rather than point to immediate solutions. They cannot hide behind economic rationality and analysis, and have to admit that they may be as lost as we are, sailing and experimenting in uncharted waters, tentatively seeking answers to what are increasingly loaded questions, and understanding increasingly the limits to their power and the 'downside' to their decisions, while still having to manage the consequences. Not surprisingly, psychologists argue that the management of cognition is inextricably linked with the management of strategic risk. Why? Because this managerial role specification has given rise to concerns about the 'cognitive limits' of managers. Are they capable of such skilful thought? It is also leading to calls for new, more intelligent (in the true sense of the word) approaches to management.

Strategy as an Imprecise Information World: the Cognitive Perspective

Early work assumed that individuals were essentially rational. It concentrated on the way they formed expectations about the outcome of their decisions, the beliefs that guided those decisions, and the way in which managers 'calculated' probabilities. There was no explicit theory of how knowledge was actually organized. The metaphor that guided understanding of the mind was one of computation. Individuals calculated the costs and benefits associated with various actions and then maximized, or at least satisfied, their own utility by choosing the most appropriate behaviour. Research then challenged this view. Early studies of the psychology of the managerial mind analysed decision processes and organizational problem solving. They showed that the way in which organizations processed information, and the quality of managerial decisions in situations when information was either uncertain or too costly to acquire, was not a rational process. By the late 1960s the 'constructionist logic' approach focused on the meanings managers attributed to the world and the ways in which they constructed managerial and organization knowledge. Reality was seen as a *social construction* in which managers actively combined their existing knowledge structures with external information and constructed their own environment. Weick (1995) developed this approach. He pursued the theme that reality within organizations is relative. Choices cannot be seen as being correct or incorrect against an abstract mathematical equation. The correctness of a decision is dependent on the point of view that is being used to evaluate it. A distinction was made between the *downstream* choice or calculation process, and the *upstream* process of sense-making (Porac et al., 1996). The strategic environment is partially dependent on the perceptions of what Weick calls 'communities of believers' who have their own 'local rationalities' or 'interpretative stances'. These local rationalities are, in turn, embedded in a larger 'system of meaning', some of which are individual and some of which are shared by the group.

Managers represent their 'information world' by employing knowledge structures (or schemata) which serve as top-down or theory-driven aids to information processing. These structures are generated largely from experience and are felt to affect a manager's ability to attend to, encode and make intelligent inferences about new information. Managers are also capable of pursuing a bottom-up, or data-driven approach, whereby they let current or novel information contexts shape their processing and inform or develop their existing schema. The knowledge structures of managers act as mental templates which can be imposed on an information environment in order to give it meaning (Walsh, 1995). These mental templates have been called many things, including attentional fields, belief structures, causal or cognitive maps, dominant logic, distilled ideologies, frames of reference, schemas and world views. They act as simplifications, helping managers to overcome the limitations of short-term memory when they search long-term memory for relevant information (Daniels et al., 1995). These individual knowledge structures must be appropriate (i.e. contain high-quality information, rich and sophisticated linkages, and are built around deep predictive constructs) and they must be utilized by highly competent managers. As is made clear by the discussion on emotional intelligence, a manager might have very effective cognition but can still lack the competence to draw benefits from this. Having rich schemata is only part of the requirement. However, appropriate knowledge structures do mean that the manager is able to attend to the most meaningful events in his or her environment, can encode and retrieve information more effectively, produce better interpretations, make more appropriate and accurate interpretations and solve problems more quickly.

However, relying on top-down knowledge structures that are not optimal can also produce many negative consequences and actually limit the manager's understanding of the environment. The liabilities include stereotypic thinking, mis-controlled information processing, inaccurate filling of data gaps, rejection of apparently discrepant but important information, refusal to disconfirm cherished hypotheses and inhibition of creative problem solving. The consequence has variously been called blind spots, collective strategic myopia, selective perception, tunnel vision and grooved thinking (Walsh, 1995). These are all problems of 'cognitive inertia' – the inability of strategists to revise their mental models quickly enough – and they revolve around managers using 'old maps' to 'navigate new environments' (Reger and Palmer, 1996). Research has looked at how managers use mental models to analyse the competitive positioning strategy of their organization and how they view the structure of their industries and markets (see, for example, Calori et al., 1994; Hodgkinson and Johnson, 1994). Managers have clear mental models of their competitive worlds and the environment, the boundaries of the competitive arena, who their rivals are, and on what basis they can compete. They use these mental models to determine appropriate strategic action. Moreover, strategists from rival firms can develop very similar mental models over time as they frequently exchange information during business interactions and share similar technical problems and problem-solving ideas. Strategists then see the world as 'socially constructed' and based on common underlying recipes that are seen to be effective (Huff, 1982). In an analysis of the volatile estate agency industry, Hodgkinson (1997) found that both the individual and collective cognitive maps of the industry remained remarkably narrow and insensitive to important cues during a period of rapid industrial restructuring. Cognitive inertia – unless challenged by periodic in-depth reviews that enable the world maps of managers to catch up with material changes in the business environment – can lead to the ultimate demise of whole industries. Work on schematic information processing shows that knowledge structures can be both enabling and crippling (Walsh, 1995). In asking whether managers (and their strategies) are rational or not, the propensity of managers to see the world through blinkered eyes should be seen simply as a source of error. It is another strategic risk that has to be managed!

The Information Overloaded Manager: a Strategic Risk

Not only is there risk in relying on the knowledge structures of managers, but managers now rarely have the time to apply, wisely, the knowledge they have. Information is defined as that which alters or reinforces understanding (Daft, 1995) but when too much information is available it has the opposite effect. The problem of information overload – and the ensuing potential for risks and error that it generates from the ill-conceived actions of overburdened managers – is one of the biggest challenges facing organizations today. Managers are faced with an increased volume and load of information, forcing them to devote much more time to the process of information search (skills that have become critically important in many roles) with too little time spent on processing or learning from the information. A key management challenge is to find ways to utilize the available brain power of the organizations' employees while not immersing them in a welter of data.

Sadly, much of the information that managers find – or are bombarded with – in their organizations is problematic, because it is: of low quality, low value, high ambiguity, and has an ever-decreasing 'half-life' in terms of the currency it carries (Sparrow, 1998). This all increases the 'information load' carried by the manager, who has to process and make sense of this problematic data. Low-quality information requires the manager to add the mental effort to make it of any worth to the issue at hand. Low-value information requires an assessment of its explanatory power in relation to other sources of information. Contradictory information requires an assessment of what must remain ambiguous and what can be deduced to be certain. Information that only has a short period of relevance requires quick processing and dissemination. Many of these actions not only waste time but carry negative properties. They can blind the manager to more important matters, divert attention to irrelevant issues, and give the manager the feeling that he or she is 'drowning' in a sea of information.

The difficulties created by the need to process vast amounts of information (called information overload, communication pollution or information anxiety) have not received much attention in the strategic management literature. At a personal level information overload is associated with feelings of inability to cope and inadequacy of knowledge and has been identified as a source of stress. The information load of most jobs is expected to increase, exacerbated by the explosion in 'electronic connectivity' and the number of 'interactions' that now surround most tasks. Research by McKinsey consultants shows that taking a conservative view of the convergence of technologies, and allowing for human limitations, the overall 'interactive capability' in developed countries is set to increase by a factor of between two and five over the next decade (Butler et al., 1997). Workers will be able to process existing interactions in less than half the time or, more realistically, will be asked to do two jobs or double their information load in the same time.

What do we know about information overload and why is it going to be a problem that will affect strategy implementation? Information load is defined as '...a complex mixture of the quantity, ambiguity and variety of information that people are forced to process. As load increases, people take increasingly strong steps to manage it' (Weick, 1995: 87). It is typically measured in terms of:

- the number and difficulty of decisions and judgements the information requires;
- the time available to act;
- the quality of information processing required; and
- the predictability of the information inputs.

Overload implies an excessive burden and encumbrance that is sustained with difficulty. People cease to operate effectively as load increases and begin to demonstrate dysfunctional behaviour. In coping with the volume of information (let alone its complexity and ambiguity) they begin to neglect large portions of it and try to 'punctuate' its flow in predictable ways. This 'punctuation' begins with omission, then greater tolerance of error, miscueing or mis-attributing the source of information, filtering its message, abstracting its meaning, attempting to use multiple channels to decode and transmit its content, and finally seeking escape! These punctuations serve to highlight the residual information, and therefore heighten the impact of misperceptions on subsequent 'sense-making'. Closely related to 'volume-induced' information overload is 'complexity-induced' overload (Huber and Daft, 1987). Uncertainty is increased because of three elements, referred to as: numerosity (the number of separate elements to be dealt with), diversity (the range of information sources and media), and interdependence (the complexity of causal relationships between the information elements). Employees may be exposed to information that conveys a greater number of diverse elements, which interact in a variety of ways. The greater the complexity, the more the untrained person searches for and relies on habitual and routine cues. This creates the potential for disaster, as in the nuclear industry, where the combination of a reliance on complex technologies, numerous transformation processes, and inexperienced operatives makes the unexpected commonplace.

The strategists, organization designers, systems analysts and ergonomists are the first to have created – and then tried to deal with – the problem of information overload. The main problems created by information overload are organizational, structural and cultural. In the UK there are only three Professors of Business History. In Japan there are over 400 (van de Vliert, 1997). The field of strategic management is replete with stories of firms repeating corporate blunders, blissfully unaware of any sense of continuity. 3M talks of the 'shadow organization'. Strategists refer to it as 'organizational' or 'corporate memory'. Organizations are highly dependent on the complex knowledge that resides within the net sum of an organization's employees'– their experiences of events, projects, knowledge of clients and contacts, their awareness of decision-making styles and their assumptions about working practices and relationships. In the west much of this intelligence has recently been 'externalized' or 'outsourced'. Today managers say 'I don't need to know that, I just need to know . . . who to ask, where to look, where to go to find out, or that it is known by others'. The need for them to have a 'good' mental model of how knowledge and information is shared across the people with whom they need to interact (in order to deliver an important business process, product or service) has never been greater. As we move towards virtual forms of organization this need becomes even more paramount (Sparrow and Daniels, 1999). Managers therefore act as information brokers, managing a web of natural 'interactions' that take place within the organization. This is called the 'intra-organizational information market'. When strategic change is implemented, the implementation usually entails a redesign of the interactions needed to operate effectively.

However, interactions also lie at the heart of information load (Norman, 1985). As well as representing an increasing proportion of the time spent in jobs, each interaction now carries a higher information load. Until recently our ability to manipulate and process information and data outstripped our ability to communicate and interact, but managing the quantity and quality of interactions is now a key strategic management skill. All interactions have the same economic purpose – the exchange of goods, services or information – but they involve different cognitive requirements for data gathering and searching, co-ordination, communication, collaborative problem solving, and monitoring of transactions. They occur in many forms and each medium is associated with a different load and richness of information. Managers have to seek the right party with whom to exchange information, arrange the presentation of the information, manage its brokerage, integrate it with other databases, and monitor the performance of the interaction. While interactions are not the only source of information overload (time spent in individual analysis and data processing plays a role) they represent the largest and most rapidly expanding element of most work. They account for 51 per cent of labour activity in the USA, the equivalent of one-third of all economic activity carried out (Butler et al., 1997). The volume of interactions varies with the type of work: peaking at 78 per cent for interpersonal knowledge workers (such as teachers and doctors), data harvesters and communicators (such as retail workers and secretaries); 42 per cent for analytic knowledge workers (engineers, scientists and technicians); and 37 per cent for data manipulators (such as back office clerks and analysts). Interactions are shaped increasingly by computing and communications technologies. Networking technologies make it more 'economic' to share a piece of information with a colleague or a group, or to work with different people inside the organization, customers or suppliers outside the organization, or parties around the world.

Competencies for the Future, or New Management Fads?

The new types of interaction and increased information load in many jobs is reinforcing the need for managers to develop new mindsets and for the organization to consider new concepts of intelligence. The ability to manage information overload and cope with information anxiety is seen as a key management competency (Wurman, 1989), but to expect all managers to improve their cognitive capabilities to cope with information overload is a route to chaos. Not all managers may be capable of such development, the organization might not have enough depth of talent capable of being developed, and even the most competent manager has cognitive limits. Organizations must also analyse some of the structural reasons why the overload has occurred. None the less, a validity study of high-performance competencies in a sample of 140 managers conducted by Cockerill and Schroder (1993) lends support to the argument that cognitive competencies – defined in a broad behavioural manner – are the most predictive of business unit performance under uncertain environmental conditions. Out of seven high-performance competency factors (information search, conceptual complexity, team facilitation, impact, charisma, proactive orientation, and achievement orientation) the assessed score of the managers on the two cognitive factors (information search and cognitive complexity) were the most predictive of subsequent business unit performance. Two cognitive competencies operationalized by Cockerill and Schroder (1993) were linked by them to constructs previously identified in Burns and Bass's Transformational Leadership studies, Boyatzis's American Management Association Competency Study, the FCEM competency study, and the Princeton complexity theory studies. Information search – defined as the ability to gather many different kinds of information and use a wide variety of sources to build a rich informational environment in preparation for decision making in the organization – correlated with business performance at $r = 0.35$, $p < 0.01$. Conceptual complexity – defined as the ability to link information to form and compare alternative conceptions of and solutions to managerial problems, issues and situations – correlated with the business performance measure at $r = 0.4$, $p < 0.001$. It consisted of two elements: concept formation (a creative and logical process of forming ideas based on a range of information and linking different kinds of information separated spatially and over time to form concepts and hypotheses) and conceptual flexibility (viewing events from multiple conceptions or perspectives simultaneously and considering the relationships between different options or strategies to arrive at decisions). Under a stable environment, the link between these cognitive management competencies and business unit performance disappeared.

There is a managerial skills agenda that cuts across the information processing perspective in this chapter. Managers believe increasingly that the rules of the past are no longer a guide to the future. We see renewed attention given to more subjective, intangible, implicit cognitive skills and a return to the analysis of 'telling' individual differences that may help managers to cut through a chaotic environment, including:

1. Investigation of less tractable areas of human cognition, such as intuition and creative processes that help managers adapt to sudden crises and major adjustments.
2. Management of emotions in organizations and the role of emotional intelligence.

However, are we looking at another set of catchy-sounding concepts, or is there any support for these new ideas? The next sections consider some of the latest work and debates.

The Intelligent Unconscious

The intuitive manager

In addition to assessing the complexity, richness and 'appropriateness' (we can never say accuracy) of a manager's worldviews or cognitive maps (such as assessing a manager's cognitive or knowledge structures), organizations must also assess the skills and competencies, and specific cognitive processes, that drive the 'intelligent unconscious'. There has long been a debate as to whether analytical expert judgements are better than intuitive judgements under situations of uncertainty. Studies comparing the accuracy of an individual's intuitive judgement with the application of some external rational rule-based analysis of the problem unsurprisingly find rational analysis to be more accurate than intuition. However, when Hammond et al. (1997) compared the use of intuitive with rational judgements *within* individuals (a group of expert highway engineers) they found that intuitive reasoning performed as well as, or better than, rational analysis. A reliance on analytical reasoning was more likely to produce extreme errors or failures, which was not the case with intuitive reasoning. Intuition was the best strategy when:

- the information presented to the manager involved a reliance on perceptual processes to interpret it (i.e. the information is carried in media that require the manager to sense it by relying unduly on vision, hearing and so on);
- the cues were multiple and appeared in parallel rather than a simple sequence; and
- many of the cues were redundant or irrelevant.

The comments on information overload suggest that these are the conditions under which strategists will work. Psychologists have explored many different ways of 'knowing' and conclude that 'we know more than we know we know' (Spender, 1998). What can we learn from intuitive and creative strategists? What do these abilities really look like, and can they help managers to cope with information overload – or manage a way through it? Is there an identifiable set of cognitive processes that are associated with intuitive or creative analyses and how might we move towards more solid assessment, training or development of such competencies?

Psychologists are resuscitating the idea of the 'intelligent unconscious' by exploring the 'implicit' or 'tacit' cognitive system. This operates at the unconscious level, reflects a combination of innate factors and learning and is seen as a rapid form of intelligence, which has a large processing capacity. We have assumed that explicit, articulate thinking is the most powerful form of cognition. 'Ways of knowing' that are hazy have been denigrated and such assumptions are now under attack. Claxton (1997, 1998) asks: 'How do we know, without knowing why?' Intuition (often referred to as 'inklings' or 'glimmerings' of understanding) is defined as a sense in which vision and immediate knowledge are identical. Intuitions are often of a fleeting quality – faintly grasped by the manager, easily dissolved and lost in the next moment. They 'arrive' in several forms: '. . . it may arrive abruptly "like a bolt from the blue", or it may emerge into consciousness much more slowly. It may be absolutely clear-cut already formulated in all essential details, or it may be much more hazy: a hunch, an inkling or a glimmering of something that cannot yet be articulated' (Claxton, 1998: 217). Without being able to articulate clearly the reason or justification, the manager finds that an answer to a question, a solution to a problem, or a suggested course of action enters his or her mind with an aura or conviction of 'rightness', plausibility or fruitfulness.

Psychologists have investigated the way people develop 'hunches' and convert them into explicit knowledge and 'know-how'. This meta-ability is called *implicit learning* or *intuitive expertise*. When people are asked to perform a complex practical task, their expertise in the task develops well before their ability to articulate, explain or even consciously detect the patterns of information they have acquired (Lewicki et al., 1992; Reber, 1993). We act intuitively before we act rationally. In the early stages of implicit learning people 'guess' even before they develop 'hunches' and these guesses often have more validity than they are given credit for. Managers, therefore, undervalue their intuitions and place more weight on systematic thinking, often in situations where research tells us that systematic analysis is not the best tool for the job. Far from being a fuzzy and inferior way of knowing, intuition is actually the functional basis for informed choice, even after conscious understanding has been developed. Karmiloff-Smith (1992) uses the anecdote of the Rubik cube to explain this. Children are remarkably good at solving the puzzle of rotating and aligning the colours of the mini-cubes by using a strategy of playing and then unknowingly learning the perceptual-motor patterns that emerge. Adults, in trying to adopt an intellectual approach to figure out the solution of what is actually too complex a problem, under-perform. Implicit learning requires the manager to tolerate a temporary state of confusion. Complex, counter-intuitive predicaments are best mastered in this state of confusion, rather than through the generation of conscious hypotheses. Those who persist in operating intuitively maintain higher levels of skilled performance. Those who fall back on conscious rationality see decrements to their performance.

We must develop our understanding of what occurs during intuitions if we are to identify how some managers are more sensitive than others to the way that intuitions 'pop' into their mind. Intuitions are characterized in two respects: the ability to make rapid access to faint stimuli; and the ability to incubate, slowly, a creative solution. Taking the first, Claxton (1998: 219) explains it by quoting Linford Christie's insistence that in order to win a 100 metres race: '... one must learn to go on the "b" of bang! If you wait 'till you've consciously heard the gunshot, you've already lost the race.' The fleeting nature of the rapid access type of intuition has a physiological reflection in the phenomenon known as 'sub-threshold priming'. Such intuitions result when a stimulus triggers some neural or biochemical activation (researchers are unclear exactly what the physical representation is), which may have nothing to do with the territory of the intuition. Often this activation is not enough to be consciously recognized. However, an associated concept is already primed, and as the neural activation spreads out from the 'epicentre', the small amount of stimulation it receives is enough for it to 'pop into your mind'. It becomes sufficient to influence the 'guess' that is produced or to bias the global assessment of a situation that the manager makes (for example, a goalkeeper who has a remarkably good record of guessing the right direction of a penalty kick).

Charles Carroll argues in his chapter that the essence of strategy is creation. Creative imagination certainly serves as a source of ideas for strategic managers, but this creativity does not just involve the generation of new ideas. Much innovation is essentially akin to 'theft' – the ideas were already in existence, but the manager finds a new 'recombination' formula that creates a new insight. Creativity, therefore, is a complex competency to understand. In fact intuition and creativity are strongly influenced by the ability of the manager to *incubate* and to draw upon the '... creative value of patience and reverie – of daring to wait and drift' (Claxton, 1998: 217). For example, studies into award winning Nobel prize laureates show that the vast majority place intuition at the heart of their success. The creative cognition approach provides an explicit account of the relevant cognitive processes and structures that lead to such insights by identifying measurable cognitive operations. Creativity is seen as the product of many types of mental process, each of which helps set the scene for subsequent insight and discovery. Attention is given among other issues to 'pre-inventive' structures. These are used and exploited by managers when they engage in creative search and exploration. Unlike mental schemata, pre-inventive structures are largely uninterpreted at the time they are initially formed and as they remain so for a considerable time they are particularly useful for associating novel, incongruous, ambiguous, divergent but implicitly meaningful information. If psychologists are ever able to reliably assess such mental processes, organizations will be able to consider recruiting, selecting and developing more intuitive and creative managers. In the meantime, they will look to another form of intelligence.

The emotionally attuned manager

David O'Donnell argues that change is a complex and intensely emotional psychosocial drama. The ability to trust your own and others' emotions has become the latest business buzzword. We have given too much attention to the hyper-rational *objective* view of intelligence, which focuses on the role of a limited set of cognitive attributes and language and the way the mind registers and stores information. The ability to be aware of one's own mental processes is key to more *subjective* definitions of intelligent behaviour. The topic of 'emotional intelligence' is also referred to as emotional quotient, personal intelligence, social intelligence and interpersonal intelligence (Goleman, 1995; Cooper, 1997, 1998; Cooper and Sawaf, 1997; Ryback, 1998). It is linked to the intelligent unconscious because it:

- operates at a preconscious level and is seen to share many common neurological processes with intuition and creativity;
- serves as a source of energy, drive and feelings that subsequently acts as a wellspring for intuitive and creative wisdom and guides people to unexpected possibilities;
- is a series of emotion-handling competencies, suggesting that some aspects of it are indirectly assessable through their reflection in behavioural competencies such as self-awareness, emotional management, empathy, relationships, communications and personal style.

However, what evidence is used to support the existence of such a meta-ability in real organizational settings? Is this just another catchy-sounding construct that will appeal to leaders convinced that this is something they surely possess, or is it a valid construct? If it is a valid construct, is it something that can realistically be assessed at the individual level? Most research has been conducted outside the work context. Psychologists are now attempting to assess emotional intelligence (EI) using traditional competency identification techniques (Dulewicz and Higgs, 1998). EI is appealing because it offers the potential to explain aspects of success at work that are overlooked by more traditional tests of intelligence and attainment. Interest has grown because alternative constructs do not explain performance outcomes. EI provides awareness of one's own cognition's. Such aptitudes are called *meta-abilities* or *meta-cognitions* and determine how well people use the other skills they have, including their intellect. It draws upon '...the ability to sense, understand and effectively apply the power and acumen of emotions as a source of human energy, information, trust, creativity, connection and influence' (Cooper, 1998: 48).

Goleman's (1995) work on EI has gained most prominence. He drew attention to the need to explore the extent to which there is both intelligence *in* the emotions, and the way in which intelligence can be brought *to* emotions. EI represents a collection of traits and abilities, defined as: '... *the ability to motivate oneself and persist in the face of frustrations; to control impulse and delay gratification; to regulate one's moods and keep distress from swamping the ability to think; to emphasize and to hope*' (Goleman, 1995: 34). Considering whether EI can be assessed, Dulewicz and Higgs (1998) note conflicting views. For Steiner (1997: 23) it is a marketing concept and not a scientific term: '...we can meaningfully speak of EQ as long as we don't claim to be able to measure it precisely'. Many of its behavioural reflections, such as empathy, are best seen (and therefore assessed) through the eyes of others. Dulewicz and Herbert (1998) conducted a longitudinal study linking managerial competency data for managers assessed in 1988/9 with subsequent career advancement and current level of seniority. Traditional competency measures were predictive of career success. They reassigned forty competency measures across three components: emotional intelligence (sensitivity, resilience, influence and adaptability, decisiveness and adaptability, energy and leadership); rational and intellectual intelligence (analysis and judgement, planning and organizing, strategic perspective and creativity and risk taking); and management process effectiveness (supervision, oral communication, business sense, and initiative and independence). Process competencies, rational and intellectual competencies, and EI competencies accounted for 16, 27 and 36 per cent, respectively, of subsequent managerial advancement.

Conclusions

A key argument has been that we must question what intelligence in modern organizations really looks like. The discussion of levels of information load, richness of a manager's required cognitive maps, and increased reliance on the intelligent unconscious suggests that cognitive skills should form the main issue in future competency profiles. The key consideration is whether the new styles of intelligence and supporting cognitive skills are something that can be developed in managers, or something best selected in (or deselected out of) the organization. The relationship between IQ and broad measures of life success is weak, and small in relationship to other characteristics brought to life (Hernstein and Murray, 1994). The validity of IQ tests in predicting executive or management competencies is low – leaders require a baseline level of intelligence to be effective and tend to be more intelligent than the average group member, but they are not the most intelligent within the group

(Bahn, 1979). Success depends on attributes beyond the rational side of management. Recent work on management competencies has led us towards a situationally specific, cognitive and behaviourally complex definition of what an intelligent manager in an organization really looks like. Managers can learn how to think in ways that maximize the opportunity for creative insight:

> There is no reason that (the) cognitive strategies that promote creativity in one domain could not be extended to other domains as long as . . . the person could recognize when an idea in the new domain was truly important . . . creative people share a basic understanding of how to go about being creative; they can then extend their creative skills into other areas as long as they know something about the relevant issues, methods and values and are sufficiently motivated to do so.   (Finke et al., 1992: 6)

It has been argued that intuitive skill, while based on years of experience and training, can also be developed as well as selected. The implications of the shift towards developing greater reliance on the intelligent unconscious within organizations are broad. As we unpack the concepts of intuition, creative cognition and emotional intelligence, psychologists will look for ways to make them more amenable to investigation, and therefore ultimately assessment. This must influence the way we think about training and educating the managers and strategists of the future.

References

Bahn, C. 1979: Can intelligence tests predict executive competency? *Personnel*, July–August, 52–8.

Butler, P., Hall, T.W., Hanna, A.M., Mendonca, L., Auguste, B., Manyika, J. and Sahay, A. 1997: A revolution in interaction. *McKinsey Quarterly*, 1, 5–24.

Calori, R., Johnson, G. and Sarnin, P. 1994: CEOs cognitive maps and the scope of the organisation. *Strategic Management Journal*, 15, 437–57.

Cassell, C. 1999: Exploring feelings in the workplace: emotion at work. *The Psychologist*, Special Issue, 12(1), 15.

Claxton, G. 1997: *Hare brain, tortoise mind: why intelligence increases when you think less.* London: Fourth Estate.

Claxton, G. 1998: Investigating human intuition: knowing without knowing why. *The Psychologist*, 11(5), 217–20.

Cockerill, A.P. and Schroder, H.M. 1993: *Validation study into the high performance managerial competencies.* London Business School Report, May. London: LBS.

Cooper, R.K. 1997: Applying emotional intelligence in the workplace. *Training and Development*, 51(12), 31–8.

Cooper, R.K. 1998: Sentimental value. *People Management*, 2 April, 48–50.

Cooper, R.K. and Sawaf, A. 1997: *Executive EQ: emotional intelligence in leadership and organisations.* New York: Grosner Putnam.

Daft, R.L. 1995: *Organisation theory and design* (5th edn). St Paul, MN: West Publishing.

Daniels, K. 1999: Affect and strategic decision making. *The Psychologist*, 12(1), 24–7.

Daniels, K., DeChernatony, L. and Johnson, G. 1995: Validating a method for mapping managers' mental models of competitive industry structures. *Human Relations*, 48(8), 975–91.

Dulewicz, V. and Herbert, P.J. 1998: Predicting advancement to senior management from competencies and personality data: a seven-year follow-up study. *British Journal of Management.*

Dulewicz, V. and Higgs, M. 1998: Emotional intelligence: can it be measured reliably and validly using competency data? *Competency,* 6(1), 28–37.

Fineman, S. 1996: Emotion and organising. In S.R. Clegg, C. Hardy and W.R. Nord (eds) *Handbook of organisation studies.* London: Sage.

Finke, R.A. and Bettle, J. 1996: *Chaotic cognition: principles and applications.* Englewood Cliffs, NJ: Lawrence Erlbaum.

Finke, R.A., Ward, T.B. and Smith, S.M. 1992: *Creative cognition: theory, research and application.* Cambridge, MA: MIT Press.

Goleman, D. 1995: *Emotional intelligence: why it can matter more than IQ.* London: Bloomsbury.

Hammond, K.R., Hamm, R.M., Grassia, J. and Person, T. 1997: Direct comparison of the efficacy of intuitive and analytical cognition in expert judgement. In W.M. Goldstein and R.M. Hogarth (eds) *Research on judgement and decision making: currents, connections and controversies.* Cambridge: Cambridge University Press.

Hernstein, R.J. and Murray, C. 1994: *The Bell Curve: intelligence and class structure in American life.* New York: Free Press.

Hodgkinson, G.P. 1997: Cognitive inertia in a turbulent market: the case of U.K. residential estate agents. *Journal of Management Studies,* 34(6), 921–45.

Hodgkinson, G.P. and Johnson, G. 1994: Exploring the mental models of competitive strategists: the case for a processual approach. *Journal of Management Studies,* 31, 525–51.

Huber, G.P. and Daft, R.L. 1987: The information environments of organisations. In F.M. Javlin, L.L. Putnam, K.H. Roberts and L.W. Porter (eds) *Handbook of organisational communication.* Newbury Park, CA: Sage.

Huff, A.S. 1982: Industry influences on strategy formulation. *Strategic Management Journal,* 3, 119–30.

Karmiloff-Smith, A. 1992: *Beyond modularity: a developmental perspective on cognitive science.* Cambridge, MA: MIT Press.

Lewicki, P., Hill, T. and Cryzewska, M. 1992: Non-conscious acquisition of information. *American Psychologist,* 47, 796–801.

Norman, D. 1985: Twelve issues for cognitive science. In A.M. Aitkenhead and J.M. Slack (eds) *Issues in cognitive modelling.* London: Lawrence Erlbaum.

Porac, J.F., Meindl, J.R. and Stubbart, C. 1996: Introduction. In J.R. Meindl, C. Stubbart and J.F. Porac (eds) *Cognition within and between organisations.* London: Sage.

Reber, A.S. 1993: Implicit learning and tacit knowledge: an essay on the cognitive unconscious. Oxford: Oxford University Press.

Reger, R.K. and Palmer, T.B. 1996: Managerial categorisation of competitors: using old maps to navigate new environments. *Organization Science,* 7, 22–39.

Ryback, D. 1998: *Putting emotional intelligence to work: successful leadership is more than IQ.* Oxford: Butterworth–Heinemann.

Sparrow, P.R. 1994: The psychology of strategic management: emerging themes of diversity and managerial cognition. In C. Cooper and I. Robertson (eds) *International review of industrial and organizational psychology,* vol. 9. Chichester: Wiley, pp. 147–81.

Sparrow, P.R. 1998: Information overload. In K. Legge, C. Clegg and S. Walsh (eds) *The experience of managing: a skills workbook.* London: Macmillan, pp. 111–18.

Sparrow, P.R. and Daniels, K. 1999: Human resource management and the virtual organization: mapping the future research issues. In C.L. Cooper and D. Rousseau (eds) *Trends in Organizational Behaviour,* vol 6. London: Wiley.

Spender, J.-C. 1998: The dynamics of individual and organizational knowledge. In C. Eden and J.-C. Spender (eds) *Managerial and organizational cognition: theory, methods and research*. London: Sage.

Steiner, C. 1997: *Achieving emotional illiteracy*. London: Bloomsbury Publishing.

Stewart, T.A. 1994: Managing in a wired company, *Fortune*, 11 July, 44–56.

van de Vliert, A. 1997: Lest we forget. *Management Today*, January, 62–3.

Walsh, J. 1995: Managerial and organisational cognition: notes from a trip down memory lane. *Organization Science*, 6(3), 280–321.

Weick, K.E. 1995: *Sensemaking in organisations*. Thousand Oaks, CA: Sage.

Wurman, R.S. 1989: *Information anxiety*. New York: Doubleday.

2

Implementing Strategic Plans through Formalized Goal Setting

STEPHEN CARROLL

Percy Barnevik, recently voted to be the top executive in Europe, and Jack Welch, described in *Business Week* as the top US executive, both agree that firm success depends on a business organization not only designing strategies that are appropriate for external and internal environments but implementing those strategies successfully (Dillon, 1998). In terms of time requirements they also seem to agree that the implementation phase takes at least 90 per cent of the total effort necessary to carry out a change programme adequately. Barnevik says that the challenge to get people to buy into, and then to accomplish, strategic direction is 95 per cent execution and that the differences in execution are what differentiates the successful companies from the less successful.

It is not surprising that implementation seems to be the critical factor in strategic planning. It often takes many years to move an organization in a new direction and may also involve thousands of people, as would be the case at GE and ABB. In addition, thousands of difficult problems associated with the thousands of implementation details may have to be solved. The desired future state itself may be realized only to some degree and in some dimensions, and environmental changes beyond the organization's control are likely to create new change imperatives.

Both GE and ABB, as well as many other effective companies such as Intel, Merck, Marriott and Walmart, seem to place a heavy reliance on the use of goal-setting processes in the implementation phases of the strategic planning process although they go about this in different ways. Let us remind ourselves why most companies use goal-setting processes to implement strategic decisions. Goals obviously help to focus attention on the activities and results needed to achieve certain desired ends. They clarify expectations, motivate by providing opportunities for achievement and are useful in holding individuals and groups accountable. To the critics of goal-setting processes who felt that they created stressful pressures, Harold Geneen (1984), CEO of ITT, once stated 'but the drudgery of the numbers will make you free'. By making explicit expectations they may make it possible to be free from day-to-day supervision and also may help in the unleashing of personal creativity in developing means to ends. They represent a means of achieving a true form of contractual management.

Despite the necessity of goals in implementing organizational strategies, it is also obvious that the goal-setting processes used in the past may have to be changed considerably in light of today's competitive realities and the structural and process changes that companies have made in response to the new competitive realities. For example, both GE and ABB are now heavily decentralized with thousands of profit centres located in most major countries. Jack Welch of GE now allows subordinate businesses to develop their own approaches to accomplishing corporate goals and also has integrated goal-setting processes with other important strategic systems such as the zero defects quality programme pioneered at Motorola (General Electric, 1977). Strategies must be implemented through a goal-setting and review process, and this is true for most organizations. A top strategic planner for the Marriott Hotel business, for example, recently said in a speech to MBA students that the company uses a management by objectives (MBO) procedure for every major new competitive initiative.

Traditional Strategic Goal Implementation Systems

It has been said that the older MBO approaches simply do not give organizations the speed and flexibility needed to operate in contemporary environments. Mintzberg (1994), for example, points to the rigidity involved in the old process of organizational planning in which objectives in strategic management were set entirely by top management and cascaded down the structural hierarchy using very formalized procedures. He also discusses how this process was effective at first, but eventually produced ineffective results when competitive conditions changed. He appears to be correct in this, and we shall look at one of the many examples that support Mintzberg's observation. In the 1960s and 1970s the author, along with Henry Tosi, worked in Black & Decker in a consulting capacity on their pioneering MBO programme which the company initially copied from General Electric who had created this system of management under a work planning and review label in 1948. In the late 1960s, Black & Decker, like many well-known large multi-nationals, used the popular SWOT approach for setting organizational goals (Tosi et al., 1970). It is now common knowledge that this involved analysing the key external environments and internal systems to identify opportunities, threats, strengths and weaknesses, which were then converted to goals and sometimes detailed plans for each major organizational component of the firm. These plans were then pushed down through the managerial and professional ranks. Next, evaluation timetables and action plans were established and implemented for each objective. Various analytical approaches were devised to help to gather the information necessary to carry out this strategic process – for example, the author worked on a global management inventory system designed to identify the strengths and weaknesses in the managerial resources that would be necessary to achieve strategic goals. This information was ultimately utilized in a performance management system.

To the company, this classical strategic planning process, and the system of management by objectives devised to implement organizational goals, seemed to work very well. For example, with respect to profit and growth goals in the first six years of Black & Decker's improved MBO programme, productivity increased 109 per cent, sales increased 252 per cent, the number of new employees increased 68 per cent, and the dollar value of sales per salesperson increased 400 per cent (Carroll and Tosi, 1976). Of course, we all know that these performance achievements may have been due to many factors other than their newly designed MBO system. However, several years later with new competition from Japan and a changing economic situation (higher interests rates, lower home sales, etc.) the company ran into serious economic difficulties and improved performance came about only through the adoption of a more flexible and open system of management. In fact, the new CEO told the author (much to the latter's distress) that the old MBO system was being abolished. Of course, with the demise of the old command and control authority system and the adoption of new horizontal organizational forms such changes are inevitable (Wally et al., 1995). The new emphasis is on integrating relatively autonomous subunits into a community of communities and breaking down functional silos. Systems which are oriented entirely towards vertical co-ordination are obviously no longer functional.

Effectiveness of Goal-Setting Systems

Although there are new systems, this does not mean that the MBO approach has no further value. Many of the most highly rated companies in the world, with excellent performance records in the 1990s – such as Intel, Merck and Walmart – have been strong advocates of the MBO approach. GE, ABB and other companies use goal-setting systems in line with the new organizational realities without necessarily using the term 'management by objectives'. The experience of these and many other companies indicates that goal-setting systems can be quite successful in implementing organizational goals and strategies. Also, the empirical research on goal-setting still demonstrates, as it has for many years, a consistent relationship between the use of goals for managers and successful company performance. This is illustrated in a study published by Martell and Carroll (1995) of 115 independent companies, all of which were affiliated with US Fortune 500 companies. Among the results of this study, the use of both quantitative and qualitative goals and objectives in evaluating managerial performance were shown to be the most consistent predictors of overall company effectiveness as compared to other predictors, including the use of various financial incentives for managers. In this study the overall company effectiveness was defined as the degree of actual performance as compared to *a priori* managerial expectations along twelve different dimensions reflecting diverse strategic goals. These included operating profits, sales growth, market share, profit-to-sales ratio, cash flow from operations, return on investment, new product development, market development, R&D activities, cost reduction and personnel development. In another recent survey of a large number of US firms, Terpstra and Rozell (1994) found that organizations that used goal setting were more profitable than those that did not. These studies are in line with very extensive prior research on MBO systems in industrial organizations that clearly demonstrated the positive relationship between the use of goal-setting systems and company performance. For example, Krondrasuk reviewed 185 studies of MBO programmes, although many of these focused on unit rather than company performance. Overall, about 91 per cent of these studies showed positive or contingent positive results (Locke and Latham, 1990). A later review by Rodgers and Hunter of MBO research studies found that 97 per cent showed positive results (Locke and Latham, 1990). The results were especially positive when there was evidence that top management in the company provided a good deal of support and commitment to the MBO programme (Rodgers and Hunter, 1991). Another review of all the MBO literature up to the mid-1980s by Carroll (1986) also showed very positive results for MBO in terms of not only performance but also of positive managerial reactions to the system.

Of course, there are always problems in interpreting the results of correlation and case studies carried out in the field with respect to causality. Improvements in company performance following the adoption of any new management system can simply reflect a changing economy, or could be due to a host of other factors unrelated to the system itself. Thus such correlation studies provide little proof that the goal-setting process variables are responsible for the higher performance. Perhaps the most comprehensive and very extensive field study that attempted to see if an introduced MBO system was in fact the causal agent in improvements in company performance and managerial satisfaction over time was carried out by Tosi et al. (1976) over a ten-year period. In this study a quite lengthy questionnaire was administered to the same sample of managers twice in one company, and three times in another company, with each administration involving a time lag of at least 18 months. In this study, several rather sophisticated statistical procedures were used to relate change scores in various MBO process variables to changes in performance and satisfaction. The large amounts of data generated by this extensive effort were then used to rule out various theoretical models of how the MBO questionnaires used in the studies might have produced the results they did. All the models examined, – which assumed that the results were due to such factors as managerial moods, – timing of the questionnaire and other factors were ruled out as unlikely, given the pattern of results obtained. This led to the acceptance of the MBO systems as the causal factor in the performance and managerial satisfaction increases observed in the data.

Why Do Goal-Setting Systems Work?

One issue of importance in use of the MBO/goal-setting approaches to implement organizational goals and to improve organizational performance is to identify the reasons why an effective or quality MBO programme is related to higher performance. An early research study with Black & Decker managers using extensive managerial interviews pointed to the positive effects of a MBO programme on clarifying performance expectations leading to a more efficient use of time and effort, on forcing a planning process helping to reduce the number problems and errors occurring, and also the forced superior-subordinate increases in communications which took place with the benefits of a higher information exchange to decision making (Tosi and Carroll, 1968). Also, the feedback system associated with this approach makes it possible to identify problems and difficulties which may be more effectively solved in their early stages. In addition, from a psychological and motivational perspective, research indicates that goals when accepted impose a burden in the form of a promise and commitment whose tension is only released when the goal is achieved (Carroll, 1986). Of course there is extensive research which indicates that effort and performance tend to be higher when organizational members know that they are to be evaluated (Shalley, 1995). These are some of the reasons why research indicates that about 75 per cent of all objectives under a MBO programme tend to be achieved (Carroll, 1986). If such objectives represent the highest returns for the use of organizational resources, it is clear why goal-setting systems can contribute significantly to higher organizational performance. Some research on goal setting for individuals also points to the importance of goals serving as the means by which many individuals satisfy their needs for achievement and validation of a self-concept of competence (Carroll, 1986). In fact there is extensive research validation for the idea that MBO systems are viewed as especially desirable by managers and professionals who are higher in self-esteem, achievement orientations and psychological maturity (Carroll and Tosi, 1970; 1973). Thus, as organizations become more selective in their hiring requirements the appeal of a goal-setting system may increase. Finally, it has been shown that goals on complex tasks such as in managerial work do lead to a search for analytical strategies which, in turn, have a rather high relationship to performance (Wood and Locke, 1990). Thus goals (if accepted) can contribute significantly to higher creativity and problem solving.

On the other hand, many goal-setting systems do not work effectively and many managers have been quite dissatisfied with them. For example, in the interview and questionnaire studies carried out by Carroll and Tosi (1973), managers reported that some of their superiors used goals as a club to force them into unreasonable work assignments, smothered them in paperwork, and made goal assignments among subordinates that were perceived to be unjust. Goals have pressured managers to perform unethical acts and activities, which have created harmful long-term consequences for organizations and units.

Variance in MBP Process Characteristics

It must be recognized that some managerial goal-setting systems do not work well as the research shows significance variance in the results obtained among different companies. Differences in the performance of management systems can be due to differences in the way they are designed as well as differences in the way they are administered. For example, differences in top management support for a goal-setting system has been found to be significantly related to its effectiveness in achieving higher levels of performance (Rodgers and Hunter, 1991).

In the Black & Decker study the positive results in performance and satisfaction were obtained after the system had been studied systematically and improved on various occasions over a period of several years. In fact questionnaires were administered four times at Black & Decker in a period of eight to ten years with the results being used to eliminate or reduce weaknesses in how the system was employed. Of course, even within a company there can be considerable variance in how a programme is carried out by different managers. In one large Fortune 500 company, the methods by which various aspects of the MBO system were carried out in different organizational units were statistically related with unit performances. It was found that only when goals were appropriately difficult and relevant to company goals – and when participation in their establishment was used and frequent feedback on goal progress was given – was there a relationship between the use of MBO and unit performance on a number of performance criteria. This study concluded that a quality (QMBO) system incorporating difficult, relevant, and participative goals, along with frequent feedback, is most likely to be related to higher performance and to account for much of the variability in goal-setting programme effectiveness (Gillen et al., 1984).

Current Approaches for Establishing Organizational Goals and Strategies

Current approaches for establishing organizational meta-goals and the strategies for achieving them, as well as establishing necessary derivative goals, are perhaps not so different from those used in the past. Most current systems also seem to focus on identifying opportunities, threats, strengths and weaknesses but go about this in a more systematic fashion and involve more managers than they did in the past. For example, General Electric, while keeping its basic processes for strategic planning and operational review, made considerable changes on how these are carried out (Elderkin and Bartlett, 1991). The operating heads of all of GE's major businesses now carry out this process with members of the office of the CEO in many informal intensive and confrontational meetings held throughout the year. The extensive inputs of staff have been eliminated or reduced, with significant reductions in corporate staff and in much of the complex and detailed paperwork associated with the older approaches. Within GE businesses, mandatory and very open 'Work Out' meetings are held over periods of two or three days, where cross-sections of employees can voice their opinions about the management of their businesses and about accumulated bad habits. Jack Welch considers these 'Work Out' sessions to be of major importance in improving the performance of GE companies and units. In addition, best practices are identified through visits to other companies by many groups of subordinate managers. Jack Welch of GE feels, for a number of reasons, that this process of establishing goals and strategies is superior to the former approach of using corporate staff for these purposes. Under the older approach those who had to implement company goals and strategies had little input into their establishment and were therefore not committed to them. In addition, the staff procedures for analysing external and internal environments was too slow and cumbersome to create the rapid response to changing conditions that is required by the competitive realities of today.

At GE, at the corporate level, the meta-goals of being number one or two in every market have been established along with the creation of an organizational culture emphasizing speed, simplicity and self-confidence. As before, there is to be an emphasis on obtaining the highest possible value from the use of all corporate resources, both human and material. Strategies or means of achieving goals are to be worked out by the separate businesses with the help of other businesses however and whenever this is required (General Electric, 1977). This strategic process appears to be quite similar to that of ABB, perhaps the leading European company at the present time.

Within a business of a larger firm, such as the mini-chip business of Motorola, a somewhat more systematic procedure is often used, again with the participation of a significant number of people who must integrate their activities for organizational goals and strategies to be achieved. For example, the 'search conference' at Motorola brings key people together to learn about the environment, to learn about the system and to produce a set of action plans to integrate the system and the environment (Cabana and Fiero, 1995: Cabana et al., 1995). More specifically, this process involves (1) establishing a desirable future, (2) documenting the external environment, (3) analysing past mistakes, making decisions as to what to keep, jettison and create, (4) setting goals to achieve the desirable future, (5) identifying the constraints, (6) developing strategies to overcome these constraints and (7) developing action goals and plans which must be implemented.

Designing and Implementing Effective Goal-Setting Systems

Goal-setting systems, like all managerial systems, may produce results which are good or bad depending on how closely the system design meets operating imperatives and realities as well as how the system's components are carried out by managers and operating personnel. With respect to MBO and similar goal-setting systems, a great deal of research has fortunately been conducted over several decades to provide guides on the characteristics of an effective system. This research can also be useful in providing guides in how such goal-setting systems should be designed in the light of the changing business environments that exist today.

Space limitations prevent the citation of the research, which has provided normative guides or principles for use in establishing formalized goal-setting systems for strategy implementation purposes. However, table 2.1 gives a sample of some of the major findings from this body of research which can be helpful in creating such a system.

Table 2.1 Some research findings on the goal-setting process for managers*

1. Lower level goals should be congruent with higher level goals.
2. Goals should be chosen that maximize the leverage of an individual's time and skills.
3. Goals should be set to reward co-operation as well as individual achievement.
4. Use a variety of motivational approaches to gain acceptance of high-performance goals.
5. Avoid using goals which create ethical dilemmas for managers.
6. The number of goals to be pursued should be limited to perhaps six.
7. One should use maintenance as well as performance improvement goals.
8. Subordinate participation in setting goals is essential if they have needed information.
9. Performance feedback is not helpful unless the path to goals is clear.
10. Subordinate participation is necessary if other motivational conditions are low.
11. Subordinate participation in action planning is especially necessary.
12. A mixture of objective and subjective goals works best.
13. Higher environmental uncertainty requires more frequent review.
14. Stretch goals work best when goal failure is not punished.
15. A belief in one's ability to reach the goals is essential for success.
16. High rewards for goal achievement can lead to negotiations for easy goals.

* See Carroll and Tosi, 1973; Carroll and Schneier, 1982; Carroll, 1986.

Strategy and Goal Acceptance

A review of research on MBO and goal-setting systems of all types reveals that research on goal acceptance is deficient. However, there has been considerable research in recent years on the topic of transformational leadership, in which investigations of the persuasiveness of leaders have been studied in a number of experiments. These studies have pointed to the importance of establishing a vision of the future which is appealing to subordinates given its congruence with their values. One well-designed research dissertation at the University of Maryland (Kirkpatrick, 1992) found that, in such persuasive efforts, the content of the message or its specific visionary elements and its congruence to listener values was more important in its effects on subsequent performance than the dynamics of the communication process itself (differences in voice, enthusiasm, style, and so on).

Sarah Moore (see chapter 3) points out that the role of visioning as an antidote to over-formalized rational-planning systems should not be underestimated. However, it is worth noting in passing that a large leadership literature exists today in which the importance of visioning as a process for uniting very diverse organizational units, elements, and members is of critical importance in gaining acceptance of organizational goals and strategies (Hesselbeing et al., 1996; Nathan, 1996). More recently we have seen surveys of the visioning process among CEOs indicating growing interest in this subject (Larwood et al., 1995).

To be effective, visioning seems to require several elements. First, the vision should be compelling and attractive; it must be perceived as feasible or possible; it should be simple enough to understand; and it should be remembered by all concerned with its attainment. For the latter aspect there probably should be a lot of repetition. The vision should also set standards of excellence, reflect high ideals, be ambitious, and reflect the uniqueness of the organization (Nanus, 1991). Again, Jack Welch of

General Electric would seem to be an exemplar in such visioning activities. His overall corporate meta-vision of creating the most effective and admired company in the world is accompanied by other derivative visions which are means to his meta-vision, such as GE becoming a truly 'boundary-less' company (Elderkin and Bartlett, 1991).

Welch is known for disseminating his vision widely. He talks to all GE managers attending the corporate university at Crotonville and the managers at all the many meetings he attends. He is also very skilled at persuasion. He makes very effective use of metaphors, such as his conceptualization of the company as a self-sustaining growth engine. He constantly uses familiar metaphors, such as the weeds that will not go away until you pull up their roots, how useless assets accumulate in the 'attics' of companies and the company has accumulated more than 100 years of closets that need to be cleaned out. He constantly tells his managers stories of unusual successes which have occurred at various GE plants around the world, and stories of his own experiences in talking to many GE managers. Other very effective CEOs seem to use a similar approach. At Intel, Andy Grove, who has built the company with a very effective MBO system, explains the whole process of achieving an organization's goals by describing the process of how Columbus discovered America in 1492 and other historical events in terms of the MBO perspective (Grove, 1983). Welch also appeals to consensual values, which is important in persuasion. He has also described what these consensual values should be at GE and takes actions to remove executives who do not share these values – which have provided a common mental perspective for GE managers. Again, Andy Grove at Intel tends to behave in similar ways and has a similar perspective. For example, he has created a culture which greatly values actual output and accomplishment rather than the mere possession of high levels of knowledge and talent (Grove, 1983).

Persuasion and visioning are not, however, only important at the top levels of an organization. Persuasion and the use of visions are needed in every unit of the organization and thus are important skills for all managers. There can be visions of a unit as well as that of a company and really effective managers are aware of this. A very important aspect of effectiveness in persuasion is, of course, the credibility of the manager. Aristotle pointed out many years ago that an audience can be persuaded by the logic of the message, by the emotions created by the message, and by the characteristics of the speaker, which include competence, reliability and integrity. Trust in the leader, built up over time through the leader's past behaviour, may be the most important factor in persuading people to accept a particular vision or organizational/unit goal.

Towards a Contemporary Goal-Setting System for Implementing Organizational Goals and Strategies

We have indicated that goal setting, accompanied with effective persuasive leadership at the top, is currently being used to attain very spectacular levels of organizational performance in several of the most widely admired companies in the world. This blending of goal setting with visioning and persuasive leadership seems to be what is needed in the new decentralized horizontal and networking organizational forms which have evolved in many of the largest companies. Of course, goal setting by itself has long been established as an effective tool for achieving higher performance if used appropriately. Research has identified an appropriate use of goals and links to organizational and individual performances. However, as we have indicated, this does not mean that the very formalized goal-setting systems such as management by objectives, which were very popular in the past, are still useful. Such systems are probably too rigid and inflexible to meet current competitive requirements of speed, simplicity and flexibility, as described by Jack Welch, Percy Barnevik and other widely quoted CEOs. In addition, older approaches would simply not fit the new horizontal rather than vertical organizational structures that emphasize decentralization and horizontal integration. Thus there is a necessity today for a far greater use of persuasion at the top through the use of transformational leadership behaviours to obtain acceptance of integrating organizational visions and meta-goals as well as in all organizational units.

With respect to the design of specific features of such goal-setting systems it would appear that all of the extensive previous research findings on MBO process variables, as well as on goal-setting experiments, can be still useful in designing such optimum systems. Virtually all of the later research studies on the effectiveness of goal-setting systems in organizations and on specific attributes of goals and feedback conditions are quite congruent with the earlier studies carried out on these issues. These goal-setting principles seem to be widespread, at least in the US culture.

Some of the new issues in goal setting are also receiving attention. For example, the issue of integrating individual and group goals (Crown and Rosse, 1995) and the issue of the effect of goals on competitive behaviours (Campbell and Furrer, 1995). There is also the fact that greater task uncertainty, which is more common now, makes it more difficult to benefit from performance feedback (Carroll et al., 1985). We now recognize the importance of having all types of performance management systems follow accepted principles of procedural justice (Taylor et al., 1995). Also, the importance of co-operative goals as well as individualistic goals (Smith et al., 1995) and the idea that goal setting in more collectivist cultures may have to be modified to be effective (Ramamoorthy and Carroll, 1997) are currently being discussed. Finally, the issue of the relationship of goal setting to ethics and social responsibility is receiving increased attention because of many past examples of how goals have contributed to corporate behaviour of questionable ethics and social responsibility (Carroll and Gannon, 1996).

The accomplishment of the more difficult goals required by performance improvement initiatives will also obviously require very well-developed human resources. Monsanto, for example, has found that development of an effective performance management programme emphasizing the development of its human resources provided then with a real competitive advantage (Jones, 1995). Also, as indicated previously, there seems to be some evidence that developing higher levels of organizational trust may be a prerequisite of the acceptance of any managerial system, no matter how effectively it is designed. In an era of downsizing and union suppression programmes this is not so easy to achieve but certain companies that have been very effective in implementing significant organizational change and performance improvements in unionized settings, such as Xerox, have demonstrated that this can be done (Foulkes, 1989; Condrey, 1995).

Although we have used business examples throughout this chapter, many effective non-profit organizations are implementing new strategic directions and even implementing them through goal-setting systems. For example, the new dean at the Smith School of Business at the University of Maryland, Howard Frank, has recently formulated a new vision of a business school which involves much more integration among the various functional academic units than existed formerly, and has made attempts to unify discipline diversity through a common emphasis or vision emphasizing the new information technologies and the topic of knowledge management. He also instituted a new formalized goal-setting system which requires each unit within the college to develop short- and long-term specific objectives that will implement the college's new integrated strategic directions.

Even in literature we see recognition of Jack Welch's epigram 'control your destiny or someone else will'. A book by the well-known V.S. Naipaul (1989), *The Bend in the River*, starts off with the lines: 'The world is as it is. Men who are nothing, who have let themselves become nothing, have no place in it.' In the book, the narrator and some of his friends who are generally passive and reactive and non-analytical, are overwhelmed to a large degree by the incredible changes they are experiencing in their world. However, some in the book are more analytical and less reactive and manage to survive quite well. Although these words appear to be an exceptionally harsh worldview perspective, it is a view that in many ways unfortunately does seem to fit present-day realities not only for organizations of all types but, as Naipaul's book indicates, also for individuals everywhere.

References

Cabana, S. and Fiero, J. 1995: Motorola, strategic planning and the search conference. *The Journal for Quality and Participation*, 18(4), July/August, 22–32.

Cabana, S., Emery, F. and Emery, M. 1995: The search for effective strategic planning is over. *The Journal for Quality and Participation*, 18(4), July/August, 10–12.

Campbell, D.J. and Furrer, D.M. 1995: Goal setting and competition as determinants of task performance. *Journal of Organizational Behavior*, 16(4), 377–90.

Carroll, S.J. 1986: Management by objectives: three decades of research and experience. In S.L. Rynes and G.T. Milkovich (eds) *Current issues in human resource management*. Plato, TX: Business Publications.

Carroll, S.J. and Gannon, M.J. 1996: *Ethical dimensions of international management*. Thousand Oaks, CA: Sage.

Carroll, S.J. and Schneier, C.E. 1982: *Performance appraisal and review systems*. Glenview, IL: Scott Foresman.

Carroll, S.J. and Tosi, H.L. 1970: Goal characteristics and personality factors in a management by objectives program. *Administrative Science Quarterly*, 15, 295–305.

Carroll, S.J. and Tosi, H.L. 1973: *Management by objectives: applications and research*. New York: Macmillan.

Carroll, S.J. and Tosi, H.L. 1976: Relationship of various motivational forces to the effects of participation in goal-setting in a management by objectives program. *Proceedings, Industrial Relations Research Association*, Atlantic City, NJ.

Carroll, S.J., Lee, C., Taylor, M.S. and Gillen, D. 1985: Task uncertainty as a moderator of the feedback–performance relationship. *Proceedings of Southern Management Association*.

Condrey, S.E. 1995: Reforming human resource management systems: exploring the importance of organizational trust. *American Review of Public Administration*, 25(4), 341–55.

Crown, D.F. and Rosse, J.G. 1995: Yours, mine, and ours: facilitating group productivity through the integration of individual and group goals. *Organizational Behavior and Human Decision Processes*, 64(2), 138–51.

Dillon, F. 1998: Barnevik's global vision. *Decision*, 3(2), 12–18.

Elderkin, K.W. and Bartlett, C.A. 1991: General Electric: Jack Welch's second wave. *Case 9–391–248. Harvard Business School*.

Foulkes, F.K. 1989: *Human resources management: cases and text*. Englewood Cliffs, NJ: Prentice-Hall.

Geneen, H. 1984: *Managing*. New York: Doubleday.

General Electric 1977: *Annual Report*.

Gillen, D., Carroll, S.J. and Fitzpatrick, B.W. 1984: QMBO and the effectiveness of organizational units. *Proceedings, Eastern Academy of Management*. Montreal, Canada.

Grove, A.S. 1983: *High output management*. New York: Random House.

Hesselbeing, F., Goldsmith, M. and Beckhard, R. (eds) 1996: *The leader of the future*. San Francisco, CA: Jossey-Bass.

Jones, T.W. 1995: Performance management in a changing context: Monsanto pioneers a competence-based developmental approach. *Human Resource Management*, 34(3), 425–43.

Kirkpatrick, S.A. 1992: *Decomposing charismatic leadership: the effects of leader content and process on follower performance, attitudes, and perceptions*. PhD Dissertation, University of Maryland.

Larwood, L., Falbe, C.M., Kriger, M.P. and Miesing, P. 1995: Structure and meaning of organizational vision. *Academy of Management Journal*, 39(3), 740–69.

Locke, E.A. and Latham, G.P. 1990: *A theory of goal setting and task performance*. Englewood Cliffs, NJ: Prentice Hall.

Martell, K. and Carroll, S.J. 1995: Which executive human resource management practices for the top management team are associated with higher firm performance? *Human Resource Management*, 34(4), 497–512.

Mintzberg, H. 1994: The fall and rise of strategic planning. *Harvard Business Review*, January/February, 107–14.

Naipaul, V.S. 1989: *The bend in the river*. New York: Random House.

Nanus, B. 1991: *Visionary leadership*. San Francisco: Jossey-Bass.

Nathan, M.L. 1996: What is organizational vision? Ask chief executives. *Academy of Management Executive*, 10(1), 82–3.

Ramamoorthy, N. and Carroll, S.J. 1997: Individualism–Collectivism orientations and reactions toward alternative human resource management practices. Human Relations, 51(5), 571–88.

Rodgers, R.C. and Hunter, J.E. 1991: The impact of management by objectives on organizational productivity. *Journal of Applied Psychology*, 76, 322–36.

Shalley, C.E. 1995: Effects of coaction, expected evaluation and goal setting. *Academy of Management Journal*, 38(2), 483–508.

Smith, K.S., Carroll, S.J. and Ashford, S.J. 1995: Intra- and inter-organizational cooperation: toward a research agenda. *Academy of Management Journal*, 39, 7–23.

Taylor, M.S., Tracy, K.B., Renard, M.K., Harrison, J.K. and Carroll, S.J. 1995: Procedural justice in performance appraisal: a field test of the due process metaphor for performance appraisal systems. *Administrative Science Quarterly*, 40, 495–523.

Terpstra, D. and Rozell, E.J. 1994: The relationship of goal setting to organizational profitability. *Group and Organization Management*, 19(3), 285–95.

Tosi, H.L. and Carroll, S.J. 1968: Managerial reactions to management by objectives. *Academy of Management Journal*, 11, 415–26.

Tosi, H.L., Rizzo, J.R. and Carroll, S.J. 1970: Setting goals in management by objectives. *California Management Review*, 12, 70–8.

Tosi, H.L., Hunter, J., Chesser, R., Tarter, J. and Carroll, S.J. 1976: How real are changes introduced by management by objectives? *Administrative Science Quarterly*, 21, 276–302.

Wally, S., Carroll, S.J. and Flood, P.C. 1996: Managing without traditional structures. In P.C., Flood, M.J. Gannon and J. Paauwe (eds) *Managing without traditional methods*. Reading, MA: Addison-Wesley.

Wood, R.E. and Locke, E.A. 1990: Goal setting and strategy effects on complex tasks. In B. Staw and L. Cummings (eds) *Research in organizational behavior*, 12, Greenwich, CT: JAI Press, pp. 73–109.

3

Analysing Strategic Activity through Narrative Analysis

SARAH MOORE

Much has been written about the current conceptual crisis in strategy research. Debates about the rationality, implementability, sequence and effectiveness of strategic behaviour have failed to reach any cohesive conclusions about how best to approach the complex tasks of strategic formulation and implementation. Perspectives on strategy have variously been attacked for being too rational or not rational enough and for creating false divisions between the thinking that is often associated with strategy formulation and the action which accompanies implementation. The dimensions of the debate are complex and numerous, reflected by many current authors and summarized in the recent words of Barry and Elmes (1997: 429):

> Mirroring longstanding concerns with competition, forecasting and fit, the field [of strategy] has itself become a highly contested and questioned site, one riddled with competing models, 'whither now' conferences and effectiveness disputes.

Despite (or perhaps because of) the debates and disagreements that exist within the field, interesting developments in theory and practice have emerged, allowing for a range of different types of strategic analyses to take place. Nevertheless a polarity still tends to persist in theoretical and practical discussions about strategy, a division which has recently put opposing views into the two broad camps of rational planning and creative visioning. While some theorists have developed more elaborate and numerous strategy definitions, the division between these two broad perspectives represents one of the many divisions in strategy research and practice. The strengths of the rational planning schools are the weaknesses of the creative visioning schools and vice versa. While rational approaches are characterized by technical realism, control and logic, they are seen to lack inspiration, novelty and innovation. Also, while visionary approaches are seen as more inspiring and involving, they are criticized for being high on rhetoric but low on realism. Creative visions may indeed be coherent statements of organizational values and long-term ideologies but too often they are seen as unfocused on detailed, actionable strategic issues, and therefore difficult to implement from a practical point of view.

These critiques of strategic approaches too often focus on differences and incompatibilities between various theoretical models of strategic behaviour. This chapter aims to provide some reconciliation between these two central approaches to strategic behaviour, perspectives that have predominated in theoretical discussions about strategy. In addition, it explores how such a synthesis can aid analytical approaches to strategic implementation.

In applied settings, no one strategic model is likely to predominate, regardless of the pure forms of strategic approaches that exist in the theoretical literature. Real-life settings, by definition, do not present 'pure' or ideal type categories of strategic behaviour. While on the one hand 'model proliferation' relating to strategy has occurred in the academic literature, on the other hand, organizations have continued to operate, plan, create visions, without ever consistently selecting and applying a single strategic model. Real life organizations are much more familiar with the grey and complex area of human experience than theoretical models are likely to capture.

Nevertheless, one of the ways in which novel and useful perspectives can emerge from existing complicated debates on strategy is when new definitions are explored and applied. By changing the definition of 'strategy' it may be possible to develop more useful insights, new and exciting avenues of investigation and to uncover hidden dynamics that might help to explain the successes and failures of strategic activity in a variety of settings. This chapter explores the two classic approaches to strategic activity and proposes that analysing organizational narrative and increasing reflection on and awareness of strategic narratives can provide a useful technique for deriving better results, higher chances of implementation and reconciling the two opposing approaches to strategic activity. By developing and building on the theme of strategy as narrative, it is also proposed that hidden or implicit functions associated with strategic behaviour can be identified more clearly. Many theorists have called for a more realistic and more grounded exploration of both the formulation and implementation of strategy. It is argued here that treating strategy as narrative can help to bridge the gaps between existing ideas, as well as create some interesting new ones.

This discussion also seeks to recognize the value of rationalist and visionary approaches to strategy, by seeking to demonstrate the contributions that such perspectives can make to a workable and inclusive analysis of strategic behaviour.

This chapter also aims to overcome some of the problems associated with understanding and managing strategic activity by suggesting how analysis of strategic conversations may be used as a key device for uncovering some powerful dynamics that influence organizational strategies. It argues the importance of attending more closely to the features and fabric of various forms of strategic narrative and shows that this can be effective in uncovering more about what strategic activity actually achieves in real organizational settings. This argument is underpinned by the increasingly widely held assumption that strategists can benefit significantly from more critical and analytical reflection of their own activities and achievements in their efforts to craft and execute effective strategies in their organizations. In addition, by bridging the gap that is frequently perceived to exist between rationality and creativity, some of the frequent and fundamental problems associated with strategy can be tackled with more confidence and more understanding than might otherwise be possible.

Two Classic Definitions of Strategy

Useful efforts have been made in the past to open up the definition of strategy and explore its dimensions as a concept from a variety of standpoints. Theorists such as Mintzberg (1980), Quinn (1988) and Hart (1992) have devoted significant time and attention over the last two decades to the exploration of diverse perspectives and to the facilitation of a multi-faceted understanding of this complex field. Since these efforts, definitions of strategy have continued to burgeon. This section provides a review of two classic and competing definitions that are relevant to current strategic settings. These definitions have long been associated with strategy research and practice and both are views that persist in influencing strategic thought in today's organizational contexts.

Both definitions highlight a different but important challenge to practitioners in their attempts to develop and to activate effective strategies for their organizations. Viewing strategy as rational planning highlights the cognitive need for order and sequence, both when making sense of past activities and in the face of future uncertainties. Academics have been telling us for some time, however, that a purely rational, planned approach to strategy often gives rise in many strategic contexts to the separation of thinking from action as well as the creation of unrealistic expectations of human capacities in the development of effective strategy. Viewing strategy as creative vision demonstrates that strategy demands a long-term and often radical futurist orientation. But while a creative and visionary approach may provide inspiring generalities and develop shared organizational principles, it may be less likely than the planning approach to give rise to a coherent network of actionable and organized first steps.

Strategy as rational planning

By now, most theorists and insightful practitioners have recognized the limitations associated with purely rationalist approaches to strategy. The 'Planning school', for example, has often been referred to as a hyper-rationalist approach to strategy that makes a series of unrealistic assumptions about the cognitive capabilities of strategists. Most strategists will automatically caution against assuming that strategic activity is based on high (or even any) levels of rationality or objectivity. On the one hand, it does make sense to lay out action in advance and to engage in formal planning so that provisions can be made to achieve such plans. On the other hand, the rational planning school of strategic thinking 'assumes intellectual capacities and sources of information that [people] simply do not possess' (Lindblom, 1959). It has long been recognized that even the most talented and insightful of strategists are vulnerable to innate cognitive limitations. In one sense, then, it is astonishing that much of today's strategic literature persists in its assumption of rational approaches to strategic activity. Lindblom's claim that strategic prescriptions tend to recommend impossibly rational, comprehensive decision procedures is as true today as it was when he proposed it decades ago.

The predominance of the rational school in both theory and practice has been explained in detail and at length in strategic literature. Psychologists show that people tend to present their activities in the form of an integrated account. Such accounts are also likely to appear cohesive, logical and linear in hindsight, even when the actions that led to them were chaotic, irrational and only very loosely sequenced, if at all. True to this psychological tendency, formulated organizational strategies are often presented to various audiences as polished, edited, structured documents, with linear sequencing, rational arguments and strong implications that such arguments have been crafted objectively, with full commitment from the entire organization (Mintzberg, 1994). Indeed, what 'outsiders' see of organizational strategy is often an apparently well conceived series of plans, which simply await implementation by a willing crew of team workers. Under this veneer of rationality may lie a hidden story. Confusion, frustration, cynicism, secrecy, power struggles, uncertainty and fear are among the negative experiences that may be encountered during strategic initiatives. Conversely, formal documents outlining either planned or achieved strategies can also conceal many positive dynamics such as humour, passion, creativity, excitement and fun. The language of formal strategy, particularly that which emerges from the rational planning school, often appears to suffer from a form of emotional anorexia (see Fineman, 1993) which fails to account for the complicated processes associated with affective, cognitive and behavioural dynamics. Over the years, organizational theorists have increasingly recognized that we ignore such dynamics at our peril. The difficulty is that finding out what these tendencies are, and how they interact with more formal and rational dynamics is by no means a straightforward process. As Weick (1990) famously contends: 'the territory is not the map'. Even the most genuinely honest account about how a strategy has taken place is merely a rough map that may hide many complex secrets about the real territory it tries to reflect. This human tendency may be the single most important reason why the rational planning school persists and survives as robustly as it does in today's strategic textbooks, organizational accounts and prescriptions. In short, many organizational plans and reports simply serve to act as 'sequentializing, sensemaking devices' (Quinn, 1992; Weick, 1995).

Such a tendency also calls into question the validity of self-report research, where strategists are directly asked to provide accounts of their strategic activities, successes and failures. Indeed, much of the rational planning school of thought is based on this type of research (Ansoff, 1977; Thune and House, 1970). Without the development of effective and creative research strategies, it might be easy for strategic researchers to continue to perpetuate certain rationalized myths within organizational theory and practice. Uncovering hidden functions and dynamics of strategic activity requires not only reading between the lines of traditional research data, but also the development and use of more innovative research devices, some of which will be discussed in more detail later in this chapter.

Viewing strategy as rational planning then, has a long and at least somewhat explicable heritage in organizational research. Its persistence, however, has failed to uncover some of the more complex and interesting dynamics of strategic activity that might provide vital new perspectives for strategists in a wide range of different settings.

Strategy as creative vision

In the 1980s, a new verb, 'visioning', was coined and popularized among strategic theorists. 'To vision' was seen to engage in a new way of creating strategy that required strategists to develop creative, radical, long-term views of their organizations. The cognitive paradox of 'starting in the future' was a device used to help participants in the strategic process to think radically, to free themselves from the limiting assumptions of the present and to be unbridled in their creative thinking. 'Visioning' was also seen to require the development of overarching values that could help to provide an important ideological framework for strategic action. In addition, the visioning concept was generally accompanied by democratic ideals, involving groups who had traditionally played little or no part in the formulation of strategy, despite being required to implement it at a later stage in the process. Developing a clear vision was seen as important, but equally important was the need for that vision to be shared among all members of the organization. The idea that all organizational members would be committed to a common organizational vision was particularly appealing to those concerned with effective implementation, but the accompanying lack of actionable first steps to the achievement of such a vision, was a common stumbling block.

On the one hand, therefore, in order to develop strategies that welcome change and more importantly develops a significant competitive edge, the vision concept can be a useful strategic definition. However, on the other hand, the long-term nature of the visioning approach also creates its own problems. Developing a long-term vision of the future of an organization usually leads to extremely generalized shared visions, if indeed such visions can be shared in large and diverse organizations. Creating a clear shared vision of an organization's future requires huge time and investment and to be successful, necessitates the initiation of multistatus, horizontal and diagonal groups (Wilson, 1992). Such efforts to develop a creative shared vision within any organization may uncover many competing world views and perspectives, which may also be irreconcilable. Yet the investment required by such initiatives can lead to the formal creation of an impression that there is a unanimous commitment to one single, cohesive vision. Written documents which report the outcomes of 'visioning' initiatives, often fail to transmit the diversity of views, the conflicts and the contingencies on which many of the emergent vision and mission statements have been based. Similarly, they do not capture the process benefits that may be accrued from engaging in such initiatives. Many participants of more democratic vision initiatives report that the outcomes of visioning exercises are too broad and general to be particularly valuable. Vision statements that are generated via brainstorming sessions and team meetings often leave people at a loss with regard to actionable first steps for the realization of this vision. However, hand, the process may be more likely to be viewed as at least in some ways rewarding, integrating and morale boosting, creating as it can a cohesiveness and interconnection among organizational members that may otherwise not have existed.

Thus, strategy as rational planning emphasizes the content of a strategy. Strategy as creative vision focuses more on the process by which a strategy is achieved.

Interactive Narrative as a Bridge between Rational Plans and Creative Visions

Viewing strategy as interactive narrative may be able to uncover hidden funct- ions and themes by exploring deeper dynamics associated with strategic activity. This in turn may highlight significant challenges as well as great opportunities associated with the non-rational, serendipitous nature of human thought and action.

Table 3.1 describes the formulation and implementation activities associated with three key approaches to strategy. Interactive narrative, which is being advanced as a bridge between rational planning and creative visioning approaches, is now dis- cussed.

Barry and Elmes (1997) have been among the first theorists to argue the usefulness of viewing strategy as interactive narrative. Strategic success in rational planning terms is assumed to require objective, comprehensive planning; in creative visioning terms, it requires the development of a long term, cohesive world view. If we define

Table 3.1 Formulation and implementation activities associated with three key approaches to strategy

Approaches	Strategy formulation	Strategy implementation
Rational planning	Formal meetings, forecasting, positioning, external evaluation, resource assessment – deriving future scenarios from current contexts	Non-iterative execution of plans conceived and elaborated at formulation phase, resource allocation, project management, negotiation of task distribution
Creative visioning	Brainstorming, team development, collaboration, consensus building, conflict management – relating to the long-term future of the organization	Testing and accomplishing actionable first steps derived from broad vision. Deriving immediate first steps from a clear, shared, long-term vision (logical incrementalism)
Interactive narrative	Participating in active narrative (i.e. talking about and listening to ideas from all levels of the organization) about past, present and future. Being reflective and aware of the major strands of organizational narrative and understanding the core and peripheral values that it reflects	Building an understanding of the organization's narrative into strategic activity at all levels in the organization. Using effective narrative to initiate actionable first steps that will realize elements of a strategic vision or execute specific strategic plans

strategy as interactive narrative, our definition of strategic success will also be different. As Barry and Elmes (1994: 443) put it:

> From a narrative perspective, the successful strategic story may depend less on such tools as comprehensive scanning, objective planning or meticulous control/feedback systems, and more on whether it stands out from other organizational stories, is persuasive and invokes retelling. What the story revolves around, how it is put together and the way it is told all determine whether it becomes one worth listening to, remembering and acting upon. Thus strategic effectiveness from a narrative perspective is intimately tied to acceptance, approval and adoption.

Viewing strategy as narrative may be an important conceptual step in bridging the gap between the present and the future of organizations. From a narrative perspective, it can be argued that in order to create a successful strategy, it must be both believable and novel (e.g. Bann and Bowlt, 1973; Lemon and Reis, 1965; Matejka and Pomorska, 1971). It could thus be argued that neither the rational planning nor the creative vision approaches can achieve both these aims, with the former being believable but not novel and the latter being novel but not believable. Successful strategic narratives take into account the need for inspiring novelty as well as the need for an anchor of credibility to hold the vision together. Analysing the narratives that occur in real organizational settings can be seen as an important way of evaluating the extent to which successful strategic stories are being told.

Identifying new levels of analysis by exploring strategic narrative

Strategic narrative can be defined as any organizational interaction that focuses on the future of the organization. The sources of narrative in organizations are extremely diverse, and rarely will any one individual or group have access to all forms and types. However, top management teams do operate in important interactive arenas, particularly with respect to an organization's strategy. They engage in spoken and written conversation which contains rich and complex information, much of which fails to be captured or attended to, even by the participants themselves. The value of any self-reflective activity is that it allows for a more considered understanding of the rationale of action. Some legal and political organizational arenas have recognized this and use transcripts of spoken interaction as part of an important tapestry of data, informing decision and action. However, in most corporate settings, much of what is spoken, even at formal meetings, fails to be captured except in the most skeletal of forms. For future organizational competitiveness, capturing and analysing the dimensions of both spoken and written strategic interaction may represent an important self-reflective tool which contains a wealth of important food for thought.

Comparing written and spoken data in corporate strategic research has the capacity to yield interesting and significant results by uncovering some of the hidden and implicit functions associated with strategic activity. Research in organizations increasingly recognizes the importance of using actual conversations as a valid source of data for exploring various dimensions of organizational activity. Ford and Ford (1995) and Donnellon (1986) have asserted that any changes in organizations can be seen as communication processes, laden with narrative. It has long been argued that organizational talk is indeed a central form of organizational action (Searle, 1969) and that studying talk and other forms of narrative (including written texts) is vital for an understanding of the context of further action (Donnellon 1986; Argyris, 1990). Most importantly, by exploring formal written strategic documents and comparing them with less formal, spoken strategic conversations the difference between the explicit and hidden functions and dynamics of strategy might be more clearly uncovered. Thus an analysis of spoken and written narrative and a comparison between the two might be a useful model for effective reflection on the strategy process in any organization. A proposed methodology for achieving this type of analysis is outlined here.

With access to written and spoken strategic transcripts (such as a written strategic plan and the conversations or meetings that contributed to the crafting of this plan), it is possible to divide such data into separate text units and analyse the similarities and differences between these two forms of narrative. Using the same coding framework, similarities and differences can be identified in the patterns of the two types of data. This framework for analysis of strategic narrative should contain at least the following four levels of analysis:

1. Strategic orientation (whether statements refer to content, process or context issues).
2. Time orientation (whether statements refer to past, present or future time frames).
3. Subject focus (the issues which form the subject of each statement).
4. Specificity (whether statements are general or specific in nature).

The rationale for creating these levels of analysis is based on an approach that combines current theoretical themes in the literature on strategy, and a grounded approach to diverse samples of strategic narrative. Each of the levels of analysis was chosen for its ability to throw light on the patterns and dynamics of strategic interaction.

With respect to level one of the research framework, the identification of the concepts of process, content and context represents a major taxonomic attempt in the field of strategy and in various theorists' attempts to understand the nature of strategic activity (Rouleau and Seguin, 1995). There is strong implicit and explicit evidence that these concepts have been seen as important dimensions of strategic activity since formal investigation into organizational theory began. These conceptual distinctions continue to be incorporated into central views and perspectives on strategy guiding data collection, analysis and interpretation in the area. Pettigrew et al. (1992: 7) continue to assert the importance of considering these three dimensions of strategy when shaping organizational change. They propose, for example, that:

> theoretically sound and practically useful research on change should involve the continuous interplay between ideas about the context of change, the process of change and the content of change.

Indeed, while traditional, predominantly rational approaches to strategy tend to focus on the content of strategy while ignoring strategic processes (Narayanan and Fahy, 1982), a holistic understanding of any strategic activity cannot be achieved by focusing only on the 'what' of strategy. For a real understanding of strategic activity, context ('why') and process ('how') issues are also important.

Time orientation is the second important theme when analysing strategic narrative. Most definitions of strategy assume that strategic activity is focused on the future and many recommendations about strategic activity have often implied the importance of taking people away from their present situation (see Schwartz, 1992; Schoemaker, 1993). Indeed, much associated work on organizational creativity suggests that a past time orientation is potentially damaging in the development of effective strategies for the future (Woodman et al., 1993). Also, the assumption that strategy is 'action laid out in advance' (Mintzberg, 1994) is one that might benefit from further critical exploration through the analysis of strategic narrative. Exploring the predominant time orientations that appear in strategic narratives may help to demonstrate the extent to which a future time orientation is actually adopted, and to understand the conditions under which various time orientations are more likely to emerge.

The rational planning approach is stereotypically more focused on the content of plans associated with strategy than it is on the process by which such plans may be achieved. It tends to derive its projections from current performance and is thus grounded in a present time orientation. Consistent with its content orientation, it is also focused on the organization and the industry within which that organization operates, and it tends to present its proposals in specific terms. Commitment levels are higher in the short term than they are in the long term.

Subject focus is the third proposed level of analysis. Familiarity with diverse strategic narratives (both spoken and written), yields the general observation that two broad strands of subject focus run through most strategic interactions. First, references to the strategic initiatives themselves and, second, references to the organizations and/or the wider industries within which the organizations operate.

The fourth valuable level analysis is the extent to which various parts of strategic narrative are either general or specific in nature. 'Specificity' is both theoretically and practically important. Collins (1981) observes that 'some conversational topics are generalized in that they refer to events and entities on some level of abstraction from the immediate and local situation . . . [and that] other conversational topics are particularlized: they refer to specific persons, places and things'. The relevance of differentiating between generalized and specific narrative has long been seen as important by sociologists (see Bernstein, 1971) but has not yet been explored in detail in the field of strategic narrative. Observing extents of specificity in strategic narrative may reveal a different set of emphases, concerns and effects within any one organizational conversation. The more, or less, generalized a series of statements are in strategic settings, the more such statements may be able to tell us about whether strategic approaches are rational or visionary in emphasis, and the extent to which different interventions need to be applied to ensure that strategy implementation will be possible to complete.

Table 3.2 A framework for analysing strategic narrative

Approach	Strategic orientation	Time orientation	Subject focus	General/ Specific orientation	Levels of commitment to implementation
Rational planning	Mainly content oriented	More frequently linked to the present	The organization	Specific	High in the short term; low in the long term
Creative visioning	Mainly process oriented	More frequently linked to the future	The strategic initiative	General	High in the long term; low in the short term

Using these levels of analysis, an exploration of strategic narrative may be able to identify more clearly the extent to which rational or visionary approaches predominate at different phases in a strategic initiative. Such an analysis would be able to highlight whether, and under what conditions, for example the rational planning or creative visioning approaches are more likely to create an effective momentum towards successful implementation. Table 3.2 provides a broad diagnostic framework for the use of such an analytical approach.

The rational planning approach is stereotypically more focused on the content of plans associated with strategy than it is on the process by which such plans may be achieved. It tends to derive its projections from current performance and is thus grounded in a present time orientation. Consistent with its content orientation, it is also focused on the organization and the industry within which that organization operates and it tends to present its proposals in specific terms. commitment levels are higher in the short term than they are in the long term.

The creative visioning approach is stereotypically process oriented, focusing as it does on involving and sharing a cohesive organizational world view. It is focused on the long-term future and may represent radical departures from current activities and foci. It is more likely to be focused on the strategic initiative and the methodologies involved. Its ideas and outcomes tend to be very broad and generalized in nature. Table 3.2 summarizes these features and shows that commitment to implementation is likely to vary according to the different approaches used.

Closer attention to strategic narrative may reveal more clearly which approaches are used, to what extent and with what effect. However, as most OD specialists recognize, it is more difficult for internal organizational participants to recognize and monitor their own patterns of strategic behaviour in a critical or remedial way. Organizational defence routines are arguably more likely to exist at senior 'strategic' levels than they are at any other level within the organization, thus making it less likely that ineffective patterns of behaviour relating to strategic activity will be rectified. If strategists could become more aware of the importance of their patterns of language and interaction, their chances of addressing ineffective but ingrained strategic routines might be significantly enhanced. Demonstrating to practitioners how much of their strategy meetings are devoted to more visionary or to more rationalist orientations represents a useful self-reflective and awareness-building technique which may help them to recognize the importance of imagination as well as pragmatism. Attending to strategic narrative is one of the important routes to enhancing the elusive possibility of strategic success. Such attention could be achieved through dedicated organizational development type interventions, using frameworks similar to that outlined above. Capturing typical strategic narrative and analysing this interaction in a critical way is capable of uncovering, within organizations, some patterns and tendencies of which participants themselves may not be explicitly aware (Prasad, 1993). Using narrative analysis, it is more likely that organizations may be able to address their strategic implementation deficiencies by developing a more energizing balance between rational and creative approaches to strategy, avoiding on the one hand, the 'accomplished mediocrity' induced by a lack of strategic imagination to which Charles Carroll refers in chapter 13, and on the other hand the groundless, unimplementable creative visions that may emerge from a focus on the future which is unaccompanied or uninformed by an understanding of the present.

Conclusions

Carrying out an analysis of the words and sentences that organizational members use in the course of their strategic conversations may reveal a variety of important features of that organization's approach to strategic thought and action. Written documents may espouse visions, whereas spoken interactions may focus on planning or vice versa. Time orientation can validly be measured for the frequency of future against present oriented-type statements in order to reveal the different approaches emerging at different stages in the strategic process. Similarly, the balance of content-oriented statements can be compared to context- or process-type statements to examine and reflect upon the extent to which a strategic team has considered these three essential dimensions when crafting their strategy. Through narrative analysis, strategic statements can also be more easily identified as general or specific in focus. Those that are identified as highly generalized strategies might benefit from a critical review and a consideration of actionable first steps; those that are highly specific might be reviewed and rebalanced with a coherent framework of guiding principles.

Essentially, the use of a narrative analytical approach does not set down absolute or normative rules about how best to manage the complex tasks of strategy formulation and implementation. It can however, facilitate a more reflexive approach to strategic activity and in the process, allow valuable lessons to be learned.

Some of the conundrums associated with the field of strategy have persisted despite decades of research. The fact that strategists often fail to achieve their objectives is not new to strategy literature. Indeed, while strategy is presented as being linear, logical, objective, rational, comprehensive and future oriented, real strategic narrative is also loaded with a variety of different chaotic dynamics like subjectivity, irrationality, selective information processing, serendipity and current time orientations.

Before managers become brilliant strategists, they need to be able to recognize the hidden tendencies associated with strategic behaviour in their organizations. Strategists can use relatively informal narrative analysis approaches by recording or noting various narrative dynamics: e.g. the proportion of past-, present- and future-oriented statements; the extent to which various discussions and documents are focused on context, content or process issues; the subjects chosen for discussion; and the extent to which recommendations or proposals are specific or general in nature.

The narrative approach can go beyond dichotomous views of strategy by using multiple levels of exploration. Narratives are not simply strategic techniques for creating strategic rhetoric; they form an important fabric around which strategic activity takes place. They exist regardless of whether organizations adopt rational or visionary approaches (or, which is more probable, a mixture of the two). They are important sources of organizational and strategic information that can help to uncover differences between the dimensions of strategic interaction and highlight the importance of listening to the real voices of strategic actors in their natural settings. It is through the direct observation and analysis of these voices that we can gain valuable access to new avenues for understanding the central dynamics associated with strategic activity.

References

Ansoff, I. 1977: Does planning pay? The effect of planning on success of acquisition in American firms. *Long Range Planning*, 3, 2–7.

Argyris, C. 1990: *Overcoming organisational defenses: facilitating organisational learning.* Boston: Allyn and Bacon.

Bann, S. and Bowlt, J. (eds) 1973: *Russian formalism.* New York: Barnes & Noble.

Barry, D. and Elmes, M. 1997: Strategy retold: toward a narrative view of strategic discourse. *Academy of Management Journal*, 22(2), 429–53.

Bernstein, B. 1971: *Class, codes and control.* London: Routledge and Kegan Paul.

Collins, R. 1981: On the microfoundations of macrosociology. *American Journal of Sociology*, 5, 984–1013.

Donnellon, A. 1986: Language and communication in organisations: bridging cognition and behaviour. In H. Sims, D. Gioia et al. (eds) *The thinking organisation: dynamics of organisational social cognition.* London: Jossey-Bass.

Donnellon, A. 1996: *Team talk: the power of language in team dynamics.* Boston: Harvard Business School Press.

Festinger, L. 1957: *A theory of cognitive dissonance.* Illinois: Row Peterson.

Fineman, S. 1993: *Emotion in organisations.* London: Sage.

Ford, J.D and Ford, L.W. 1995: The role of conversations in producing intentional change in organisations. *Academy of Management Review*, 20(3), 541–70.

Hart, S.L. 1992: An integrative framework for strategy making processes. *Academy of Management Review*, 17(2), 327–52.

Lemon, L. and Reis, M. (trans.) 1965: *Russian formalist criticism: four essays.* Nebraska: University of Nebraska Press.

Lindblom, C.E. 1959: The science of muddling through. *Public Administration Review*, 19(2).

Matejka, L. and Pomorska, K. (eds) 1971: *Readings in Russian poetics: formalist and structuralist views*. Cambridge, MA: MIT Press.

Mintzberg, H. 1980: Opening up the definition of strategy. *Strategy formation*, vol. 1. Schools of Thought.

Mintzberg, H. 1994: *The rise and fall of strategic planning*. Hemel Hempstead: Prentice Hall.

Narayanan, V.K. and Fahy, L. 1982: The micro politics of strategy formulation. *Academy of Management Review*, 17(1), 25–34.

Pettigrew, A., Ferlie, E. and McKee, L. 1992: *Shaping strategic change*. London: Sage.

Quinn, J.B. 1988: Strategies for change. In J.B. Quinn, H. Mintzberg and R.M. James (eds) *The strategy process: concepts, contexts and cases*. Englewood Cliffs, NJ: Prentice-Hall.

Quinn, J.B. 1992: *The intelligent enterprise: a knowledge and service based paradigm for industry*. New York: Free Press.

Rouleau, L. and Seguin, F. 1995: Strategy and organisational theories: common forms of discourse. *Journal of Management Studies*, 32(1), 101–17.

Schoemaker, P. 1993: Multiple scenario development: its conceptual and behavioural foundations. *Strategic Management Journal*, 14(3), 193–213.

Schwartz, P. 1992: Composing a plot for your scenario. *Planning Review*, 20(2), 4–8.

Searle, J.R. 1969: *The construction of social reality*. New York: Free Press.

Senge, P. 1990: *The fifth discipline: the art and practice of the learning organisation*. New York: Doubleday

Thune, S. and House, R.J. 1970: Where long range planning pays off. *Business Horizons*, 13(4), 81–7.

Weick, K. 1990. Cartographic myths in organisations. In A. Huff (ed.) *Mapping strategic thought*. London: Wiley.

Wilson, D.O. 1992: Diagonal communication links within organisations. *Journal of Business Communication*, 29(2), 129–42.

Woodman, R.W., Sawyer, J.E. and Griffin, R. 1993: Toward a theory of organisational creativity. *Academy of Management Review*, 18(2), 293–321.

4

Strategy Implementation and Polarity Management

TONY DROMGOOLE AND DAVID MULLINS

Many of the strategy implementation and change management models have a deceptive lure. The unstated hypothesis goes 'follow this approach and successful implementation will follow'. The road map points the way from A to B. This assumes we are at A and have decided we need to get to B. But what if there is a difficulty in defining B? And what if it is unclear as to whether we are in fact at A?

The most striking difference between the change initiatives embarked upon by managers over the past twenty years is the quantum increase in uncertainty surrounding every aspect of these initiatives – uncertainty regarding a clear future state, uncertainty regarding the best change strategy to move towards that fuzzy picture of the future and, even more alarmingly, uncertainty regarding the very reason for change (the problem which is giving rise to the change). At the core of this observation is the contention that the process of change is itself changing, and in its wake the traditional approaches to strategy formulation and implementation need to be revisited. This in turn comes about as a result of the exponential increases in the rate of change and as a result of the increasing frequency at which discontinuities or radical environmental shifts are occurring.

This increase in the pace and nature of change gives rise to two phenomena. Firstly, as incremental and discontinuous changes overlap, the intensity and complexity of change generates significant ambiguity as organizations' efforts to respond begin to overlap one another. One change effort overlaps itself on another leaving it difficult to decipher current and future states, with the result that present and future states become blurred. Secondly, the efficacy of classic incremental change strategies and approaches is significantly reduced. By the time the strategies are being implemented, the original problem has changed and new and significantly different challenges have emerged. Approaches to strategy often assume that incremental change approaches will suffice, but in a world where the 'goalposts' of the present and future are in continuous flux these assumptions are increasingly flawed. McCaskey (1988: 2) captures this dilemma:

I was thinking of installing one of those automatic garage door openers over the weekend. The directions say, 'make certain the garage door is square and straight and that the garage floor is level'. Directions always read like that. Is everything in your house straight, square and level? If my house was straight, square and level, I would never have to fix anything. What we all need are directions that tell us what to do when everything is crooked, off-centre and all screwed up.

Managers must act in ambiguous situations. Again, McCaskey (1988: 2) captures the situation they face:

Managers do not enjoy many greenfield problems, where the site is flat and clear. More often they face a mess with a significant history, entangled in past mistakes and cover-ups, confounded by power struggles, questionable motives and conflicting agenda.

Managers face 'messy' situations, and this chapter attempts to illustrate the difficulties in forming and implementing a durable strategy in a rapidly shifting environment. We shall use the case study of a medium-sized electronics company to demonstrate how a manufacturer shifted its strategy only to find that the pace of change had rendered the intervention ineffective. We shall then describe a framework for examining the apparently contradictory, or at least confusing, pulls on a manufacturing organization and suggest a process for continuous evaluation and evolution of strategy in this context. The second author was production director of the electronics company, 'Extronics', in the time period in which the case is set.

We propose that at the core of this case is an organization grappling not with a problem to solve but rather with a paradox to manage. This chapter contends that at the core of strategy formulation and implementation in 'messy situations' is the mindset of its leaders. Through this case the writers hope to portray a 'conventional' mindset and go on to outline a polarity approach that may be critical to managing change and strategy implementation.

The Company: Extronics

The sequence of changes over a period of two years in the company is explained below.

Stage 1: The context

Extronics began life as the Irish manufacturing subsidiary of a multinational. It supplied the parent with electronic subassemblies. The main distinguishing characteristic at this stage was the stability of work from the parent. Wheelwright (1984) introduces the concept of dominant orientation. Some companies are clearly market oriented. They consider their primary expertise to be the ability to understand and respond effectively to the needs of a particular market or consumer group. Another group of firms ('steel companies' or 'oil companies') are clearly oriented to materials or products, and a further group (electronics companies) are technologically oriented. The important point is that companies often experience considerable trauma when they venture outside their dominant orientation.

In its earlier existence, Extronics had a dominant process orientation and a distinctive competence in the manufacture of electronic subassemblies for its parent, its sole customer. During the late 1980s, the parent embarked upon a phased process of withdrawal, and Extronics began to substitute work for the parent with subcontract work for other multinationals (manufacturing printed circuit boards).

Stage 2: The drive for diversification

As the date for final withdrawal neared, a decision was taken to move into total product manufacture to offset the dependence on erratic subcontract business. Subsequently there was an addition of further products and customers, with Extronics becoming the manufacturing arm for a number of marketing and design companies.

Using the notion of dominant orientation, the company adopted a strategy with a dominant product/market orientation in an attempt to develop as a self-sufficient indigenous Irish business. This shift in dominant orientation to product/market yielded much needed increases in turnover and a diversified business portfolio of new customers and business opportunities. However, the strategic reorientation gave rise to a series of knock-on effects, in particular a proliferation of products and services.

Stage 3: The unintended consequences of change

The effect of this product and service proliferation was a significant increase in overhead to handle the complexity it brought. The addition of new products and customers demanded a plethora of additional skills. As a result, Extronics was obliged to offer services for which it had not developed a distinctive competence. The product proliferation gave rise to complexity, and service departments expanded in terms of size and function to keep pace with the increasing scope of the business. Engineering and materials fragmented to support the growth in both customer function and alternative technologies, while finance and marketing departments grew as customer groups expanded.

In the rush to expand, Extronics had moved before its distinctive competences were developed to support it, and, as it diversified, the original process focus of its earlier days became diffused. During this period Extronics gave little or no attention to criteria for accepting or rejecting orders – growth being its primary motivating factor. Whether a business was high or low volume, price sensitive or insensitive, Extronics quoted for it, and only after the contract was signed was the impact on manufacturing considered. Cost and quality suffered. Priorities shifted from one day to the next, with the latest project demanding and usually getting most attention. This created a management blindspot that saw growth through product acquisition as an end in itself, without considering the subsequent effects on manufacturing. This resulted in a gradual but significant fragmentation of competitive priorities (see table 4.1).

Table 4.1   Fragmentation of Extronics' competitive priorities

Business	Customer	Dominant competitive priority
Subassembly	Original MNC parent	Dependability and quality
Subassembly	Other MNCs	Dependability and quality
Subassembly	Company A	Price and volume flexibility
Subassembly	Company B	Product flexibility, quality
Subassembly	Company C	Volume and product flexibility
Total product	Company D	Product flexibility, quality
Total product	Company E	Cost, volume, flexibility, quality

Extronics had developed a syndrome of 'success breeding failure' – success in acquiring new business coupled with failure to deal effectively with these business additions. It was losing money. Added to this, significant capital was required to cope with the requirements of new technologies. Eventually, a management buy-out was effected in 1990, backed by a number of financial institutions. Extronics moved to a new, enlarged premises.

The cumulative effect of this change, following a decade of relative calm, left the organization bruised and shell-shocked. In order to satisfy the financial investors' demands, further products were acquired in an attempt to increase turnover, to support the increasing overhead and to achieve breakeven. The phenomenon identified as 'creeping breakeven' (Hayes and Wheelwright, 1984) eventually set in, and the rationalization programme that was put in place during 1991 involved laying off 100 employees from a workforce of just over 300.

Stage 4:   The need to address complexity

By mid-1991 a fall-off in business coupled with spiralling costs led to a total re-evaluation of the company's resources and mission. It reconfigured the organization to emphasize a 'process' orientation to balance the original 'product market' orientation (Kaplan and Murdoch, 1991). The company focused on a reduction of lead times (with a subsequent reduction in stock levels), quality improvement (thereby reducing rework) and cost containment (spending controls). Accepting too many contracts had ironically brought about a drop in business activity because of quality and lead-time problems. Despite these problems, the management team agreed to modify its pursuit of new business to enable the company to implement improvements to its manufacturing system. The net effect of the interventions (too detailed to describe here) was that effectiveness and efficiency improved greatly.

In the second half of 1991, a 54 per cent reduction in faults was reported, and, in the same period, test yields improved from 70 per cent to over 90 per cent. Between 1990 and 1991 overheads reduced by almost 20 per cent, manufacturing lead times were reduced from 18 days to 8 days, and inventory levels dropped by 28 per cent.

Stage 5: The intervention revisited

Despite the improvements in operating performance, a number of problems remained. The environment continued to be erratic due to the recession. The nature of the customer base (five-year contracts typically lasting 12–18 months!) gave rise to a sharp decline in core business shortly after the intervention, and the company was forced to seek new contracts to fill the gap. The pendulum was swinging back towards the original product market orientation. The number of competitors increased dramatically in the year after the intervention, causing downward pressure on pricing for contracts, which had the effect of requiring a manufacturing process that was both finely tuned and cost effective. If Extronics was to survive, the issue was no longer one of dominant orientation in either process or product market but a *combination of both*. The problem had been reframed.

A Framework for Extronics: An Early Approach to Managing 'Messy' Situations

Pascale (1990) proposes that to deal with dramatic change in an organization's internal and external environment, a transformation in the managerial mindset or paradigm is required. He proposes that we have traditionally treated trade-offs as irreconcilable dilemmas. He suggests instead that all of these paradoxical qualities be viewed as a whole, powering the engine of an enquiry-generating system. Properly channelled they fuel enough pain to stimulate change and adaptation. Yet to harness this fuel requires a different mindset – a shift in paradigm. He uses Hegel's dialectic to illustrate the point. Hegel's central idea is that one entity (thesis) when juxtaposed with its opposite (antithesis) can generate a new configuration that both includes and transcends the two foundational elements (synthesis). This notion suggests a means of resolving problems beyond the old simplistic mindset of right and wrong. Consistent with this mindset Extronics could have considered the apparent polar opposites of process and product market orientation not as opposite ends of a continuum, but as nodes of elliptical orbits – a phenomenon that never comes to rest, like particles around a nucleus.

The initial positive results of the intervention described earlier led the management team to conclude, with some justification, that they had chosen well. Looked at from the old mindset, such a conclusion is valid. But there is a weakness. While an organizational mindset with an emphasis on right and wrong did improve organizational effectiveness in the short term, in the longer term it left the organization very vulnerable to environmental change.

McCaskey (1988) describes a framework for dealing with such 'messy' situations. The characteristics of such situations, three of which were present in the Extronics case, are defined as follows:

1. The problem is – what is the problem?
2. Different value orientations lead to political and emotional clashes.

3. Contradictions and paradoxes begin to appear.

He identifies a set of managerial attitudes and skills for coping with situations that contain paradoxes. He also identifies a framework for channelling these skills towards dealing with situations posing conflicting demands and he refers to this framework as 'dialectical reasoning'. The concept of dialectical reasoning is explained by McCaskey (1988: 12–14) in the following way.

The development of an action plan is normally thought of as occurring in a linear sequence:

$$Assumptions \rightarrow Data \rightarrow Plan$$

Assumptions and prior expectations lead managers to recognize certain data to be important. These data are related to each other in a plan. In reality, a plan can be more accurately described as a circle of related elements. Typically, someone in the management group begins to explain a particular situation, pointing out its significant features. Embedded in those data are assumptions. Alternatively, the situation is described so that the data are reviewed with an eye towards a favoured plan. Once a plan is formulated, the search begins among the plentiful array of assumptions that each of us holds for those that give logical closure. The elements lock tight to reinforce each other in an A–D–P circle, as shown:

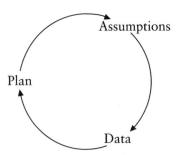

The framework was put to work in Extronics with three groups in the management team being selected for a specific function in solving a particular problem. The first group developed a plan for solving the problem. They elaborated on their assumptions, the data they used, and their proposed plan of action. They then compiled a short list of the key assumptions underlying the plan. The second group received this list of key assumptions from group 1. This group was then responsible for developing a counter-plan or antithesis to the first plan. Group 2 took each assumption and if possible invented a plausible counter-assumption. The group searched beyond surface appearances and was even suspicious of the intuitively obvious. Group 2 used its counter-assumptions to surface new data about the problem, or to interpret the old data in a fresh way. Combining counter-assumptions and new data, the group formulated a new plan. The managing director was part of the third group. Groups 1 and 2 made vigorous presentations of their plans to the third group, outlining the data they considered important and the assumptions on which their plans rested. Each group probed the weaknesses of the other groups' plans, generating a good deal of constructive tension. It was important for group 3 to remain alert for assumptions that were not on the lists of the other teams but which might be central to conceptualizing the problem. Through this iterative process, all the assumptions that figured prominently were pooled. Led by group 3, everyone examined the list and weeded out those assumptions that were, by agreement, unrealistic. This kind of process can be viewed as constructive conflict. The Extronics management team became more confident as they developed the discipline of looking at problems in this way and saw their efforts producing successful results. This dialectical process renders maps more visible to a manager and thus more amenable to revision and improvement.

Polarity Management

The Extronics case demonstrates the need for devising and formulating frameworks in the area of strategy formation and implementation that confront the issue of how managers can transcend the treadmill of chasing environmental and organizational change in what can often appear to be a zero-sum game. How can we make sense of situations in which a solution to one problem gives rise to a set of unintended consequences which, in turn, requires a response? This very response can itself give rise to a further set of unintended consequences. The result is that strategy formation lurches from solution to solution, often doubling back on itself over time.

Johnson (1992) grapples with these issues. He contends that at the core of the issue is our perspective on dealing with difficulties. When confronted with difficulties we invariably identify them as problems and proceed to attempt to solve them. However, as in the case of Extronics in 'messy' situations, we are often deep in the solution mode when the unintended consequences of our 'solution' forces us back to look at the problem again. As McCaskey succinctly states in observing messy situations: The problem is – what is the problem?

In the case of Extronics, the shift from the dominant product-market focus to the process focus is a good example. While providing initial relief from the original set of difficulties the 'solution' masked another set of problems (see figure 4.1).

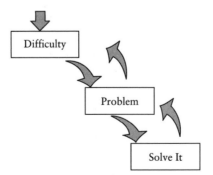

Figure 4.1   The 'classic' approach to dealing with difficulties (adapted from Johnson 1992)

Johnson asserts that we should take a further step back and look at the nature of the difficulty itself. He proposes another typology of difficulty-mutually interdependent opposites or polarities, that is, solutions that are apparently contradictory but need to be addressed concurrently. In order to clarify this definition let us juxtapose the attributes of problems and polarities in table 4.2.

Because of the fundamental differences between problems and polarities, applying problem-solving skills to polarities that should be *managed* gives rise to the pendulum or lurching effect in strategy formation, as in Extronics. The issue with Extronics was not *either* product market focus *or* process focus, which had been the managerial mindset, but rather how to attain product-market *and* process focus simultaneously. It is this challenge that is at the heart of strategy formation in messy situations, and it is this issue that polarity management attempts to address (see figure 4.2).

Polarities thus challenge and change the fundamental paradigm of problem solving from 'either-or' to 'and'. While this issue is discussed widely in the literature on leadership, it is also fundamental to strategy formation and implementation for discontinuous and complex change. Because our mental lenses are trained to see all difficulties as problems we continue to attempt to solve a problem which, in fact, is a polarity that requires managing. We shall now discuss how this error of judgement might be corrected.

Table 4.2 A typology of difficulties and their attributes (adapted from Johnson 1992)

Difficulties

Attributes of problems	*Attributes of polarities*
• Have a defined solution	• Are insoluble but can be managed
• Resolve a set of *independent* alternatives	• Represent a set of *interdependent* alternatives
• Are time bounded	• Are ongoing
• Can stand alone	• Cannot stand alone
• There is no need to include an alternative to work	• The alternatives need each other to optimize the situation over time
• Often contain mutually exclusive opposites	• Always contain mutually inclusive opposites
Examples	*Examples*
• Should we promote Bill?	• Reduce cost *and* improve quality
• What should we include in our customer survey?	• Centralized co-ordination *and* decentralized initiatives
• Should we buy the 200-ton press?	• Stability *and* change
• Should we upgrade the system?	• Recognize the individual *and* recognize the team
• Should we remove one level of management?	• Taking care of the customer (product-market focus) *and* taking care of the organization (process focus)

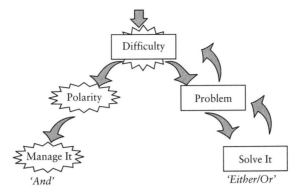

Figure 4.2   The hidden side of messy situations – polarities (adapted from Johnson 1992)

The application of polarity management

Understanding the necessity of distinguishing between problems to be solved and polarities to be managed maybe fundamental to strategy formation, but it remains a conceptual construct. The acid test of the usefulness of a framework or construct is the extent to which it enables us to describe such situations and tells us how to handle them. A technique suggested by Johnson (1992) for disentangling such 'messy' situations is 'polarity mapping'. In this section we shall apply the technique in retrospect to the Extronics case study and describe the steps involved in con-structing a polarity map, showing how it can facilitate strategy formation–implementation in 'messy' situations.

Polarity mapping allows us to disassemble a set of contending opposites (polar-ities) and look at their dynamics so that we can better manage them concurrently. It begins with identifying the difficulty to be addressed and deciding whether it is a problem to solve or a polarity to be managed. This is done by applying the criteria shown in table 4.3.

Having identified the polarity (in Extronics, achieving both product-market and process focus) we begin to build the map itself. The map consists of a number of components which allow us to identify the real goal of strategy formation in messy or polarized situations. This is, to manage *both upsides*. Polarity mapping when used with a management team during a strategy formation process can allow them to see clearly the difficulty to be addressed and to identify the potential threats or down-sides to a series of opposite but interdependent strategies. The final stage is mapping the dynamics of the polarity.

This final map shows the 'normal flow' of a polarity (Johnson, 1992). Figure 4.3 describes the predicament of Extronics as outlined in the case study. Initially Extronics experienced the upside of working for a single parent company, essentially a process focus. However, over time a series of unintended consequences or down-sides emerged – in particular, too narrow a business scope to have long-term viability with the parent. These downsides drove Extronics to pursue the upsides of a product-market focus as it attempted to minimize its dependency on its parent and

Table 4.3 Components of a polarity map

Higher purpose

What can we achieve for managing the upsides of Poles 1 and 2 concurrently; for example, *competitive advantage* through structured flexibility

Pole 1	Pole 2
This is one side of the polarity to be managed; for example, achieving *product-market focus*	This is the other side of the polarity to be managed; for example, achieving *process focus*

Upside of Pole 1	*Upside of Pole 2*
This quadrant describes the benefits of achieving the goal; for example, for *product-market focus* this may be, increased turnover, improved customer satisfaction and retention, greater growth potential	This quadrant describes the benefits of achieving the goal; for example, for *process focus* this may be reduced inventories, increased efficiency, improved delivery on time and quality, reduced costs

Downside of Pole 1	*Downside of Pole 2*
This quadrant describes the potential negative consequences of achieving this goal; for example, spiralling costs due to the complexity of many customers, creeping breakeven, inefficient processes	This quadrant describes the potential negative consequences of achieving this goal; for example, inflexible processes, unresponsive business, overdependency on fewer customers

Deeper fear
Inefficient processes coupled with creeping breakeven

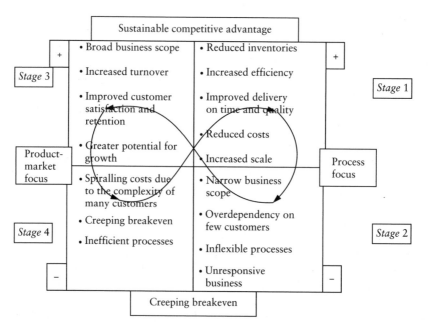

Figure 4.3 The 'normal flow' of a polarity applied to Extronics

improve its long-term viability. Having made the transition to a product-market focus, Extronics briefly experienced the upside of increased turnover, but this was rapidly followed by the downsides of this pole, specifically spiralling costs and complexity as it developed its customer portfolio. In an attempt to address this problem it once more moved back towards a process focus in an attempt to regain the upside of the process pole. The results it enjoyed temporarily were outlined above. The case ends with Extronics beginning to experience the downsides of the process focus pole.

Summary

This, then, is a classic example of strategy formation caught in the horns of a dilemma. Indeed, this story is resonant of many of the problems experienced in both strategy formation and implementation. Whether it be centralization and decentralization, or team focus and individual focus, or growth and consolidation, all too often strategy implementation seems to move first in one direction, then the other, only to arrive back at its original position.

What is interesting about the normal flow, as described, is that it follows an infinity loop, doubling back on itself over time. It is only when we reframe the difficulty of using a technique such as polarity management that we can be more deliberate about strategy implementation in messy situations. As we move into the next millennium the intensity and complexity of change will no doubt increasingly surface many such polarities. Polarities require managing, and we believe that the techniques and skills associated with this conception of strategy formation–implementation will be critical in helping managers deal with ambiguity and enable them implement strategies by managing polarities.

Conclusions

Many leaders and managers already know and practise the principles of polarity management intuitively. The intention of this chapter is to argue for making this process more explicit and deliberate, so that this capability can be shared with more managers and leaders. It works.

The Extronics case illustrates the point made by Weick (1969) that when we analyse an organization we do so at a point in time. What in fact we are looking at is a portion of a process of organizing. This can be likened to taking a photograph of a moving object. It gives us a picture of the object at a point in time but does not capture the action of movement itself. Polarity management offers users a glimpse of the process of organizing over time and thus makes strategy formation and implementation in challenging and very often messy circumstances a more deliberate and understandable process. As we approach the millennium with the rate of change continually increasing, this case illustrates that by the time managers understand their strategy and its fit or lack of fit with the environment, the environment may have 'shifted its goal posts'. The trick appears to be, like a surfer, to ride one wave and have the flexibility and confidence to move on to another before the first one breaks.

Polarity management is a technique for developing continuous renewal of the strategic effort to deal with a complex and turbulent environment. It aims to offer a framework for developing one's own place and one's own unique perspective. However, considerable work needs to be done to develop it fully in any organization facing 'messy' change – and especially to develop the skills of the management team selected to undertake such a process.

References

Hayes, R. and Wheelwright, S. 1984: *Restoring our competitive edge*. New York: Wiley.

Johnson, B. 1992: *Polarity management: identifying and managing unsolvable problems*. Human Resource Development Press.

Kaplan, R. and Murdoch, L. 1991: Core process redesign. *McKinsey Quarterly*, 2.

McCaskey, M.B. 1988: The challenge of managing ambiguity and change. In L.R. Pondy, R.J. Boland and H. Thomas (eds) *Managing ambiguity and change*. New York: Wiley.

Pascale, R.T. 1990: *Managing on the edge*. London: Viking Penguin.

Pondy, L.R., Boland, R.J. and Thomas, H. 1988: *Managing ambiguity and change*. New York: Wiley.

Weick, K.E. 1969: *The social psychology of organising*. Reading, MA: Addison-Wesley.

Wheelwright, S.C. 1984: Manufacturing strategy: defining the missing link. *Strategic Management Journal*, 5, 77–91.

Part 2

Behavioural Barriers and Problems in Strategy Implementation

5. The Emotional World of Strategy Implementation
   David O'Donnell

6. Change Management and Stress
   Carol Borrill and Sharon Parker

7. Strategy Implementation in Public Sector Organizations
   David McKevitt

8. Leading and Managing the Uncertainty of Strategic Change
   Jean Hartley

5

The Emotional World of Strategy Implementation

DAVID O'DONNELL

*The less a person understands his own feelings, the
more he will fall prey to them.
Howard Gardner (1993: 255)*

Introduction

The experiences of both life and work are obviously saturated with emotion or
'emotionality' (Ashforth and Humphrey, 1995; Fineman, 1993), with important
issues, and major change initiatives in particular, being typically 'emotionally
laden' (Beer and Eisenstat, 1996). These emotional reactions, however, are too
often ignored or thought to be unscientific as they do not fit the logical or rational
form of many approaches to social reality or the research methods on which they are
based. Tom Peters (1996) notes that emotion receives 'short shrift' in most business
writing but that it receives 'long shrift' in the most successful companies. Borrowing
a metaphor from Gestalt therapy, we argue here that 'unfinished business' (Perls et
al., 1951), which basically refers to the blocking, repression or denial of emotions, is
detrimental to both strategy implementation processes and to implementing middle
managers in particular. All contributors to this section attempt to move beyond the
one-sidedness inherent in all overly rationalist models of management highlighted by
Paul Sparrow in chapter 1 of this book.

Whatever the strategy type – traditional top-down or emergent bottom-up –
reformulating and implementing organizational strategy in the context of continuous organizational realignment, learning and change presents an awesome managerial prospect. It requires a delicate balance to be struck between individual
and collective action, and necessitates managing both the content and process of
strategic change whatever the contextual setting, climate or culture (Argyris, 1992;
Beer and Eisenstat, 1996; Kanter et al., 1992; Pettigrew, 1987; Stace and Dunphy,

1996). In a turbulent era, it is little wonder that frustration appears to be the central emotion in the middle manager's – or strategy implementer's – working life. The key argument introduced here, and developed in the following chapters, is that considerations of both *emotionality* and rationality are central to implementing such processes successfully. This key argument can be summed up in the following two hypotheses.

1. Considerations of both emotionality and rationality are central to effectively managing strategy implementation processes.
2. Acknowledging, planning for, and managing emotionality issues will result in weak strategy implementation situations becoming stronger, and thus potentially more effective and successful.

The people involved in the strategic psychodrama within the organization are the strategists, implementers and recipients (Kanter et al., 1992). An approach from social psychology recognizes that it is people who are the causal agency and not the organization as an 'overperson' (Katz, 1986). People *think*, *feel* and *do* in time, place and space. Rationality, emotionality, actions and particular strategy implementation situations are interlinked. This emotional world, which is too often neglected in the 'overrationalized' (Morgan, 1986) conception of organizational life, is almost certainly the primary source of the 'defensive routines' identified by Chris Argyris (1992) as the most important causes of failure in strategy implementation. Any change process requires new learning, and defensive routines, at any level, are anti-learning. Defensive routines require attention at the emotional level and purely rational approaches to overcoming them will, in most cases, fail. In this brief and pragmatic introductory chapter to this section of the book, the concept of emotionality is considered in fairly broad terms and I emphasize its power. I then provide some broad indicators of how aspects of emotionality can be linked at the organizational level to different approaches to business strategy. I conclude that considerations of emotionality are central to managing successfully the process of implementing strategic change.

The Power of Emotionality

Ashforth and Humphrey (1995) define emotionality in fairly broad, inclusive and pragmatic terms as simply a subjective feeling state which includes the basic emotions (such as joy, love, anger, fear), social emotions (such as shame, guilt, jealousy), as well as such related constructs as affect, sentiment and mood. Such feeling states vary widely in terms of their intensity, duration, consistency, valence and motivating force. Almost thirty years ago Paul McClean coined the term 'The Triune Brain' to emphasize the main divisions in our most important human resource (Giles, 1994).

The 'first brain' controls the very basic instinctive responses such as 'fight or flight'. The 'second brain' or limbic system controls the emotions and can be visualized as the main home of emotionality; it is linked to the 'third brain' in complex ways. The 'third brain', or neo-cortex, controls intellectual processing and can be visualized as the main home of rationality. At a basic level, the connections between our second and third brains link emotionality to rationality, thus demonstrating that both learning and change have an emotional dimension. Strategy implementation is about the institutionalization of change processes and all change requires new learning, often of an initially emotionally distressing or threatening nature. Defensive routines (Argyris, 1992) and aspects of 'unfinished business' (Perls et al., 1951) can be visualized here as mainly second-brain phenomena and cannot therefore be overcome using a purely rational or third-brain approach. These must be surfaced, felt, faced, acknowledged, accepted and discussed as a prerequisite to overcoming them and changing them. Block uses the concept 'ego resilience' rather than 'emotional intelligence', but notes that its main components include emotional self-regulation, an adaptive impulse control, a sense of self-efficacy, and social intelligence (Goleman, 1995). From a longitudinal analysis, Block finds a modest correlation between IQ and ego resilience, but the two are independent constructs. Rationality and emotionality are distinct yet interpenetrate and complement each other.

The behaviourist psychological paradigm, which in many ways paralleled the bureaucratic-control paradigm in mass production which sought to eliminate emotion from the work equation, has dominated psychology and, to a significant extent, management training for a large part of this century. Hierarchy, bureaucracy and traditional methods of management are, however, now undergoing major change (Flood et al., 1995). Structural changes, owing to the changing nature of economic forces, have thus allowed emotionality to 'come back in' to the work equation. Managerial competence, in this sense, has interlinked dimensions of both rationality and emotionality heralding a shift from directive to more consultative and persuasive management styles. As Stephen Carroll points out in chapter 2, this requires a much greater emphasis on, and awareness of, emotionality than previously. After years in controlling hierarchical and systems-driven organizations with perhaps little experience of spontaneous frontline initiative and entrepreneurship, many managers may lack the basis on which to make the type of emotional commitment that the emerging decentralized and individualized organization requires (Ghoshal and Bartlett, 1998). Implementation is about the institutionalization of change, and any change process may cause positive (joy, release, satisfaction, accomplishment) or negative (fear, threat, anger, resentment, anxiety, frustration) aspects of emotionality to surface. Change is a complex psychosocial drama in which the personalities of the individuals involved, the roles they play, the situation where interpersonal interactions occur, and the prevailing political climate crucially affect both the nature and the form of the implementation process. Paying attention to the emotional aspects of this profoundly complex process is critical to implementing sound strategy.

Alan Church (1997), using data based on the multirater or 360-degree feedback system, provides evidence to support the growing belief that enhanced managerial self-awareness leads to improved performance. Church's results consistently indicated that high-performance managers were able to assess more accurately their own behaviours in the workplace and were more self-aware than average-performing managers. Learning the softer and more experiential skills of emotional awareness, however, is probably much tougher than learning the cognitive skills of rational analysis which tend to dominate most management development programmes. Dealing with 'unfinished business' as an aspect of critical reflection may be particularly difficult, threatening, uncomfortable and anxiety provoking. Instead of allowing themselves to fully experience feelings which accompany traumatic events – for example, massive layoffs during a downsizing with its resultant anger, resentment and tensions, or a change in role from a strongly directive middle manager to a more consultative and facilitative team leader – individuals with unfinished business inhibit them, and are often unwilling to acknowledge and experience the pain, anxiety and frustration they feel, and move forward (see chapter 6 on Stress by Carol Borrill and Sharon Parker; and Kets de Vries and Balazs, 1997). During traumatic, directive and sometimes coercive turnarounds, implementers may experience self-criticism, blame, guilt, judgements related to self and others, resentments, anger and countless tensions which can affect not only their work lives, health and general effectiveness but can overspill into their family and social lives.

The characteristics and roles of strategists, implementers and recipients, and situational forces interpenetrate in very complex ways to affect organizational performance substantially. From an interactionist perspective, actions may be viewed as a function of both internal (character, personality) and external (situation, environment) factors. Different kinds of behaviour may be expected from different people in different situations. Mischel (1977) classifies situations as either 'strong' or 'weak' and argues that the nature of the situation helps to predict the relative prepotency of the contributions of internal and external factors to behaviour (Waldersee and Sheather, 1996). Strong situations are characterized by a high degree of certainty, clear guidelines, historical norms or generally accepted patterns of behaviour. Weak situations, however, are characterized by a much greater degree of uncertainty where no such clear guidelines exist. In strong situations emotionality may play a relatively small role as these lead people to construe events in similar ways, produce uniform expectations for role performance and incentive patterns, and provide the requisite skills. Weak situations, however, are not interpreted or construed in similar ways, do not provide uniform expectations about performance and incentives, and may not provide the requisite skills. In weak situations, individual differences related to emotionality and other aspects of personality can be expected to exert a greater and perhaps more unpredictable influence on behaviour.

This begs the question: Are strategy implementation situations strong or weak? Strategy implementation has at least some of the elements of a strong situation in that there is usually some degree of uniformity in the way some changes are encoded and therefore in the perception of the appropriateness of different implementation actions (Waldersee and Sheather, 1996). This can refer to hard rational aspects such as a new organizational structure, new performance or financial targets, or a decision to enter a new market segment. From this perspective strategies carry strong implementation imperatives. However, the fact that most of the weakness in the strategy field seems to be attributable to strategy implementation rather than formulation leads us to suggest that most implementation situations are relatively weak and that part of the reason for this 'weakness' may lie in the pervasive neglect of emotionality. Were such implementation situations to be predictably strong, then we would expect much greater congruence between intended strategy formulation, implementation and realized strategy than recent business history and the relevant literature would suggest. The core argument presented here is that paying more attention to emotionality will result in weak strategy implementation situations becoming stronger, and thus potentially more effective and successful.

Mapping the Emotional World

Stace and Dunphy (1996) suggest that change strategies are best chosen for their 'situational specificity' and their linkage with the business strategy, rather than their universal appeal. Implementation must be part of a change programme's earliest formulation as strategists must pay attention to all the constituents that are to be sold on change, and not just to what should be changed (Kanter et al., 1992). I believe that an understanding of emotionality as it relates to all stakeholders is central not only to good strategy formulation and pragmatic crafting of the implementer's role by the key strategists, but is probably one of the most critical determinants in successfully implementing an intended strategy or facilitating an emergent strategy. Beer and Eisenstat (1996) suggest three broad principles that should characterize change processes if they are to result in effective strategy implementation.

1. First, the change process should be systemic. As organizations are complex and highly interdependent open systems, unidimensional interventions will usually fail. The soft elements of people, leaders and values and the harder elements of strategy, structure and technology must be appropriately aligned. The change process must 'focus on both strategy and organization, structure and behaviour, analysis and emotion, internal organizational arrangements and the context in which the organization operates'.

2. Second, the change process should encourage the open discussion of barriers to effective strategy implementation and adaptation. This principle is crucial to our discussion here. People cannot develop realistic and implementable plans for change unless all impediments are taken into account – issues which are normally hidden because they are threatening or embarrassing, such as related to internal politics and defensive routines, must be surfaced and dealt with. This is, however, very frequently ignored in practice for often very emotional reasons. Argyris (1992) proposes four fundamental rules within the 'master programmes' that people use to avoid dealing with embarrass-ment or threat: (1) bypass embarrassment or threat whenever possible; (2) act as if you are not bypassing them; (3) don't discuss the first two while they are happening; and (4) don't discuss the undiscussability of the undiscussable! Overcoming these master programmes is no easy task.

3. The third principle is that the change process should, where possible, develop a partnership among all relevant stakeholders.

These principles, despite their plausibility and existing research support, are rarely reflected in actual intervention practice (Beer and Eisenstat, 1996) and I argue

Table 5.1 Typology of change strategies

	Incremental change strategies	Transformative change strategies
Collaborative/ consultative mode	**Participative evolution** Use when organization is in fit but needs minor adjustment, or is out of fit but time is available and key interest groups favour change	**Charismatic change strategies** Use when organization is out of fit, there is little time for extensive participation but there is support for radical change within the organization
	Positive emotionality	*Positive emotionality*
Directive/ coercive mode	**Forced evolution** Use when organization is in fit but needs minor adjustment, or is out of fit but time is available, but key interest groups oppose change	**Dictatorial transformation** Use when organization is out of fit, there is no time for extensive participation and no support within the organization for radical change, but radical change is vital to organizational survival and fulfilment of basic mission
	Somewhat negative emotionality	*Strongly negative emotionality*

Source: Adapted from Stace and Dunphy (1996).

strongly here that inadequate attention to emotionality may well be part of the answer. Estimating the costs and risks of different tactics for dealing with organized or structural resistance and passive or covert resistance, motivating, persuading and negotiating situational definitions are all emotionally highly demanding managerial activities. All strategy implementation must, in turn, eventually result in change at the level of the individual employee, the main strategy recipient. Employees are too often cited merely as sources of resistance but we argue that it is vital that implementers understand how employees perceive and experience the change and that this is considered by strategists when crafting the implementer's role.

It is difficult to speak about a universal model of change as the context, business strategy, type of change and ideological or societal approach differs. Stace and Dunphy's (1996) typology is used here (table 5.1) to demonstrate that the scale of change (incremental or transformative) and change management style (collaborative, consultative, directive, coercive) emphasize quite different emotional worlds of strategy implementation. Strategies and tactics related to different emotional worlds can therefore be identified and planned for, and relevant training and development undertaken which can complement the usual emphasis placed on the hard rational financial and operational aspects of the implementation process.

At one end, we can observe the empowering, communicative and affectionate world of a developmental transition with a 'participative evolution' change strategy where Beer and Eisenstat's third principle of partnership between strategists, implementers, recipients and, perhaps, trade union representatives (see chapter 15), should definitely be possible. At the other end, we can almost sense and feel the mud, blood, conflict, slaughter, frustration and fear of more turbulent shareholder-led re-engineering, cost-cutting and downsizing turnarounds using a 'dictatorial trans-formation' change strategy. This model illustrates that useful guidelines and baseline maps can be constructed within which to place the emotional world in relation to specific business strategies and change strategies at the organizational level. These, in turn, have decisive impacts for emotionality at the level of the implementer and the employee. The interactional interplay between the affective–emotional dimen-sion of personality, the role of the implementer, and situational factors can be carefully thought through and planned for as they would be expected to occur in specific strategy implementation contexts. It is, therefore, possible to map and identify in broad terms how linkages between business strategies, changes in busi-ness strategies, type of change process (participative evolution; charismatic transfor-mation; forced evolution; dictatorial transformation), scale of change (incremental, transformative), and style of change management (collaborative, consultative, direct-ive, coercive) can be related to emotionality. In this way strategists and implementers can plan for the management of different emotional worlds and in the process make weak strategy implementation situations stronger.

Box 5.1   Common-sense principles for strategy implementers, middle managers

- Don't crucify yourself on the cross of perfection. Expect to be criticized, to make mistakes, to feel dissatisfied, frustrated and disappointed at times. Any manager who expects to please himself or herself as well as strategists and recipients 100 per cent of the time is guaranteed at least an ulcer!
- Communicate the object of the change strategy, the criteria governing success, and the needs identified as important.
- Involve people wherever and whenever possible.
- Be flexible and adaptable – there is no one best way. No textbook model or consultant's blueprint has any universally innate validity.
- Ground your workshops, training and counselling exercises on real-life issues and real life emotional concerns.
- Be your own methodologist – don't be afraid to do it yourself and follow your own gut instincts. Give your heart its head occasionally. Follow your second brain!
- Finally, and most importantly, give yourself a break every now and then.

Source: Broadly following Brookfield (1986)

Conclusion

Throughout, the complementarity and interpenetration of rationality and emotion-ality have been emphasized. At a basic individual level, it is unwise to ignore these aspects of the emotional world; to do so at an organizational level at a time of turbulent strategic change may be a recipe for almost certain failure. Rather than viewing emotion as the 'dysfunctional antithesis of rationality' we endorse both Ashforth and Humphrey's (1995) argument that researchers and management practitioners need to recognize the 'functional complementarity of emotionality and rationality' and Paul Sparrow's pragmatic recognition (see chapter 1) that managers may need training in emotional management. In particular, we argue that the emotional world of strategy implementation should be given *long shrift*. This attention to situational emotionality is, I believe, critical. Following Brookfield's (1986) ideas (see box 5.1), I stress that group workshops for professional development must be built around the real life problems and frustrations that implementers face; they must be built around specific emotional worlds. In such workshops managers can engage in a collaborative analysis and exploration of experiences (see Dromgoole and Gorman on 'action learning', chapter 14). Methods can include discussion, T-group work, role play, simulation, and small group analysis of case studies. Ethical dilemmas can be explored with peers in a confidential and safe setting. Defensive routines can be surfaced, acknowledged and worked on thus increasing managerial self-awareness. The following chapters in this section of the book develop this argument further. If, as Chris Argyris argues, defensive routines are the primary source of failure in implementing sound strategy, then the emotional world of strategy implementation must be taken seriously for both very personal and very economic reasons. I conclude that defensive routines and unfinished business are basically bad for business in general and for strategy implementation and implementing middle managers in particular.

References

Argyris, C. 1992: *On organizational learning*. Oxford: Blackwell.

Ashforth, B.E. and Humphrey, R.H. 1995: Emotion in the workplace: a reappraisal. *Human Relations*, 48(2), 97–126.

Beer, M. and Eisenstat, R.A. 1996: Developing an organisation capable of implementing strategy and learning. *Human Relations*, 49(5), 597–619.

Bennis, W. 1996: A conversation with Warren Bennis: on leadership in the midst of downsizing, by Richard M. Hodgetts. *Organizational Dynamics*, Summer, 72–8.

Brookfield, S.D. 1986: *Understanding and facilitating adult learning*. Milton Keynes: Open University Press.

Church, A.H. 1997: Managerial self-awareness in high-performing individuals in organizations. *Journal of Applied Psychology*, 82(2), 281–92.

Flood, P.C., Gannon, M.J. and Paauwe, J. 1995: *Managing without traditional methods*. Wokingham and Reading, MA: Addison-Wesley.

Gardner, H. 1993: *Frames of mind* (2nd edn). New York: Basic Books.

Ghoshal, S. and Bartlett, C.A. 1998: *The individualized corporation*. London: Heinemann.

Giles, J. 1994: Learning how we learn. In J. Prior (ed.) *Gower handbook of training and development*. Aldershot: Gower, pp. 259–73.

Goleman, D. 1995: *Emotional intelligence*. New York: Bantam.

Kanter, R.M., Stein, A. and Jick, T.D. 1992: *The challenge of organizational change*. New York: Free Press.

Katz, D. 1986: The social psychological approach to the study of organizations. *International Review of Applied Psychology*, 35, 17–37.

Mischel, W. 1977: The interaction of person and situation. In D. Magnusson and N.S. Endler (eds) *Personality at the crossroads: current issues in interactional psychology*. Mahwah, NJ: Evelbaum, pp. 333–52.

Morgan, G. 1986: *Images of organization*. Beverly Hills, CA: Sage.

Perls, F., Hefferline, R. and Goodman, P. 1951: *Gestalt therapy*. New York: Julian Press.

Peters, T. 1996: We hold these truths to be self-evident (more or less). *Organizational Dynamics*, Summer, 27–32.

Pettigrew, A.M. 1987: Context and action in the transformation of the firm. *Journal of Management Studies*, 24(6), 649–70.

Stace, D. and Dunphy, D. 1996: Translating business strategies into action: managing strategic change. In D. Hussey (ed.) *The implementation challenge*. Chichester: Wiley 69–86.

Waldersee, R. and Sheather, S. 1996: The effects of strategy type on strategy implementation actions. *Human Relations*, 49(1), 105–22.

6

Change Management and Stress

Carol borrill and Sharon parker

Organizations are increasingly facing difficult and demanding environmental conditions: competitive pressures, deregulation, technological changes, increased legal demands, externally imposed standards, and more differentiated and demanding markets (Salaman, 1995). Responding to these pressures and maintaining competitive advantage requires constant, substantial and wide-ranging change within organizations – for example, changes in strategy, orientation, structure, work organization, management arrangements, work roles and reward systems. These changes can have a substantial impact on the stress levels experienced by people working within organizations – both those implementing the change and those whose working lives are different as a result of the change.

This chapter is divided into two sections. In the first we describe stress, its consequences for organizations and individuals, and its causes. The second section discusses approaches to the management of change that can help to reduce the possibility that employees will experience stress. Finally, we present guidelines for managing change to reduce dysfunctional stress consequences for employees.

The Organizational Demands which Create Stress

The staff employed by an organization are increasingly being considered its biggest asset, particularly in companies which are labour intensive rather than capital intensive. Therefore, how to take care of employees, including the measures required to reduce the possibility that they will experience stress, is an important issue for organizations. At the same time, there is increasing awareness and concern about the extent to which the workplace can cause stress – that is, features of the work environment which create the demands that initiate the stress process. Prominent legal cases, which have resulted in employees receiving compensation for work-related stress (see Howard, 1995), and recent initiatives in the field of health and safety in Europe and elsewhere, have served to raise awareness. In fact, more than 90 per cent of the largest companies in the USA now have stress management programmes (*Business Week*, 1985) as a result of these legal liabilities.

About stress

The term 'stress' refers to an affective state characterized by such features as feelings of strain, depression, inability to cope and anxiety. 'Stress' is also referred to as strain and poor mental health. The absence of stress has variously been described as well-being and mental health. The experience of stress does not come from a single event but arises from a process. The first major aspect of the stress process is an environmental demand on an individual (for example, a tight deadline at work). The second aspect is how an individual perceives the demand. There are considerable individual differences: one person may perceive a tight deadline to be a challenge, but to another it may be a daunting task. The third aspect of the stress process is the response; how an individual behaves (for example, working harder to meet the deadline, or taking avoidance action), what he or she thinks and feels about it, and the physiological responses, increased heart rate, headaches and so on.

The costs of stress at work

The consequences for individuals experiencing dysfunctional stress can be severe not only for them but also for their work, organizations, etc. Individuals who are stressed can experience feelings of strain, anxiety and depression, the behavioural manifestations of which can be irritability, sleeping difficulties, lack of concentration, aggression, reduced attention span and impaired memory, which in turn can affect performance at work. There can also be physical effects such as raised heart rate, gastro-intestinal and skin conditions, headaches, and reduced resistance to infection. The long-term consequences of stress can be more severe mental health problems and physical ill health.

Stress also has considerable organizational consequences; it is one of the top three causes of certified sickness absence, and is the primary cause of reduced productivity and staff turnover. Banham (1992) estimated that the cost to industry of sickness absence, turnover and poor performance at work is £5.3 billion annually. It is estimated that 80 million working days are lost annually as a result of sickness absence arising from anxiety and depression, as well as labour turnover, poor performance and accidents at work. Research by Borrill et al. (1998) carried out in the health service found that those people who were stressed subsequently had significantly higher rates of sickness absence from work and were more likely to leave the organization. In addition, those who reported experiencing stress also reported that they performed their job significantly less effectively than those who were less affected.

There is also research evidence that indicates the benefits that organizations can gain when attention is given to the welfare of staff. Patterson et al. (1997), for example, found that investment in good human resource management practices (selection, training and development, appraisal and work design) predicted the company's future financial performance. This research also shows that there is a relationship between the job satisfaction of staff and company performance; the higher the level of job satisfaction the better the productivity levels and the financial performance of the company two years later. Similar relationships between human resource management and company performance have been reported by Huselid (1995). Thus, on the basis of the research evidence discussed, there is a strong case for organizations taking seriously the issue of how to protect employees from undue stress.

Causes of stress at work

The factors associated with stress in the workplace have been grouped into five main categories relating to the work context (Cartwright and Cooper, 1994): factors intrinsic to the job; role in the organization; relationships at work; career development; and organizational structure and climate. The home–work interface creates a sixth possible factor, and all these factrors are summarized in figure 6.1.

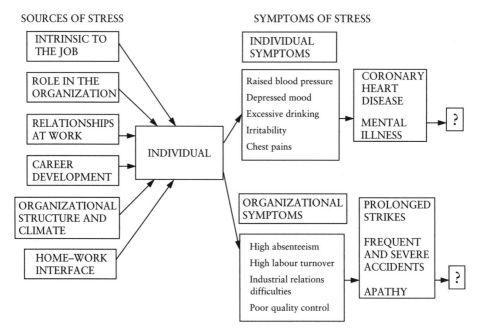

Figure 6.1   The Cooper and Cartwright model of stress factors
Source: Cooper, C. & Cartwright. S (1994)

Factors *intrinsic to the job* include working conditions, long working hours and shifts, work overload or underload, poor job design, risk and danger in the workplace, and new technology. *Role in the organization* refers to both individuals' position/status, and specific work role factors, such as the extent to which they are clear about the tasks and duties they have to perform in their work role, experience conflicting demands, the amount of responsibility they are given, and access to resources. *Relationships at work*, including staff, colleagues and superiors, can cause stress (as a result of interpersonal conflicts), although work relationships can also be an important source of practical and emotional support which buffers individuals against the factors associated with stress. The absence of support and interpersonal contact at work can also cause stress. The *career development* factors associated with stress can vary with the stage in working life; for example, in early career, factors such as unmet expectations, ambiguity, and establishing a clear role identity can be sources of stress. In later career, stress can result from managing the tensions between work and private life commitments and concerns about job security. *Organizational structure and climate* associated with stress include decision-making and communication processes. And last but not least is the *home–work interface*.

The stress consequences of change

Change in organizations comes in many shapes and forms (Hartley, 1996); the focus may be on organizational structure, culture and/or work design. The change may be introduced proactively to meet new challenges or can be a reactive response to new demands and threats; it may potentially affect a small part of the organization or be organization wide. Whatever the type of change, those affected by it may experience stress for two main reasons. First, the change being introduced may have a detrimental impact on the aspects which support a healthy workplace (for example, work design, people management/HRM functions and wider organizational factors). Second, research evidence suggests that change of any kind, even if it ultimately has positive benefits, can trigger a stress reaction (see figure 6.2).

Research studies of life changes suggests that any disruptions to our accustomed way of life can trigger a predictable cycle of psychological reactions and feelings (Sugarman, 1986), as individuals go through a transition process which enables them to accommodate to the change. The reactions (see figure 6.2) are set in motion by an event (change), or by a non-event (something that is expected to happen but does not transpire), even if these have positive implications.

The psychological reactions and feelings in the initial sequences of the change cycle, triggered by negative change, are associated with stress: immobilization or shock, characterized by a sense of being overwhelmed; emotional reactions ranging from disappointment to despair; and self-doubt and feelings of depression, anxiety, anger as the individual begins to accept the reality of the change, before moving through the other stage of the cycle to integration.

However, although change can be stressful, there are considerable individual differences in the way people react to change. The severity and duration of the reaction

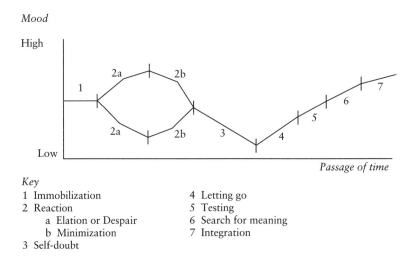

Key

1 Immobilization
2 Reaction
   a Elation or Despair
   b Minimization
3 Self-doubt

4 Letting go
5 Testing
6 Search for meaning
7 Integration

Figure 6.2   Seven-phase model of stages accompanying transition

depends on the perceived implications of the change, which varies from one individual to another. It is also influenced by individuals' ability to cope with change. Coping styles vary with factors such as personality, age, gender and life stage, and are dependent on the extent to which social support is available during the period of change. There are also considerable differences in how long it takes individuals to progress through the change cycle: some rapidly move to acceptance and integration, while others never move beyond self-doubt (Sugarman, 1986).

Of course, this is not to say that change inevitably incurs stress. The relationship between work change and employee stress depends on a number of factors, such as the way the change is introduced, individual differences (e.g. the coping style of the individual), and the role of the individual in the change process. Regarding the latter, for example, Kanter et al. (1992) argued that the experience of change varies depending on whether the individual is primarily a change strategist (concerned with connection between the organization and its environment), a change implementer (responsible for the detailed development of the change initiative) or a change recipient (on the receiving end of change). Much has been written about change management and strategy from the perspective of the change strategist/change implementer themes, and are developed later in this book. Mark Fenton-O'Creevy in chapter 11, for example, considers theoretical accounts and explanations of resistance to change among middle managers, while Philip Styles, in chapter 12, highlights the important role played by middle managers in the implementation of change. Our concern in this chapter includes the effect that change has on the change recipients, who are often those most affected but who often have least opportunity to control the introduction of change or to influence the change plan.

Illustrative changes that can cause stress

Changes at the organizational level which can result in employees experiencing stress include mergers and acquisitions, delayering and downsizing. There has been a proliferation of mergers and acquisitions during the 1990s, rising to transactions totalling $2.4 trillion in 1998, a 50 per cent increase on 1997 (*The Economist*, 1999). This dramatic increase has occurred, despite evidence that mergers often do not produce the expected and desired outcomes (Kets de Vries and Balazs, 1997), and despite evidence about the human cost. Gill and Foulder (1978) found that employees in companies that had been through mergers, or who were working in a company which had been acquired, experienced increased uncertainty and threat, loss of personal and organizational identities and feelings of conflict. Cartwright and Cooper (1993) found that even when the merger did take place between two organizations with similar cultures, middle managers experienced it as a stressful life event. Cartwright and Cooper observed that it was the expectancy of change and fears of future survival, rather than the actual change itself, which triggered merger stress. Marks and Mervis (1985) found what they termed the 'merger syndrome', which is where crisis management takes over and managers respond by sealing themselves off.

Delayering, when organizations become 'meaner and leaner' (Hirschorn, 1983), can subject staff to various sources of stress (Jick, 1983), including role confusion, job insecurity, work overload, career plateauing and poor incentives. A flatter organization can also result in 'occupational locking-in' among managers who have almost no opportunity to move from their present job. Wolpin and Burke (1986) found that this resulted in greater negative states and less life satisfaction. Kets de Vries and Balazs (1997) report that during and after downsizing, there are casualties across the entire organization. The 'victims' (those who leave the organization as a result of the downsizing), the 'survivors' (those who remain in the organization) and the 'executioners' (senior managers who plan and implement the downsizing) are all affected, and can suffer varying pathologies as a consequence.

When organizations go through mergers, delayering and downsizing, a major consequence can be increased job insecurity among employees who survive the changes and remain in the organization while their colleagues leave, or who believe their job content is insecure (because of the changes going on around them), even though job losses do not occur. Feelings of job insecurity are associated with stress (Hartley, 1996). In addition, job insecurity has other organizational implications (Hartley, 1997). Employees who feel insecure are more likely to be resistant to and oppose any changes being introduced, and because they are feeling stressed this will impact on the organizational effectiveness and efficiency (Greenhaugh and Sutton, 1991). Managers who are feeling insecure may make short-term safe decisions, which are not in the companies best interests in the long term (Whetten, 1980).

As well as the types of organizational changes described above (mergers, downsizing), modern management techniques (e.g. just-in-time, team working, business process re-engineering) and new technologies (e.g. information technologies, advanced manufacturing technologies) can have implications for employee jobs and hence employee stress. Some commentators see wholly positive consequences of new techniques and technologies for jobs and employees, arguing for example that they will mean the end of Taylorism and job simplification (Wood, 1990) and that they expand employees' opportunity for learning and development (Lawler, 1992). The argument is that, in factories, 'brawn' is replaced by 'brain'; in offices, routine work (such as processing accounts) is absorbed by information technology, leaving more complex and challenging work for employees. However, in contrast to these positive views, other commentators believe that the new technologies and techniques will de-skill and intensify work, and will ultimately lead to increased employee stress. For example, it has been argued that initiatives which remove buffer stocks between production processes (just-in-time) reduce employees' discretion to leave the work station thus 'recreating the rhythm of assembly-line pacing' (Turnbull, 1988). Similarly, case study evidence suggests that stress levels can be increased by the greater visibility of employees' performance, such as 'traffic light' systems of quality control, that are often associated with modern production initiatives (Sewell and Wilkinson, 1992).

How do we reconcile these conflicting perspectives on the effect of various modern initiatives on employee jobs and stress? Parker and Wall (1998) argued that both views are partly correct, and that the effect of modern initiatives of jobs 'depends on the nature of the new systems involved, the organizational context, and the choices made in organizing work'. For example, although just-in-time clearly has the potential to take away employee discretion, this is not always the case. In a longitudinal study of just-in-time implementation within an electronics company, operators reported higher levels of group autonomy, no detriment to their individual autonomy, and no change in stress levels after the change (Mullarkey et al., 1995). The authors attributed this outcome to the highly participative way in which the new initiative was introduced (see also Parker et al., 1995). Thus, as we discuss further in the next section, organizations can intervene to minimize the potentially stressful consequences of change.

Managing Change to Reduce the Risks to Mental Health

An important first step in managing change to reduce the possibility that employees experience stress is to recognize that change *does* have the potential to cause stress, and that stress among employees has a number of organizational costs. If the changes implemented increase the sources of organizational and work stress (for example, resulting in longer working hours, increased uncertainty, insecurity, lack of clarity, reduced training opportunities, poorer communication) the stress consequences can be severe. In addition, coping with change in itself can be stressful. Those responsible for planning and implementing change must therefore proactively and strategically consider how to minimize any potential stressful effects of new initiatives. The following comment on downsizing by Kets de Vries and Balazs (1997) can be applied to the implementation of any change:

Even executives who have a detailed strategic plan generally stumble when they set-out to realize that plan; they fail to take into account one of the most significant determinants of the success or failure of their efforts: the behaviour of the people involved. However, by acknowledging from the beginning that downsizing is an emotionally fraught process for all concerned, and by actively preparing themselves and their subordinates for the various psychological reactions that are likely to emerge during the process, the executives have the possibility to significantly limit the likelihood of disaster.

In the next section we first present an outline of the conditions required to develop and maintain a healthy workplace. Second, we present evidence from studies which demonstrate how change can be implemented without resulting in increased stress among employees, and on the consequences of inappropriate change. Third, we present a summary of steps to manage change.

Creating and maintaining a healthy workplace

As described above, there are many sources of stress in the workplace, all of which can be addressed and acted upon before and during change to minimize employee strain. For example, research shows that a major cause of stress is 'work demand' (Borrill et al., 1998; Wall et al., 1997*), which is when individuals perceive that they do not have the time or resources to carry out their job effectively. Stress is especially likely to occur when high demands exist in combination with low job control because employees lack the discretion to manage the demands (Karasek, 1979). Thus, to sustain a healthy workplace, one needs to ensure that jobs are designed so that employees have control over the demands made on them, and that work demands are manageable.

Creating and maintaining a healthy workplace requires addressing issues at a wide range of levels. These are summarized in figure 6. 3.

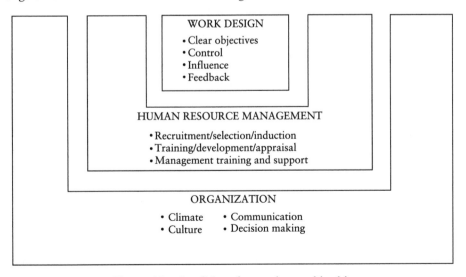

Figure 6.3 Conditions for good mental health

First, at the level of a job, employees need to have clear understanding of their objectives, have influence over decisions made about work, and receive feedback on performance. Second, the people management/HRM strategies should ensure: (1) that jobs have clear objectives and are designed so that individuals can use their skills and knowledge to best effect; (2) that the people with the required skills and knowledge are recruited into the company; and (3) that people are supported in these jobs through development, training, performance management, appraisal and reward mechanisms. Third, the organizational structure, policies and procedures should be designed to support people in their jobs, and the people management/ HRM function should facilitate communication, effective decision making and the appropriate use of resources.

Examples of managing change successfully and unsuccessfully

Earlier, we described how organizational changes such as downsizing and mergers have the potential to increase the levels of stress experienced by 'survivors' (those employees who remain in the organization). However, there are several steps that organizations can take to minimize potential negative effects for their workforce. A series of studies by Brockner and colleagues have shown the survivors' reactions to downsizing depends partly on the perceived fairness of the layoff procedures. For example, survivors react better if they feel that layoff victims are compensated and if the organization explains the reasoning behind the downsizing. (Brockner et al., 1990) The effect of downsizing on survivors can also depend on how work design is affected, as shown in the study of downsizing in a chemical processing company described below.

Parker et al. (1997) examined the effects of downsizing on survivors' jobs and mental health in a chemical company over a four-year period. The company took a 'strategic' approach to downsize the workforce by 40 per cent, rather than the most common 'reactive' approach in which reductions in the workforce are under-taken in response to short-term needs, typically involving compulsory redundancies (Kozlowski et al., 1993). The company adopted a planned approach that was in line with the long-term organizational strategy and which involved efforts to min-imize negative impacts on people. For those employees leaving the organization, the company minimized compulsory redundancies, gave advance communication about the need for and reasons underpinning the downsizing, and ensured that all leavers were offered the opportunity for out-placement counselling, and so on. For those remaining in the organization, there was a deliberate strategy to 'empower' the workforce by removing management layers and increasing multi-skilling.

Findings showed that, although employees reported an increase in work demands as might be expected (because the same number of tasks were distributed across fewer people), there was no increase in employees' or managers' stress levels. Indeed, managers reported reduced levels of stress. Results showed that the potential stress-ful effects of high work demands were offset by improvements to work design that arose from the empowerment initiative introduced in parallel with the downsizing.

In particular, increased levels of job autonomy (brought about, for example, by managers delegating tasks), increased clarity about role requirements, and more employee participation in decision making were shown to be important factors in promoting employee mental health. This study shows that by adopting a strategic approach to downsizing – for example, paying attention to the design of work – an organization can reduce head count without the survivors incurring severe negative long-term stress consequences. The fact that the company also showed performance improvements over the study period (such as increased tonnage per operator) suggests that such a strategic approach is also likely to benefit the bottom line.

Another very popular initiative in today's organization is team working. Fifty-four per cent of UK manufacturing organizations currently use some form of team working, at least to a moderate extent, and 62 per cent report that they are likely to use team working in the future (Waterson et al., 1998). Research suggests that, if appropriately implemented, team-working initiatives can have great benefits for both organizations and employees, especially if it involves enhanced employee autonomy (as in the case of autonomous work groups, or self-managing teams; see Parker and Wall, 1998). However, introducing team working does not automatically bring about benefits. A recent study conducted in a wire-manufacturing company showed that the effect of team working on employee mental health depends on the suitability of the context for this initiative (Sprigg et al., 1999; Jackson et al., in press).

On the advice of a leading consultancy, the company introduced team working across its multiple sites. This initiative was very successful in the rope-making area (where strands of wire are woven together to make rope), but there were few performance gains in the wire-drawing areas. These areas also differed in their levels of job stress: rope makers had stress levels that were lower than average, whereas wire drawers had higher than average stress. Our investigation of this situation showed that these differences between the groups were attributable to the difference in 'interdependence'. Thus, in the rope-making area, the production processes were interdependent and there was value in employees co-operating together to weave the ropes. However, wire-drawing jobs are much more 'one-person' jobs with little benefit where employees co-operated. Indeed, the noise, combined with the fact that machines were sometimes almost 60 metres apart and operators seldom saw each other, meant that it was almost impossible for employees to assist each other. The conflict between the reality and management expectations caused stress, as shown by one operator's comment:

> I don't think teams can work, I just don't think they're possible. What they want us to do with helping each other, like if I'm stood I can go and help him, it's not possible. It's just not possible yet they're expecting it.

This study shows that it is important that companies do not just 'jump on the team-working bandwagon', as is too often the case, but carefully consider the suitability of their environment for this initiative. If it is not appropriate, team working – usually a very positive change for employees – can incur stress and is unlikely to achieve the anticipated performance benefits. In these circumstances, other sorts of initiatives (such as individual job enrichment) are likely to be more beneficial to employees and the company.

A further example of introducing change is given by Parker and Sprigg (1998). To reduce lead time and to enhance product quality, a large-vehicle manufacturing company introduced a 'moving assembly line'. Prior to the installation of the moving line, groups of skilled fitters assembled a whole vehicle part; but after the change, fitters carried out narrower tasks, and the timing of the work flow was tightly regulated. The line moved continuously and it was not possible for operators to affect its pace or to stop the line. Using a longitudinal research design, the researchers showed how the moving line negatively affected employees' jobs and mental health. After its installation, employees had significantly poorer job designs (less autonomy, less variety), higher levels of job stress, and less ownership of production goals. Analysis of accident data also suggested potential negative implications for safety. Thus, any short-term performance benefits of the line were achieved at considerable cost to employees' mental health. Some limited recommendations from the researchers to improve the job design of operators on the line (allowing employees to rotate jobs, for example) were taken up by management, but more substantive suggestions to improve employees' jobs (such as giving operator control over the stopping of the line) were not acted upon. This research illustrates how companies often introduce technical change without paying sufficient attention to work design and other human and organizational issues, with consequent costs for employees' mental health.

Managing change to minimize stress

The studies of positive and negative instances of change discussed above illustrate how the effect of change on employee stress is not predetermined but depends on choices made by the organization. Although these examples are based in manufacturing (see Parker et al., 1998, for more detail), the same principles apply to white collar and professional employees. For example, research carried out in the British National Health Service (Borrill et al., 1998) found evidence that measures to improve support mechanisms can reduce stress. In the health service, lack of social support, and lack of support from top managers, resulted in significantly higher levels of stress among managers than among other staff groups. A management development intervention carried out by the health service (Borrill and Haynes, 1999) enabled managers to attend management skills workshops. Managers reported benefits from the opportunity to discuss and reflect on current work practices with colleagues in similar jobs, and to learn from each other's experiences.

Teasdale and McKeown (1994) describe an example of an effective stress management programme carried out in a pharmaceuticals company at a time of considerable change. As a first step the chief executive officer sent all department heads a letter discussing the stress associated with increasing business demands. The aim was to raise awareness about the seriousness of stress, and emphasize the need to monitor the presence of factors associated with stress; for example, high workloads, unclear priorities. The second step was to implement a six-level stress-management strategy which included:

- providing treatment and support for staff already identified as suffering from stress;
- surveying all staff to identify the extent of the problem within the company;
- taking steps to legitimize stress as a concern for senior managers;
- increasing general awareness of stress;
- providing training in stress management;
- introducing a strategy to improve the organizational culture.

Teasdale and McKeown (1994) report demonstrable benefits from the interventions which were taken to reduce the stress consequences of change in the pharmaceuticals company; stress levels reduced over time and referrals to psychiatrists and psychologists decreased.

Drawing on the literature, we now suggest the following principles for managing change in such a way as to protect employees from experiencing undue stress (see Murphy, 1995 and Quick et al., 1998, for more detail).

Recommendations for managing change and minimizing stress

It is important to involve key stakeholders from across the organization in the change process. An approach that has been shown to be successful is to form joint union and management structures which deal with issues such as technological change, job design issues and employee morale. (Appelbaum, Simpson & Shapiro, 1987). There are a number of ways that key stakeholders can be involved in the change process; for example, setting up steering groups which have representatives from stakeholder groups to plan and oversee the change. There are two main benefits from the inclusion of all stakeholders: they can not only contribute to the shaping of the change, but are more likely to accept ownership of it, which contributes to reducing the stress consequences and resistance in the change process. It is also important to maintain effective communication within the organization throughout the change planning and implementation process, so that all staff have access to information.

It is important to adopt a planned, strategic approach in which the implications of the change for employees are carefully examined. In other words, ensure that human issues (such as work roles, training, communication systems) are proactively considered when change is introduced. Too often a 'technocratic' approach is taken in which all the resources and time are concerned with technical aspects rather than people aspects, ultimately resulting in the failure of the initiative to achieve the expected benefits. It is also important to plan how to manage effectively this 'emotionally fraught process' (Kets de Vries and Balazs, 1997).

The company must ensure that any changes introduced are necessary and appropriate to the organizational and work context. Companies should beware of 'jumping on the band wagon' and should only introduce changes that align with the strategic goals and the organizational context. For example, as described above, introducing team working when there is little need for employees to co-operate with each other to get the job done can do more harm than good.

The organization should aim to prevent stress rather than 'fixing' it when it occurs. Too often, stress is identified as an issue after it has occurred, for example, when prolonged high sickness absence is observed. It is much more cost-effective to prevent stress in the first place. Known workplace stressors (such as poor work design, role conflict) should be monitored to ensure that the workplace is a psychologically healthy one, and that the conditions for a healthy workplace outlined in figure 6.3 are maintained.

It is important to prepare for change by assessing any aspects of work that already cause employees stress (that is, consider all those factors in figure 6.1, conducting a stress audit), and then develop interventions to improve the situation. For example, ensure that:

- employees have autonomy in their jobs as well as the opportunity to develop new skills;
- workloads are not excessive;
- roles are clear;
- a participatory approach to decision-making is adopted.

Part of recognizing that the process of change is likely to cause stress is providing support for those staff who suffer the consequences. It is important that senior managers in the organization demonstrate that they recognize that change can be stressful and support initiatives to prevent or reduce stress. The organization should ensure that independent counselling services are available during times of change. This will provide a 'safety valve' for the system. However, workplace stress is caused by organizational factors which must be addressed if the workplace is to be a healthy one. It is entirely inadequate to treat work stress as a 'personal problem'. For this reason, the provision of stress counselling to individuals is an important step towards maintaining organizational health, but is not sufficient on its own. Managers and employees should be trained in stress management, such as recognizing the early symptoms of stress. Supervisors and managers should also be trained to understand that workplace stress is an organizational issue, and that they are responsible for designing and maintaining a healthy workforce.

In conclusion, we argue that the effects of change should be systematically evaluated. This is important to ensure that the change has not increased stress (highlighting the need to take action) and to show any benefits of the change. No matter how small, benefits and advantages are a sign of progress and an indication that the upheaval of the change process was worth while. Regular review sessions and time given for reflection and consideration need to be built into any change process. Ideally, the evaluation should be conducted by a group that is independent of the change process and does not have any vested interest in demonstrating a particular outcome.

References

Appelbaum, S.H., Simpson, R. and Shapiro, B.T. 1987: The tough test of downsizing. *Organizational Dynamics* 15(2), 68–79.

Banham, J. 1992: The costs of mental ill health to business. In R. Jenkins and N. Coney (eds) *Prevention of ill-health at work: a conference*. London: HMSO, pp. 24–9.

Borrill, C.S. and Haynes, C.E. 1999: Health service managers. In R. Payne and J. Firth-Cozens (eds) *Stress in health care professionals*. Chichester: Wiley.

Borrill, C.S, Wall, T.D. West, M.A., Hardy, G.E., Shapiro, D.A., Haynes, C.E., Stride, C.B., Woods, D. and Carter, A.J. 1998: *Stress among staff in NHS Trusts. Final Report for Department of Health*. Institute of Work Psychology, University of Sheffield.

Business Week 1985: Stress claims are making business jumpy. October 14, 152–3.

Brockner, J., Dewitt, R.L., Grover, S. and Reed, T. S. 1990: When it is especially important to explain why: factors affecting the relationship between managers' explanations of a layoff and survivors' reactions to layoff. *Journal of Experimental Social Psychology*, Vol. 26, 389–407.

Cartwright, S. and Cooper, C.L. 1993: The psychological impact of merger and acquisition on the individual: a study of building society managers. *Human Relations*, 46, 327–47.

Cartwright, S. and Cooper, C.L. 1994: *No hassle: taking the stress out of work*. London: Century Books.

Cooper, C.L. and Cartwright, S., 1994: Healthy mind; healthy organisation – a proactive approach to occupational stress, *Human Relations*, 47(4), 445–71.

Gill, J. and Foulder, I. 1978: Managing a merger: the acquisition and its aftermath. *Personnel Management*, 10, 14–17.

Greenhaugh, L. and Sutton, R.I. 1991: In J.F. Hartley, D. Jacobson, B. Klandermans and T. van Vuuren (eds) *Job insecurity: coping with jobs at risk*. London: Sage.

Hartley, J. 1996: Models of job insecurity, and coping strategies by organisations. In M. Marmot, J. Ferrie and E. Zigilio (eds) *Labour market changes and job insecurity: a challenge for social welfare and health promotion*. Copenhagen: World Health Organization.

Hartley, J. 1997: Organisational change. In P. Warr (ed.) *Psychology at Work*. Harmondsworth: Penguin.

Hirschorn, L. 1983: *Cutting back*. San Francisco: Jossey-Bass.

Howard, G. 1995: *Stress and the law*. Occupational Health – Watching Brief, February.

Huselid, M.A. 1995: The impact of human resource management: an agenda for the 1990s. *International Journal of Human Resource Management*, 1(1), 17–43.

Jackson, P.R., Sprigg, C.A. and Parker, S.K. (in press): Interdependence as a key requirement for the successful introduction of team working: a case study. In S. Proctor and F. Mueller (eds) *Team working: issues, concepts, and problems*. New York: Macmillan.

Jick, T.D. 1983: The stressful effects of budget cuts in organisations. In L.A. Rosen (ed.) *Topics in managerial accounting*. New York: McGraw-Hill.

Kanter, R., Stein, B. and Jick, T. 1992: *The challenge of organisational change*. New York: Free Press.

Karasek, R.A. 1979: Job demands, job decision latitude and mental strain: implications for job redesign. *Administrative Science Quarterly*, 24, 285–308.

Kets de Vries, M.F.R. and Balazs, K. 1997: The downside of downsizing. *Human Relations*, 50(1), 11–50.

Kozlowski, S.W.J., Chao, G.T., Smith, E.M. and Hedlund, J. 1993: Organizational downsizing: strategies, interventions, and research implications. In C.L. Cooper and I.T. Robertson (eds) *International review of industrial and organizational psychology*. Chichester: Wiley.

Lawler, E.E. 1992: *The ultimate advantage: creating the high involvement organisation*. San Francisco: Jossey-Bass.

Mark, M.L. and Mervis, P.H. 1985: Merger syndrome: managing a crisis. *Mergers and Acquisitions*, 20, 10–76.

Mullarkey, S., Jackson, P.R. and Parker, S.K. 1995: Introducing JIT within product-based work-teams. *International Journal of Operations and Production Management*, 15, 62–79.

Murphy, L.R. 1995: Occupational stress management: current status and future directions. In C.L. Cooper and D.M. Rousseau (eds) *Trends in Organisational Behaviour*, Vol. 2, Chichester: Wiley.

Murphy, L.R. (1999) Organisational interventions to reduce stress in health care professionals. In R. Payne and J. Firth-Cozens (eds) *Stress in health care professionals*. Chichester: Wiley.

Parker, S.K. and Sprigg, C.A. 1997: A move backwards? The introduction of a moving assembly line. *Proceedings of the Occupational Psychology Conference*, Eastbourne, UK, pp. 139–44.

Parker, S.K. and Wall, T.D. 1998: *Job and work design: organizing work to promote well-being and effectiveness*. London: Sage.

Parker, S.K., Chmiel, N. and Wall, T.D. 1997: Work characteristics and employee well-being with a context of strategic downsizing. *Journal of Occupational Health Psychology*, 2, 289–303.

Parker, S.K., Jackson, P.R, Sprigg, C. and Whybrow, A. 1998: *Organisational interventions to reduce the impact of poor work design*. Norwich: HSE Books.

Parker, S.K., Myers, C. and Wall, T.D. 1995: The effects of a manufacturing initiative on employee jobs and strain. In S.A. Robertson (ed.) *Contemporary ergonomics*. London: Taylor & Francis, pp. 37–42.

Patterson, M.G., West, M.A., Lawthom, R. and Nickell, S. 1997: *Impact of people management practices on business performance*. Institute of Personnel Development.

Quick, D., Campbell Quick, J. and Nelson, D. 1998: The theory of preventative stress management in organisations. In C.L. Cooper (ed.) *Theories of organisational stress*. Oxford: Oxford University Press.

Salaman, G.S. 1995: *Managing*. Buckingham: Open University Press.

Sewell, G. and Wilkinson, B. 1992: Empowerment or emasculation? Shopfloor surveillance in a total quality organisation. In P. Blyton and P. Turnbull (eds) *Reassessing human resource management*. London: Sage.

Sprigg, C.A., Jackson, P.R., and Parker, S.K. (1999): Production team working: the importance of interdependence and autonomy for employee strain and satisfaction. Manuscript submitted for publication.

Sugarman, L. 1986: *Life-span development: concepts, theories and interventions*. New York: Routledge.

Teasdale, E.L. and McKeown, S. 1994: Managing stress at work: the ICI-Zeneca Pharmaceuticals experience 1986–1993. In C.L. Cooper and W. Williams (eds) *Creating healthy work organisations*. Chichester: Wiley.

The Economist, 1999: How to merger: after the deal. *The Economist*, January.

Turnbull, P.J. 1988: The limits to 'Japanisation': just-in-time, labour relations, and the UK automotive industry. *New Technology, Work and Employment*, 3, 7–20.

Wall, T.D., Bolden, R.I., Borill, C.S., Carter, A.J., Golya, D.A., Hardy, G.E., Haynes, C.E., Rick, J.E., Shapiro, D.A. and West, M.A. 1997: Minor psychiatric disorder in NHS trust staff: occupational and gender differences. *British Journal of Psychiatry*, 171, 519–23.

Whetten, D. 1980: Organisational decline: sources, responses and effects. In J. Kimberley and R. Miles (eds) *The organisational life cycle*. San Francisco: Jossey-Bass.

Wolpin, I. and Burke, R.J. 1986. Occupational locking-in: some correlates and consequences. *International Review of Applied Psychology*, 35, 327–45.

Wood, S. 1990: Tacit skills, the Japanese model and new technology. *Applied Psychology: An International Review*, 39, 169–90.

7

Strategy Implementation in Public Sector Organizations

David McKevitt

Introduction

This chapter concerns the implementation of large-scale strategic change in public sector organizations. Our primary focus is Ireland; however, comparative observations are made from New Zealand, Sweden and the United Kingdom experience. A model is presented – the Street Level Public Organization (SLPO) – to help to analyse the environment of the public sector and to locate sources of implementation failure. The environment organization models of Bruce Scott (1962) and Lawrence and Lorsch (1967) of the Harvard Business School are used to illustrate these issues. These models highlight the relationship between the effects of the external environment and internal features of the organization such as structures including workings of subunits as they are differentially impacted, and the control, staff and task effects of environmental change. Our model is also congruent with general normative models of effective strategic change programmes such as those which Pettigrew and Whipp (1991) identify as present in organizations that have been successful in strategic change.

Since space does not allow an exploration of all aspects of one model, attention in this chapter will be focused on the importance of the capability and skill of employees and their willingness to implement strategic change decided by the strategic apex of the organization. In both public and private sectors, employees, especially those with a professional education and training, are not passive observers of the implementation process; indeed in many cases such employees have the capability to blunt the change process if they deem it inimical of their interests. The public sector professional (doctor, teacher, architect) has his or her counterpart in the 'knowledge workers' of private sector service industries. One of the leading challenges in these complex socio-technical environments is to engage the commitment of professional staff to the implementation process. Mintzberg (1979) in his study of strategic change in professional bureaucracies, talks of 'change seeping in' rather than sweeping into the organization. Change has to be negotiated and legitimized outside of the organization and be congruent with the professional's education and accreditation process prior to its acceptance within the organization. Thus, professional educational institutions throughout the world have an important role to play in successful strategic change in any nation.

The Street Level Public Organization

The SLPO model outlined below grew out of the field research in a number of countries and is an attempt to describe and understand the conflicting forces in the environment of public service organizations; a fuller description of the research and intellectual support of the model can be found elsewhere (McKevitt, 1998). The specific components of the model are clearly aligned with, and characteristic of, a public sector environment. The relative strengths and weaknesses of specific components will vary from country to country, and, indeed, between different types of public services (e.g. health care and education).

Using this model, and noting from the data gathered in field research in the UK, Sweden, New Zealand and Germany that service delivery in the area of social welfare is a managed process, we can move now to examine the essence of the management task involved, that is, relating a street level public organization to its environment (see figure 7.1).

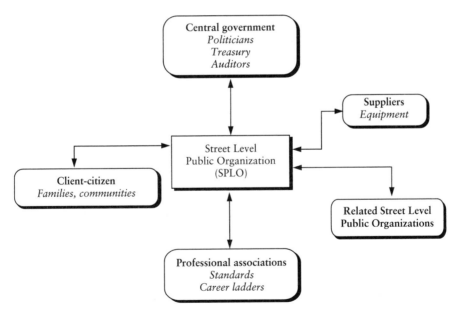

Figure 7.1   The Street Level Public Organization in its Environment

Source: McKevitt (1998)

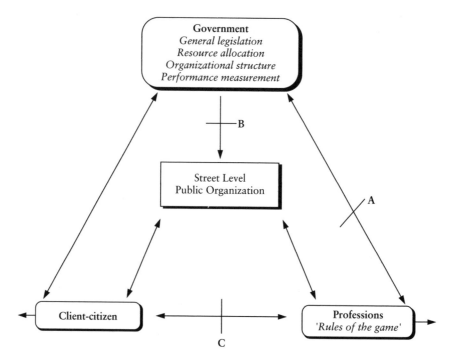

Figure 7.2   Tensions in the SLPO Environment

Source: Adapted from Wrigley and McKevitt (1995)

The question then is: What are the key points of tension in the environment itself? It is in this respect that data from field research, over a period of time in a number of countries are vital. Figure 7.2 represents our research finding of the recurring tension points in the environment of street level public organizations.

It will be noted that the immediate source of recurring tensions is point A – the relations between central government and the professions. The model enables us to see an essential fact. Street level public organizations are under a dual set of influences. From central government there are four modes of influence – general legislation, allocation of resources, organizational structure, and performance measurement – each of which is powerful, and the four when taken together are extremely powerful.

However, without established, accepted and enforced rules of the game, as we know from research on private enterprise, the effect of these four powerful modes of influence can cause the activities of street level public organizations to run wild and undirected. Because each of these four modes of influence play mainly on individual self-interest, it is the rules of the game, the ethical codes, which are needed to harness the forces of self-interest to social goals. Rules of the game really are important and it cannot be overemphasized that these rules are established by a quite different kind of institution, namely the professions. If there is a solid relationship between government and the professions, the inevitable tensions at point A can be resolved without adverse impact on the street level public organization. If, however, the relationship is poor, then the tension at point A will debilitate the whole system of service delivery as research in the UK makes quite clear (McKevitt, 1998). In the social welfare area of the public sector, good relations between government and the professions are important for success in quality service delivery.

The field research reported below shows the importance of understanding the dynamics of government–professional relations. In the health care study, government and public managers have adopted a 'hands-off' model of control, legally expressed in the position of general practitioner as self-employed contractors for state-funded patients. In the absence of explicit performance measures in their contracts of employment (apart from indicative prescription formulae) control is left primarily to the ethical base of medical training.

Such a model of control places the citizen-client in a weak position due to the differential information which exists in patient–doctor relationships and the lack of exit for over one-third of the population for state-funded medical care. *Quis custodiet ipsos custodies?* – Who is minding the minders? The case study also shows how the presumption of citizen involvement in influencing service delivery relies heavily on responsive management of the SLPO itself. That is, if public managers cede undue influence to the professionals, what role is there for the citizen-client?

Moreover, government influence on street level public organizations may be fundamentally impaired by problems in general legislation, as at point B in figure 7.2. In a study of health care policy in Ireland, McKevitt (1989) used a comparative approach whereby, in certain crucial aspects, Ireland was compared with other developed countries, including Sweden and Holland. McKevitt then explained:

> The Swedish and Dutch systems, in contrast to Ireland, share common features in their concern for explicitness in legislation, their attendance to the sovereign importance of measurement and control systems and their willingness to adapt and modify their control system to refocus their investment decisions.

From this view, we can see that any defect in the legislative framework which impairs the process of resource allocation will lead to recurring tensions of a fundamental kind between central government and professional associations in the environment of street level public organizations. But central government may not be the only fundamental source of recurring tensions.

Indeed, we can reflect that the absence of a legislative strategy to underpin some of the major UK policy shifts in education and health care probably accounts for their relative lack of success. We do not, of course, propose the view that legislation, even if it is cast in a strategic dimension such as found in Swedish health care is a guarantee of strategic control. Clearly such legislation will assist in aligning the strategic orientation of the organization and its day-to-day operational concerns. This is an important criterion identified earlier by Pettigrew and Whipp (1991) as contributing to successful strategic change.

Policy makers have numerous and conflicting demands on their attention and legislation can also be viewed as partly a symbolic act which represents good intentions rather than administrative clarity. Our research indicates that another fundamental source of the tension may well lie at point C in figure 7.2, namely a break in the natural relationship between the community of citizens and the professional bodies. In English-speaking countries, at least, the professions can and sometimes do in their practices go too far ahead of social sentiment, thereby essentially becoming isolated bodies in the environment. Governments cannot do this because of the democratic system. Professional bodies, however, can do so particularly in the Anglo-Saxon countries where the prevailing culture may feature individualism.

Thus, in the English-speaking countries, the 'rules of the game', the code of professional ethics, may evolve in ways that go too far off the boundaries provided by social sentiment, and therefore present a fundamental source of tension in the environment between client-citizens and the professions. The most conspicuous example in the early 1990s of such tension in the United Kingdom is provided by the system of primary education.

In the event, the fact that for street level public organizations, the rules of the game are provided from a different source than the other modes of influence does mean there will be tensions, and these tensions will not go away. The case study demonstrates the importance of understanding the 'rules of the game' in professional-led public service delivery. In health care the doctor is granted wide autonomy, both medical and administrative; in such circumstances what is meant by the term 'managing health care delivery'? We now report on the Irish experience and reflect on its implications for citizen participation. We also consider whether lessons can be drawn from the Irish case that will give insight into the balancing of potential conflicts within the SLPO environment.

One of the advantages of having a general strategy model of the public service environment (and understanding the source of tensions in that environment) is that it assists us in comparative analysis of strategic change. Thus, for example, in Sweden and Germany where public service professionals are primarily state employees, there is considerably more alignment between them and the managers of service provision. In Germany teacher–state relations are, by and large, harmonious and decentralized unlike the adversarial, centralist experience of England (McKevitt, 1998). The management of strategic change requires an understanding of the specific environment in which change is sought; for example, in New Zealand the 'contract model' and purchaser–provider relationship dominated change across all public sector activities, from privatization to welfare. It is hardly surprising, therefore, that senior managers admitted to great uncertainty as to the efficacy or appropriateness of this model (McKevitt, 1998). The need to understand external environmental conditions is clearly a significant part of the implementation process and constitutes one of the underpinnings of success. Governments, no less than businesses, require this strategic awareness.

The Strategic Management Initiative in Irish Public Management

The current restructuring of Irish public management owes its origin to both political and civil service initiatives. Politically, the Strategic Management Initiative (SMI) was initiated through the 1996 publication of *Delivering Better Government*,

Box 7.1 Features of the Strategic Management Institute

Delivering a quality customer service – A quality service will be actively promoted throughout the civil service and departments and offices will be expected to follow certain practices.

Reducing red tape – The regulatory environment will be examined to see where red tape could be reduced or improved in the public interest.

Delegating authority and accountability – Authority and accountability will be shifted to the person making the decision or carrying out that decision. With authority comes accountability and officials will be accountable for decisions taken at their own level.

Introducing a new approach to human resource management – The approach to managing and developing people will be more proactive and will be broadened to include improvements in personnel development programmes, workload distribution, career planning, organizational skills planning, job satisfaction and performance management.

Ensuring value for money – Financial management systems will continue to be developed to improve controls on public spending and to ensure that, where money has to be spent, the best returns for that money is achieved.

Supporting change with information technology – Improved use of information technology will be the key to this by facilitating increased organizational and management effectiveness, more efficient work processes and better information management.

the government's proposal for change and renewal in Irish public management. The primary components of the change programme are shown in Box 7.1.

Civil service thinking on reform was first publicly formed through the publication by a group of senior civil servants on reform initiatives in New Zealand and Australia (New South Wales), and their applicability to the Irish context (McKevitt, 1995). In one sense, the civil servants' approach was deliberate in their evaluation of specific strategic change in other countries. In another respect, the authors favoured an emergent process, and rejected early legislation to guide the change process, observing that it would introduce 'significant elements of inflexibility which are better avoided'. McKevitt (1995), in a critique of the civil servants' report, found that the prescriptions for reform lacked awareness of the strategic importance of legislation in guiding public sector change (see below) and noted the absence of a clear conceptual basis for the reform proposals. Indeed, this latter criticism will be revisited when we examine the Irish case studies for evidence of consistency between the espoused strategy and the operational management of the SLPO. In the event, legislation – The Public Service Management Act, 1996 – was used to underpin strategic change in Ireland.

How then can we characterize the SMI change process and the likely consequences for managing the implementation project in a professional–bureaucratic context? It is certainly a planned, deliberate, top-down process of change driven largely by civil servants, albeit supported through a legislative framework. If we examine the external environment of change at the SLPO level we can see that it is complex and changing, driven by EU regulation and international business cycles. In such an environment, where the internal context is professional–bureaucratic, how successful is a planned, deliberate, strategy likely to be? It is here that we focus in particular on the coherence and consistency of change, the internal capability of the organization and the integration of the strategic and operational. These are the attributes of successful change we examined earlier in this chapter.

The citizen-client and strategy implementation: the case of primary health care

The health care study involved the evaluation of patient satisfaction questionnaires as a mechanism for managerial control of general practitioners and as an instrument of client-citizen satisfaction. Both performance measurement and user satisfaction are espoused components of current Irish health care strategy. The study assessed the level of patient satisfaction with their general practitioners (GPs) from a population of 522,027 covering seven counties in two provinces. Six thousand questionnaires were distributed to patients in the area and 2,170 were returned. The survey scrutinized the non-medical dimensions of general practice. The average satisfaction level for the study was 74 per cent (see table 7.1). The study also sought the views of health care managers and professional service providers regarding consumer involvement in performance measurement of professionals and managerial control of professionals (Millar, 1998).

Regarding the role of client-citizen in the performance measurement, the views of managers and professionals were similar. There was a consensus held by both groups that a limited role is appropriate for the consumer in assessing the service provided by the professional. One of the obvious demarcations set by both groups was the emphasis that patients may only be involved in measuring the non-technical performance of GPs. This argument is obvious, as differential information is what

Table 7.1 Summary of patient satisfaction and dissatisfaction levels across the dimensions

Dimension of general practice	% of respondents satisfied	% of respondents dissatisfied
General satisfaction	81.2	10
Access	74.4	10
Appointments and availability	58.6	29.4
Communication	83.7	8.7
Premises	75	14.7

separates the consumer or patient from the professional service provider. Why else would the former seek the latter's services? However, this is not a justification for not introducing consumer-based performance measurement of public services. Donabedian (1980) argues that patients are clearly the best judges of the interpersonal relationship they have with the doctor and often the sole judges of the surroundings in which care is given. The GPs interviewed were very open to the fact that the patients' involvement in assessing the service they provide would enable them to see the 'lump on their neck'.

The most significant issue arising from consumer participation in general practice is the strongly held belief that 'the doctor knows best'. Vuori's (1995) work highlights the belief that patients and professionals may have different goals for care. Professionals may find the goals of the patient to be at variance with their 'best interest' and therefore not worth pursuing. This view is certainly seen in the data collected in this study. Many of the professional service providers warned that increased consumer involvement cannot imply giving patients 'everything they want'; they still require 'a little bit of what they need as well'. Thus, if the professional service provider believes that he or she knows best, what credence will be paid to the findings of a patient satisfaction questionnaire?

The 'professional' view of physicians in the Irish General Medical Services

In general, few of the GPs interviewed endorse the introduction of management-led performance measurement and few of the doctors disagreed with the concept entirely. It is accurate to say that the professional service providers view performance measurement as inevitable. However, they do have numerous issues arising from such an assessment that need to be addressed prior to the initiation of any such programme.

The data in this study suggest that if performance review of professional service providers is to be introduced in the Irish health care system it will not be passively accepted by the GPs. Neither would the GPs be totally adverse to performance measurement, but the ideal would be a joint auditing mechanism – that is, a performance measurement programme designed, constructed and executed by the managers and the professional representative bodies. The professional service providers see the introduction of performance measurement within the Irish health care system as inevitable and know that they must accept it 'albeit reluctantly'.

The acknowledgement by GPs that performance measurement is inescapable arises from their understanding that the public are not content to allow professionals to operate solely in a self-regulating manner. Most of the GPs interviewed were very aware of the existence of performance measurement in other health care systems, most significantly in the UK. There were, however, two main stipulations laid down by the GPs with regard to the introduction of performance measurement; first, that they should be all-encompassing, that is to say, that all facets of general practice be subject to performance measurement. Secondly, that they should not be designed by management alone. With regard to the first issue, the GPs believe that if performance measurement is to be implemented, all elements of performance must be measured and not just those that are easy to measure. In addition, performance indicators must include both process and outcome.

The reactions of the GPs as to who designs and implements performance measurement shows the collegiality of the professional service providers, who warned that the external imposition of performance measurement would ensure that the indicators as such are looked after, but that would not necessarily ensure that the service would improve.

Resistance to management-imposed performance measurement by the GPs suggests that if the evaluation is not a joint exercise there is no guarantee that the programme would ensure a better or improved service. This is the reassertion by the GPs of their power and autonomy over managers. It was never overtly said by any of the GPs that they would resist any initiatives by managers to introduce performance measurement. Nevertheless, there were many implicit suggestions in the data collected that if the GPs and their representative bodies are not co-operatively involved, then indices will not be accurate and real change and improvement in service provision will not occur.

The views of professionals in this study are in keeping with the traditional paradigm of professionalism in that their assertion that professionals measure their own performance – self-regulation – and only they can decide what is satisfactory performance. The professionals' power is their assertion that if the managers wish to improve the service delivered to the patient, the GPs must be to the fore of the process; if not, there are no guarantees that the service will improve.

Public managers and 'hands-off' control

One of the most significant findings of the qualitative research conducted for this study is the attitude of managers to their role in control; it was one of aversion and anxiety. They considered that GPs would not 'appreciate' being regulated by management and that they cannot measure the performance of GPs as external providers. The fear of some of the managers that the GPs, as members of a self-regulating body, would not accept their performance being assessed by managers was evident.

The reluctance to engage in performance measurement and control by managers is linked to their assessment that GPs 'do a good job' and there is no requirement on their part to 'control GPs'. One manager bluntly stated that: 'It is possible for us to measure and to utilize patient satisfaction questionnaires; however, given the good service provided by the GPs, they are not so necessary.' The qualitative data collected clearly show that managers hesitate and are uncertain vis-à-vis their control over the general practitioners. Their reasons for this uncertainty could stem from two sources; first, the absence of managerial control of professionals in the organization and, secondly, the fact that the superior–subordinate relationship within the organizational hierarchy does not legitimize the authority relationship between management and the professional service provider.

The first concept, the absence of managerial control over GPs, is significant. From a historical perspective, it is evident that any difficulties that were present within the system were linked to budgetary control, so managers sensed that change was necessary. Moreover, budgetary modifications were within their capacity as budgetary controllers.

However, the status quo was changed or modified on the basis of consultation and negotiation with the GPs and their representative bodies. Change was management-led but established on the basis of consensus between them and the professional service provider. Arising from this experience is management's belief – evident in the data – that there is no need to control GPs because there are no problems in the system. This is based on the premise that problems which did exist have been ironed out. Does this suggest, then, that management see control as 'bringing in the fire brigade' in the sense that management control is exerted when the fire is burning rather than taking preventive measures before things become out-of-control?

The second possibility is that a superior–subordinate relationship within the organizational hierarchy does not legitimize the authority relationship between them and the professional service provider. A sense of apprehension was evident as the managers believed that GPs would not 'appreciate' being regulated by managers, which would be anathema to their ethos of self-regulation. This apprehension is linked to what McClelland (1991) labels as the second face of autonomy – that is, the autonomy professional service providers possess in the face of other reference groups. If one accepts that professional service providers hold 'autonomy' over management, then the management function of control and the relationship between these two organizational groups is not classified as superior–subordinate. Within this relationship managers are hierarchically superior to GPs. If one is to follow Dunsire's (1978) framework, which argues that authority of command always rests on the willingness of the subordinate to accept the command of a superior as authoritative, then one must ask how willing is the GP to accept the command of the manager as authoritative?

If the professional service provider holds autonomy over managerial authority and the management operates on this premise, then the latter will not enforce a command which will impinge on the autonomy of the professional service provider. It could be argued that managers realize, and accept, that if they were to enforce performance measurement, this would lead to conflict, as the superior is not familiar with the subject matter of the subordinate's work. Dunsire argues that in this type of situation the superior will be conscious that he or she lacks authority and hierarchical authority will not be sufficient to ensure compliance.

As government strategy seeks to 'review performance', it must change its relationship with the professional service providers. The state has granted to the professional service provider self-regulation without interference, and this is accepted by both the managers and the GPs. It is obvious from the research data that managers anticipate an unfavourable reaction from the GPs if they seek to impose performance measurement. Hence, the message from the managers is that it will only happen if the GPs are involved in the design and implementation. Moreover, the consent of the professional service provider is required.

Main research findings

Health care managers and the professional service provider view the role of the client-citizen in health care as a limited one. This is based on the presumption that the doctor knows best and patients cannot get everything they want. While budgetary or financial control has always been evident in the Irish health care system, quality control has not been. There is a hesitation and uncertainty among health care managers *vis-à-vis* controlling the general practitioners, as there is an acceptance by the former of the dominance by the latter. If government strategy aims to 'review performance', a modification in the relationship between the state and professional service providers is necessary. The ideal method of 'performance review' for both managers and professionals would be a joint auditory mechanism.

Some Strategy Implementation Implications

The primary care example demonstrates some key characteristics of the strategy implementation process. Clearly, there is a lack of alignment between management goals (economic efficiency) and the professionals' adherence to independence of action and decision making. Indeed, as we have seen, management seem reluctant to intervene in the overall process, thereby creating a 'hands-off' model of control, where individual ethics determine system choice. The Irish case is not unique – see, for example, Carter's (1996) work on performance measurement in the United Kingdom. A countervailing influence to professional power can be found in situations where government seeks to impose mechanistic control on professional behaviour; that is, an alliance of citizen-client with professionals.

McKevitt and Lawton (1994) report on a growing trend in this area whereby blunt instruments of performance measures are countervailed by growing alliances between providers and clients. An extended analysis of this trend, in respect of primary education in New Zealand, can be found in McKevitt (1998). What is of importance to implementing successful strategic change is the need for alignment between providers and senior managers, between espoused values and operational reality.

Evaluation and Conclusion

How do we make sense of the data reported earlier and what are the implications for future implementation efforts in the public sector? Clearly one of the first findings of significance is that the problems of managing strategic change are common to both the private and public sectors. The common themes, identified by Pettigrew and Whipp (1991), of environmental sensing, linking strategy and operations are clearly evident in the case reported. That is, managing the SLPO requires sensitivity to the values and culture of the service providers; in the health care example, perhaps too much attention was paid to the professional and this resulted in a 'hands-off' model of control. This sensitivity to the 'whole-part' dynamic of strategic change is a primary requirement for strategic success.

Performance measures form another important component of the change process. At its simplest, strategic change requires that people will do things differently; measuring that desired change and reinforcing it is an important facet of change. We have seen in our example that, despite the new espoused strategic values (citizen orientation), there were no real changes in the performance measures. There was, therefore, a disjunction between the strategic and the operational. The operating core of the SLPO will not perform differently unless they see an incentive/reward in so doing. Recalling Alexander's (1989) list of common implementation problems, it is evident that the public sector case did not involve providing staff with the required new skills.

The management of strategic change requires a sensitivity to organizational context (the 'where' of strategy) as much as it demands attention to the content of strategy. Public sector organizations tend towards deliberate planned strategies albeit in a context of professional service deliverers. This requires emergent, consensual, strategies of change which can be at odds with hierarchical, top-down, implementation. It is clear, therefore, that public organizations need to attend to the processes underlying strategic change that support consensual implementation.

References

Alexander, L.D. 1989: Successfully implementing strategic decision. In D. Asch and C. Bowman (eds) *Readings in Strategic Management*. Macmillan, pp. 388–96.

Burns, T. and Stalker, G. 1994: *The management of innovation* (rev. edn). Oxford: Oxford University Press.

Carter, N. 1996: Performance indicators: 'backseat driving' on 'hands-off' control. In D. McKevitt and A. Lawton (eds) *Public sector management*. Sage, pp. 208–19.

Donabedian, A. 1980: *The definition of quality and approaches to its assessment*, vol. 1. Health Administration Press, pp. 25–9.

Dunsire, A. 1978: *Control in a bureaucracy*, vol. 2. Martin Robertson.

Dunsire, A., Hartley, K. and Parker, D. 1991: Organisational status and performance: summary of the findings. *Public Administration*, 69, Spring, 21–40.

Kanter, R. and Summers, D. 1996: Doing well while doing good. In D. McKevitt and A. Lawton (eds) *Public Sector Management*. Sage, pp. 220–36.

Lawrence, P. and Lorsch, J. 1967: *Organisation and environment: managing differentiation and integration*. Cambridge, MA: Harvard University Press.

McClelland, C.E. 1991: *The German experience of professionalisation*. Cambridge: Cambridge University Press.

McKevitt, D. 1989: *Irish health care policy, 1989*. Hibernian University Press.

McKevitt, D. 1995: Strategic management in the Irish Civil Service; Prometheus unbound or Phoenix redux? *Administration*, 43(4), 34–50.

McKevitt, D. 1998: *Managing Core Public Services*. Oxford: Blackwell.

McKevitt, D. and Lawton, A. 1994: The manager, the citizen, the politician and performance measures. *Public Money and Management*, 16(3), 49–55.

Millar, M. 1998: *Organisation control in the public sector: the case of general practitioners and performance measurement.* Unpublished PhD thesis, University of Limerick.

Mintzberg, H. 1979: *The structuring of organisations.* Englewood Cliffs, NJ: Prentice-Hall.

Pettigrew, A. 1985: *The awakening giant.* Oxford: Blackwell.

Pettigrew, A. and Whipp, R. 1991: *Managing change for competitive success.* Oxford: Blackwell.

Powell, W. and Di Maggio, P. 1991: *The new institutionalism in organisational analysis.* University of Chicage Press.

Scott, B.R. 1962: *An open systems model.* Unpublished DBA, Harvard University.

Vuori, H. 1995: *Patient as arbiter of the quality of care.* Inaugural Meeting of ISQH, Dublin.

Wrigley, L. and McKevitt, D. 1995: Professional ethics, government agenda and differential information. Open Business School Research, Working Paper 95/5.

8

Leading and Managing the Uncertainty of Strategic Change

Jean Hartley

Introduction

All organizations contain politics, whether this is formal, accountable and largely transparent, as in parts of the public sector, or informal and often secretive as in many private sector organizations. Many accounts in the management and organizational behaviour field suggest that managers try to reduce or manage the politics associated with uncertainty, creating some degree of order out of incipient chaos and maximizing predictability and order where they can. This chapter challenges the assumption that uncertainty is necessarily a bad thing and suggests rather that uncertainty can be tolerated or even usefully harnessed in some circumstances. Research in the public service sector is used to examine the role of senior politicians and senior managers in managing the uncertainties of organizational change. The argument is advanced that uncertainty is, broadly, approached in a different way by politicians compared with managers. By examining and contrasting approaches of these actors to uncertainty, we can explore the underpinnings of rationality and action in the leadership and management of organizations in conditions of uncertainty as strategy is actually implemented.

Uncertainty for organizations

There is increasing recognition that uncertainty is a key characteristic of organizational life, both in the environment and inside the organization (e.g. Grint, 1997; Sparrow, in this volume; Brown and Eisenhardt, 1998). The scale, scope and pace of change means that more attention needs to be paid to researching and understanding uncertainty and discontinuity. Chaos theory and complexity theory are becoming of greater interest (e.g. Wheatley, 1994; Waldrop, 1992: Kaufmann, 1995) to organizational researchers. Such theories have been used as metaphors to understand the turbulent context of organizations (e.g. Grint, 1997) but the concept of uncertainty is often used in an undefined or ambiguous way.

The concept of uncertainty has been widely used in organization theory, for example in analysing some of the key challenges facing organizations and those who work within them. It remains a key concept in organization theory but still remains surprisingly under-theorized and conceptualized. There are numerous references to the role of uncertainty in organizational change (e.g. Dopson and Neumann, 1998; Brown and Eisenhardt, 1998) but the concept is more often assumed rather than defined and examined.

Some definitions of uncertainty

To reduce the vagueness about the concept of uncertainty we begin by looking at some definitions. Galbraith (1977: 36–7) takes an explicitly information-processing approach to uncertainty, defining it as 'the difference between the amount of information required to perform the task and the amount of information already possessed by the organization'. However, this concentrates on information-processing and possession and appears to ignore the role of judgement, values or politics in the estimation of uncertainty.

Burns and Stalker (1961: 112) defined uncertainty as 'the ignorance of the person who is confronted with a choice about the future in general, and in particular about the outcomes which may follow from any of his possible lines of action'. This definition has a stronger emphasis on choices by the person (and by extension to the organization) and is able to encompass values.

March (1994: 174) describes uncertainty as 'imprecision in estimates of future consequences conditional on present actions'. This last definition may be particularly useful because it emphasizes that uncertainty is not necessarily an objective reality but is an interaction between perceptions of the context and beliefs about the impact of actions. The definitions of Burns and Stalker (1961) and March (1994) both emphasize the perceptual and behavioural aspects of uncertainty and are future oriented.

We also need to clear the decks by contrasting uncertainty with ambiguity. Ambiguity is sometimes used interchangeably with or in tandem with the concept of uncertainty but Weick (1995) notes that the concept of ambiguity is inherently problematic. It can refer either to the presence of two or more interpretations of a situation or to a lack of clarity (and in this latter sense, he argues it can be quite close to uncertainty as a concept). Therefore, we focus here on uncertainty in order to avoid this confusion.

In organization theory, the concept of uncertainty has largely (though not exclusively) been applied to analysing the external environment. Emery and Trist (1965) developed a typology of environmental conditions (which they termed causal textures), ranging from placid, predictable environments to those which are highly turbulent and uncertain. Child (1984), reviewing both open systems and contingency theory, summarized two key dimensions for organizations: variability (the difficulty of predicting changes in the environment, and departures from previous conditions) and complexity (the degree of diversity in the environment). A central concept of open systems theory is that of uncertainty and its related terms of instability, turbulence and indeterminacy. Other writers have drawn on the characterization of uncertainty to analyse environmental conditions and organizational response (e.g. Thompson, 1967; Morgan, 1986; Scott, 1992; Thompson and McHugh, 1995), suggesting that contingencies in the external environment constrain or influence internal organizational design.

Uncertainty and organizational effectiveness

A critical issue for organizational researchers and for managers is the relationship between uncertainty and organizational effectiveness. Contingency theory (e.g. Burns and Stalker, 1961; Lawrence and Lorsch, 1967; Galbraith, 1977) argues, with different emphases, for the fit between organization and type of environment. They argue that in stable or predictable environments the more effective organizations tend to have routinized systems, structures and processes (the mechanistic or bureaucratic type organization), while in environments with rapid change, uncertain markets or complex technologies organizations need to have more organic, flexible and responsive structures and processes to be effective. This distinction is also evident in the literature on 'high-velocity' environments (e.g. Eisenhardt and Tabrizi, 1995; Brown and Eisenhardt, 1998; Gersick, 1994). The environmental fit approach places a strong emphasis on strategic choice and leadership (e.g. Child, 1972; Eisenhardt, 1989; Wiersema and Bantel, 1993). Some theorists have also related this to the pace of change. For example, Tushman and Romanelli (1985), in punctuated equilibrium theory, argue that during periods of crisis and major uncertainty, organizations may develop more radical transformation than during periods of more benign environmental change, when incremental organizational change is more likely.

However, we may need more complex assessments of uncertainty. Milliken (1987) specifies three types of environmental uncertainty, which are useful in understanding approaches to strategic change. State uncertainty refers to difficulties in predicting how the environment itself may be changing. Effect uncertainty refers to difficulties in predicting the impact of environmental events on the organization, while response uncertainty refers to the difficulty in assessing what responses or options are available to the organization. Milliken's approach is useful because it emphasizes that uncertainty is not unidimensional, nor is it solely an objective characteristic of the environment but is shaped by perceptions of those in the organization, especially those responsible for strategic choices (see March, 1994). It also suggests that different capabilities may be needed to cope with the different types of uncertainty (Milliken, 1990). It suggests, as does Weick's (1995) work on sense making in organizations, that uncertainty arises from difficulties in extrapolating from a current situation into the future, which in part relates to the capacities, experiences and resources within the organization. This implies that different individuals and different groups in organizations may interpret and experience uncertainty differently and may therefore behave differently. Individuals and groups can vary in their tolerance of and engagement with uncertainty (e.g. Hartley et al., 1991).

The typology of Friend and Jessop (1969), developed and extended by Friend and Hickling (1997), also elaborates the concept of uncertainty. They suggest that those making strategic choices in organizations have to make judgements about the balance between uncertainties in the external environment; uncertainties about the guiding values (which affect how much emphasis to place on particular strategic choices) and uncertainties about related decisions (i.e. the uncertainties which occur where choices are affected by other decisions and events). Friend and Hickling (1997) suggest that choices can be considered on a dimension from trying to reduce or trying to accommodate uncertainty.

Contingencies, Information Seeking and Sense Making: How Organizations Respond to Uncertainty

A key question concerns *how* external environmental uncertainty affects organizational functioning and response. On the basis of the management and organizational literature, we suggest that there are three main types of responses reported. The first is the *contingency effect*, where an uncertain environment creates the need for, or is associated with, more flexible structures in order to increase responsiveness (e.g. Burns and Stalker, 1961; Thompson, 1967). For example, 'we suggest that organizations cope with uncertainty by creating certain parts specifically to deal with it, specializing other parts in operating under conditions of certainty or near certainty' (Thompson, 1967:13). The 'law of requisite variety' (Ashby, 1960) argues that organizations need to develop greater complexity where they are facing uncertain or turbulent environments. More recently, academics have described the semi-structured organization (e.g. Brown and Eisenhardt, 1998) which has some elements of structure to maximize order and predictability but is partly unstructured to maximize responsiveness. The proposal that rapidly changing environments engender organizations which are more organic in structure and activity is perhaps one of the truisms of organization theory (Morgan, 1986). On this basis, the organization attempts to reduce the surprises or the effects of uncertainty by developing flexible approaches including environmental scanning and rapid action in response to change.

The second approach to environmental uncertainty by the organization is *information seeking*. In this strategy, the aim is to seek out more and/or better information. Those leaders and managers concerned with the strategic focus and direction of the organization seek more information to reduce uncertainty by increasing predictability (e.g. Stinchcombe, 1990; Daft and Weick, 1984; Thompson, 1967). This is the approach taken by Galbraith (1977) referred to earlier, where uncertainty is defined in terms of an information deficit. Organizations develop strategies and activities to collect, analyse and use more or better information on the assumption that this will help them deal with the environmental uncertainty and also help to clarify the choices open to them. The organization uses information to increase its capacity for prediction, thereby aiming to reduce uncertainty.

The third response to uncertainty is *sense-making behaviours*, because 'interpretation, sense-making and social construction are most influential in settings of uncertainty' (Weick, 1995: 177). This approach recognizes that more or better information in itself may not be sufficient to reduce uncertainty but rather how the organization uses and interprets the data that it already possesses or that it acquires. This is about meaning as well as information. Part of the value of a sense-making approach in conditions of uncertainty may be, as Eisenhardt (1989) suggests, that taking a problem-solving approach not only enables a faster and concurrent assessment of alternative responses and scenarios to uncertainty but also can reduce anxiety and boost confidence for senior managers. This is another attempt by the organization to reduce uncertainty by gaining a different quality of information, by exploring meanings and choices and by strengthening and supporting the confidence to act in conditions of uncertainty.

Overall, research has led to the view that 'each organization needs to design the structures or processes in a manner which reduces uncertainty or adapts to the degree of environmental stability' (Thompson and McHugh, 1995: 63; see also Downey et al., 1975). However, the three approaches to responding to uncertainty all start from the assumption that uncertainty is problematic for the organization and that managers and others will always strive to reduce and/or contain uncertainty. But is this the case? This is a key issue and a critical assumption that deserves testing. Can we assume that organizations approach uncertainty in these ways. There are circumstances in which organizational leaders and managers may seek to increase or prolong uncertainty. In particular, we suggest that an organization's leadership may seek to prolong uncertainty where it enhances cohesion among key stakeholders and/or maintains the current power structure.

Leadership and Strategy Implementation in the Context of Uncertainty

Leadership and management are important for effective strategy development and implementation (Child, 1972; Mohrman et al., 1989), especially in a context of environmental turbulence and uncertainty (Pfeffer, 1992; Weick, 1995; Schuler, 1997). By organizational strategy is meant the choices about corporate long-term goals, objectives and priorities which are used broadly to guide future actions, taking account of the environmental pressures, opportunities and responsibilities of the organization. The focus here is on strategy at the whole-organization or corporate level rather than examining the strategic choices of particular functions, services or departments (see Hartley, 1998a).

In the public service sector the corporate strategic centre includes not only the chief executive and senior, corporate managers (with corporate policy support) but also the political core concerned with setting and developing strategies and policies for the organization (Campbell, 1991; Hartley and Benington, 1993). In civil service organizations (such as the large departments of state) political engagement will come from ministers while in local government local politicians are elected to lead the council and are intimately engaged with the strategy for the authority. There are equivalent political or representative bodies for the police, health services and so forth. Political leadership has to be sensitive to influences from central government and from local communities in developing and implementing strategies (Chapman, 1991).

In politically-led organizations, classical administrative theory assumes different roles for leadership as carried out by politicians compared with managers. Politicians are supposed to create and develop policies with managers acting as the executive for these policy makers. In practice, relations are both more complex and more interactive (Baier et al., 1986; Wilson and Game, 1998; Leach et al., 1998; Hartley et al., 1995). In addition, new pressures and opportunities for strategy formulation and development in a context of external uncertainty and change requires considerable collaboration between politicians and managers in environmental scanning, decision-shaping and strategic choices and in a wider set of policy networks (Benington and Harvey, 1999), though roles and accountability remain distinguishable (Leach et al., 1998).

Leadership can be viewed as the processes by which groups and organizations are able to confront and deal with novel and/or complex problems and opportunities or which require responses beyond routine, standardized ways of behaving. In this sense, leadership is an activity (see Heifetz, 1994). Leadership is also seen to be the processes occurring between the leader and the members of the team, group or organization who are the focus of influence (Schein, 1992; Yukl, 1994; Bryman, 1992).

Do managers and politicians differ in approach to the management of uncertainty? Are there differences in the tasks and activities of political compared with managerial leadership activities? On the basis of the literature about uncertainty we have reviewed, it might be expected that senior managers are concerned to reduce or contain uncertainty, through the organizational mechanisms described. However, it is not so clear that politicians will be motivated in the same way in part because their accountability lies not only within the organization but also to their political party, to the electorate and to a complex array of national and local stakeholders. If politics (as opposed to 'politicking') is concerned with processes to resolve or channel different interests (Crick, 1982), then politicians may approach uncertainty in different ways. In particular politicians may be motivated to prolong uncertainty in order to enhance cohesion within and between groups with different interests and to maintain their power base.

The Politics and Management of Uncertainty in the Public Service Sector

One (inaccurate) stereotype of public service organizations is that they are havens of predictability, control and order, undisturbed by the turbulence and uncertainty of commercial and competitive market environments. However, public service organizations have to manage uncertainty on a number of fronts as they monitor, cope with and sometimes try to shape major shifts in the external environment and new challenges to governance and service delivery. At a fundamental level, the role of elections in public service organizations means that political control and priorities for policy making may change on a punctuated basis. The degree of uncertainty is high – political leaders and their policies may fall overnight, sometimes predictably and sometimes surprisingly. Politicians and managers, especially those in senior or corporate positions, may have to adjust rapidly to changed political control and policy priorities (Hartley et al., 1997). In addition, the priorities of governing and delivering services may change as the local communities and the local economy change.

Furthermore, in the last two decades there have been major shifts and challenges in the external environment (Osborne and Gaebler, 1993; Benington and Stoker, 1989; Ferlie et al., 1996; Lawton and McKevitt, 1995). Sources of uncertainty facing public service organizations derive from political, economic, social and technological forces. These pressures may be exerted from above (legislative and financial pressures from regional, national and supra-national governments), from below (changing demographic characteristics and citizen/user/community expectations) and from lateral influences and relationships (other organizations engaged in complex partnership and contractual interrelationships between the public, private and voluntary sectors, including financing and service contracting) (Ranson and Stewart, 1988; Benington, 1997; Flynn, 1997).

The public sector is both responding to and anticipating some of the fundamental and long-term shifts which are taking place in society. The increasing complexity of issues which communities are facing (such as social regeneration, community safety or public health) means that traditional service delivery by public sector organizations has to be re-thought and that more collaborative working with local communities and other organizations is crucial for effective problem solving (Flynn, 1997; Hartley, 1998b).

The Consequences of Uncertainty: Some Longitudinal Case Evidence

What are the consequences for politicians and for managers of these high levels of uncertainty in the environment – and in organizational capacity? Here we draw on a longitudinal case study, taking place in real time over nearly four years, of organizational and cultural change in a major UK local authority employing more than 27,000 staff (reported in greater detail in Hartley and Benington, 1998). In more than 200 interviews and observations, with high-level privileged and intimate access to the 'corridors of power' including political controlling group meetings and the corporate management team meetings, the researchers tracked the antecedents, processes and consequences of major changes in the environment, including the uncertainties created by the threatened abolition of the organization for national political reasons arising from intense conflict between central and local government (Leach, 1996; Davis, 1997a, 1997b). Local government reorganization, occurring on a national scale, meant that Midshire County Council (pseudonym) faced nearly a decade (1991–98) of uncertainty occasioned by review, re-review, and eventual negotiated settlement on the transfer of some territory and 30 per cent of staff and resources to another local authority. This also resulted in the reduction in political representation of 25 per cent (with the number of councillors reducing from 88 to 63) and heralding potential changes in the balance of power within and between political groups.

In addition, the continuing budget cuts, economic decline and challenges locally, and legislative changes also contributed to uncertainty and change (Hartley, 1998c; Davis, 1997b). There was no pattern or predictability at a national or local level to the fortunes of Midshire or other local authorities in this period (Davis, 1997a). The changes were not only uncertain but also highly complex, leading to the decision to restructure the departments substantially (from eight to five). However the political structures and processes were unchanged.

The case study is based on dividing up the period of change into six phases based on the degree of external uncertainty and key external events (see Hartley and Benington, 1998, for a fuller account). In each period the key tasks of political and managerial leadership were examined, providing twelve units of analysis (six phases and two leadership roles). Within each phase the role of the political and managerial leadership in steering the organization through a period of profound uncertainty was analysed. There is insufficient space within this chapter to give full details of our analysis and so we summarize some of the key issues.

The senior management team (chief executive and eight senior managers) initially perceived the external challenges to the existence and functioning of the organization as requiring minor adaptation and adjustment. Initially response uncertainty (Milliken, 1987) was not seen to be problematic, and fully within the capability and capacity of the organization. However, by the second phase the management team was grappling with how to lead and manage a transformational change which would involve a steep, step change for the organization and where uncertainty was recognized to be an overarching concern, with uncertainty about the type of external challenges, uncertainty about what the changes would mean for the organization (abolition or restructure) and uncertainty about how the organization should respond (scaling down or reorientation of strategic priorities). Over several months of intensive work, information gathering, discussion and analysis, both among themselves, between themselves and the politicians, and taking account of the local communities, the management team forged a new set of priorities for the organization. This included a strategy for the transition and for the building of the new organization post-transition, including the major and very substantial restructuring of departments and detailed allocation of staff.

In undertaking this immense task, the corporate management team used the tools and techniques at its disposal to reduce or manage external and internal uncertainty including through information gathering, sense-making in and outside meetings, clarifying possibilities and priorities with politicians. The overall aim was to match environmental uncertainty with internal capacities, in the process developing a more flexible and more responsive organization which would not only cope with present uncertainties but also have the longer-term capacity to perceive and respond to external changes and challenges. The corporate management team commissioned and engaged in considerable work to analyse the strategic context of the organization, to analyse longer-term trends globally, nationally, regionally and locally and to gather, refine and test out information and scenarios. The corporate management team over the course of several months gradually developed a set of plans and procedures, targets and timetables for implementation to which the whole corporate management team could sign up. This was not an easy or straightforward course but the analysis across the six phases shows these means of reducing or managing uncertainty.

What is striking from the case study is that the political leadership did not approach uncertainty in this way. While the core group of senior politicians ('front-benchers' consisting of the leader, deputy leader, chairs of committees, chief whip and group secretary) worked with the senior managers to develop and implement a restructured organization, the same rationale was not applied to *political structures and processes* though these are as critical to the effective functioning of a public service organization. Initially, it may seem surprising that the politicians did not lead change in this way. Indeed, the research shows that across all six phases there was a consistent pattern: there were several occasions on which the opportunity to engage in debate or discussion about the political structures, processes and strategies was avoided, downplayed, shuffled off or indefinitely deferred.

It was not that the politicians did not notice or care about external and organizational uncertainty. They discussed it among themselves (though rarely in formal meetings), especially how to influence national and local events external to the organization (state and effect uncertainty). Indeed, they acted to reduce uncertainty when external circumstances favoured a decisive, winnable response, and they shaped the course of the national debate on reorganization. But they did nothing to settle the uncertainty about internal political structures and processes inside the organization.

Nor does the explanation lie in an organization which was ineffective either politically or managerially. On the contrary, this organization has been successful over a period of turbulence, uncertainty and change. First, the political leadership survived and held on to power (despite some challenges). The approach of the political leadership to the reorganization drew positive comments from across the political spectrum at both local and national level and there was considerable respect for the dignity and experience of the leader in handling the period of conflict with central government and uncertainty locally. Although the leadership did not succeed in preventing downsizing, they did stave off abolition and so did not fare as badly as some other organizations in reorganization (see Game, 1997). The new strategy for the post-transition organization was launched with a distinctive social and corporate agenda and set of objectives. But still, the transformational change which rocked the administrative and managerial structures had not touched the political structures.

This assessment suggests that the behaviours of the political leadership cannot be dismissed as an ineffective response to uncertainty. The approach of the political leadership becomes more interpretable when considering that its role may not be to reduce uncertainty but to maintain it in some circumstances.

Throughout the period of change, the cohesion and stability of the controlling group of politicians could not at any stage be taken for granted but had to be worked for. Retaining cohesion during a period of response uncertainty (Milliken, 1987) was a key issue for the political leadership.

By not reaching or postponing a final view or decision, internal and cross-party cohesion can be maintained because values are not overtly in conflict or contention at this stage. The organizational changes created many different views, values, interests and tensions within the controlling group, between political parties, between politicians and managers and between the organization and its network of local partner organizations. If the political leadership had reviewed the political structures and decision-making processes, this might have surfaced different view-points and interests. As it was, the decision to postpone taking a final decision on political structures can be seen as a particular approach to the management of uncertainty. Part of a politician's power and skill lies in building coalitions across different interests – this power can dissipate when a decision is reached because who loses and who gains becomes apparent. This is political power through active non-decision making (cf. Brunsson, 1985; Heifetz and Sinder, 1988) and it can be aided by the existence of uncertainty. Uncertainty supports the maintenance of cohesion in a potentially fragmenting context, and the maintenance of existing power balances. Reducing uncertainty could dissipate this and could even create opposition.

Politicians not only have to address internal tensions and issues but must also reflect the diverse range of issues of external stakeholders, such as the electorate, local communities, partner agencies (whether public, private or voluntary), the media and so forth. They are engaged in a complex web of relationships and interests outside as well as inside the organization. This contrasts with the position of senior managers who are primarily accountable to those inside the organization.

For these reasons, politicians may be able to live with uncertainty for longer periods and in greater force than managers. This is not to suggest that politicians are incapable of reducing or managing uncertainty as there are many occasions, both in the case study and more generally, where politicians have taken the lead in making decisive choices which reduce uncertainty.

Our research suggests that whether uncertainty is reduced or maintained may depend on the interests of the stakeholder group. It tentatively suggests that manage-rial leadership may often have an incentive to reduce uncertainty (through informa-tion gathering, sense making and planning) and that part of the focus is on managing event and response uncertainty. The managerial leadership has to manage and reduce internal uncertainty (as well as deal with external uncertainty). Rational planning can help to achieve this. However, the political leadership is driven by values (whether these are political values or the values attached to retaining power). Part of the role of the political leadership is to maintain cohesion and commitment among diverse groups with varied interests (as well as among the controlling group itself) and so there may be advantages to behaving in ways which maintain uncer-tainty.

Rationality and Values: Wider Lessons

The public sector is a large sector and thus, quite separately from any wider general-izations, the evidence is worthy of interest in its own right. The public sector employs more than five million people in the UK (Flynn, 1997). Whether or not the framework developed here has wider applicability, it is of interest in developing theories and approaches which reflect the realities of the public sector.

What are the lessons beyond the specific circumstances of the public service sector? Is there anything of interest to researchers and managers trying to understand and operate in the private sector? Our analysis suggests that there are several reasons for interest in the *processes* of managing uncertainty, even though the organizational form will be sector-specific.

The case study has shown that the assumption among organizational behaviour specialists that uncertainty is matched, mirrored or reduced by the organization and its actors does not apply in all spheres. The role of politicians in the case study shows that there are or can be advantages to maintaining or even enhancing uncertainty in some circumstances. This may be less to do with their formal roles (politician versus manager) than what they are trying to achieve (build consensus and act to make and implement choices). If this is true, then we would expect to find occasions when managers are acting politically and where it is convenient to maintain or enhance uncertainty. And politicians may want to make and implement choices which require the reduction of uncertainty. This recognizes that organizations consist not only of rational plans, choices and strategies, but also of values, interests and power. Thus, this analysis derived from the public sector can have much wider repercussions for organizations across all sectors. We have presented a case study based on formal and explicit power and politics but it is potentially relevant to understanding the informal political processes which occur in all organizations (see Morgan, 1986; Coopey and Burgoyne, 1999; Hartley, 1989).

Politically led organizations such as local authorities may provide useful insights because the responsibility to be democratically accountable to the public means that political decision making has to be explicit and transparent to a greater extent than occurs in the private sector. Decision making under conditions of uncertainty and change therefore has potential lessons of more general interest (see also Huff, 1988; Hartley et al., 1983; Lucas, 1987). Brunsson (1985; 1986) argues:

> [Political organizations] expose fundamental problems connected with rationality and action and can teach us a great deal about fundamental problems and solutions in organizations...they deserve more attention that organizational theorists have given them hitherto.

Brown and Eisenhardt (1998) have argued for the need for organizational theory to break out of theories largely constructed in the 1970s when the environment was more stable and to crystallize the key properties of continuously changing organizations. The growing interest in complexity theory (Waldrop, 1992), in punctuated equilibrium theory (Tushman and Romanelli, 1985) and in time-paced strategic change (Gersick, 1994) suggests that the field of management research will benefit from more dynamic theories, including how organizations address uncertainty. We cannot continue to assume that uncertainty is a negative feature which leaders and managers will always seek to banish, manage or reduce. There is a need to examine further the advantages in maintaining or even enhancing uncertainty in strategy formulation and implementation.

Acknowledgement

This chapter is based on research undertaken in conjunction with John Benington. I would like to thank John for helpful comments on this chapter.

References

Ashby, R. 1960: *An introduction to cybernetics*. London: Chapman & Hall.

Baier, V., March, J. and Saetren, H. 1986: Implementation and ambiguity. *Scandinavian Journal of Management*, 179–212.

Benington, J. 1997: New paradigms and practices for local government: capacity building within civil society. In S. Kraemer and J. Roberts (eds) *The politics of attachment*. London: Free Association Books.

Benington, J. and Harvey, J. (1999): Networking in Europe. In G. Stoker (ed.) *The new management of British local governance*. London: Macmillan.

Benington, J. and Stoker, G. 1989: Local government in the firing line. In N. Buchan and T. Sumner (eds) *Glasnost in Britain?* London: Macmillan.

Brown, S. and Eisenhardt, K. 1998: *Competing on the edge*. Boston, MA: Harvard Business School Press.

Brunsson, N. 1985: *The irrational organization: irrationality as a basis for organizational action and change*. Chichester: Wiley

Bryman, A. 1992: *Charisma and leadership in organisations*. London: Sage.

Burns, T. and Stalker, G.M. 1961: *The management of innovation*. London: Tavistock.

Campbell, A. 1991: *The role of the centre: the need for review*. Luton: Local Government Management Board.

Chapman, R.A. 1991: Concepts and issues in public sector reform: the experience of the United Kingdom in the 1990s. *Public Policy and Administration*, 6(2), 1–19.

Child, J. 1972: Organization structure, environment and performance: the role of strategic choice. *Sociology*, 6, 1–22.

Child, J. 1984: *Organization: a guide to problems and practice* (2nd edn). London: Harper & Row.

Coopey, J. and Burgoyne, J. 1999: *Politics and learning*. Unpublished paper, University of Lancaster.

Crick, B. 1982: *In defence of politics*. Harmondsworth: Penguin.

Daft, R.L. and Weick, K.E. 1984: Toward a model of organizations as interpretation systems. *Academy of Management Review*, 9, 284–95.

Davis, H. 1997a: Reviewing the review. *Local Government Studies*, 23(3), 5–17.

Davis, H. 1997b: England under review: local government structures in the English shires. *Public and Social Policy*, Paper 1. University of Birmingham/British Library.

Dopson, S. and Neumann, J.E. 1998: Uncertainty, contrariness and the double-bind: middle managers' reactions to changing contracts. *British Journal of Management*, 9 (Special issue), S53–S70.

Downey, K.H., Hellriegel, L.D. and Slocum, J.W. 1975: Environmental uncertainty: the construct and its application. *Administrative Science Quarterly*, 20, 613–29.

Eisenhardt, K. 1989: Making fast strategic decisions in high velocity environments. *Academy of Management Journal*, 32, 543–76.

Eisenhardt, K. and Tabrizi, J. 1995: Accelerating adaptive processes: product innovation in the global computer industry. *Administrative Science Quarterly*, 40, 84–110.

Emery, F.E. and Trist, E.L. 1965: The causal texture of environments. *Human Relations*, 18, 21–32.

Ferlie, E., Ashburner, L., Fitzgerald, L. and Pettigrew, A. 1996: *The new public management in action*. Oxford: Oxford University Press.

Flynn, N. 1997: *Public sector management*. London: Prentice Hall.

Friend, J. and Jessop, W.N. 1969: *Local government and strategic choice*. London: Tavistock.

Friend, J. and Hickling, A. 1997: *Planning under pressure* (2nd edn). Oxford: Butterworth-Heinemann.

Galbraith, J.R. 1977: *Organization design*. Reading, MA: Addison-Wesley.

Game, C. 1997: How many, when, where and how? Taking stock of local government reorganisation. *Local Government Policy Making*, 23(4), 3–15.

Gersick, C. 1994: Pacing strategic change: the case of a new venture. *Academy of Management Journal*, 37, 9–45.

Grint, K. 1997: *Fuzzy management*. Oxford: Oxford University Press.

Hartley, J.F. 1989: Leadership and decision-making in a strike organization. In B. Klandermans (ed.) *Organising for change: social movement organizations in Europe and the United States*. Greenwich, CT: JAI Press, pp. 241–65.

Hartley, J.F. 1998a: Organization-wide approaches to best value. *Warwick/DETR paper no. 10 on Best Value*. London: DETR.

Hartley, J.F. 1998b: *Competencies for community leadership*. London: Local Government Management Board.

Hartley, J.F. 1998c: *Preparing for the future: report of an employee survey on organisational and cultural change*. Research paper. Coventry: University of Warwick.

Hartley, J. and Benington, J. 1993: *The role of the corporate core in local authorities*. Research paper. Warwick University Local Authorities Research Consortium, University of Warwick.

Hartley, J. and Benington, J. 1998: *Leading and managing organizational change in conditions of uncertainty*. Research paper. Warwick University Local Authorities Research Consortium, University of Warwick.

Hartley, J. Benington, J. and Binns, P. 1997: Researching the role of internal change agents in the management of organizational change. *British Journal of Management*, 8, 61–73.

Hartley, J., Cordingley, P. and Benington, J. 1995: *Managing organisational and cultural change*. London: Local Government Management Board.

Hartley, J., Kelly, J. and Nicholson, N. 1983: *Steel strike*. London: Batsford Academic.

Hartley, J., Jacobson, D., Klandermans, B. and van Vuuren, T. 1991: *Job insecurity: coping with jobs at risk*. London: Sage.

Heifetz, R. 1994: *Leadership without easy answers*. Cambridge, MA: Harvard University Press.

Heifetz, R. and Sinder, R. 1988: Political leadership: managing the public's problem-solving. In R. Reich (ed.) *The power of public ideas*. Cambridge, MA: Harvard University Press.

Huff, A. 1988: Politics and argument as a means of coping with ambiguity and change. In L.R. Pondy, R.J. Boland and H. Thomas (eds) *Managing ambiguity and change*. New York: Wiley, pp. 79–90.

Kaufmann, S. 1995: *At home in the universe*. New York: Oxford University Press.

Lawrence, P.R. and Lorsch, J.W. 1967: *Organization and environment*. Cambridge, MA: Harvard University Press.

Lawton, A. and McKevitt, D. 1995: Strategic change in local government management: comparative case studies. *Local Government Studies*, 21, 46–64.

Leach, S. 1996: Local government reorganisation: a test case. In S. Leach, H. Davis et al. (eds) *Enabling or disabling local government*. Milton Keynes: Open University Press.

Leach, S., Pratchett, L., Wilson, D. and Wingfield, M. 1998: *All you need is trust? The changing relationship between members and officers*. London: Local Government Management Board .

Lucas, R. 1987: Political-cultural analysis of organizations. *Academy of Management Review*, 12, 144–56.

March, J.G. 1994: *A primer on decision-making*. New York: Free Press.

Milliken, F.J. 1987: Three types of perceived uncertainty about the environment: stage, effect and response uncertainty. *Academy of Management Review*, 12, 133–43.

Milliken, F.J. 1990: Perceiving and interpreting environmental change: an examination of college administrators' interpretation of changing demographics. *Academy of Management Journal*, 33, 42–63.

Mohrman, A., Mohrman, S., Ledford, G., Cummings, T. and Lawler, E. 1989: *Large-scale organizational change*. San Francisco: Jossey-Bass.

Morgan, G. 1986: *Images of organization*. London: Sage.

Osborne, D. and Gaebler T. 1993: *Reinventing government: how the entrepreneurial spirit is transforming the public sector*. New York: Plume.

Pfeffer, J. 1992: *Managing with power: politics and influence in organizations*. Boston, MA: Harvard Business School Press.

Ranson, S. and Stewart, J. 1988: Management in the public domain. *Public Money and Management*, Spring/Summer, 13–18.

Schein, E. 1992: *Organizational culture and leadership*. San Francisco: Jossey-Bass.

Schuler, R. 1997: A strategic perspective for organizational behavior. In C.L. Cooper and S. Jackson (eds) *Creating tomorrow's organizations*. Chichester: Wiley.

Scott, W.R. 1992: *Organizations: rational, natural and open systems*. Englewood Cliffs, NJ: Prentice-Hall.

Stinchcombe, A.L. 1990: *Information and organizations*. Berkeley: University of California Press.

Thompson, J.D. 1967: *Organizations in action*. New York: McGraw-Hill.

Thompson, P. and McHugh, D. 1995: *Work organizations: a critical introduction*. London: Macmillan.

Tushman, M.L. and Romanelli, E. 1985: Organizational evolution: a metamorphosis model of convergence and reorientation. In B. Staw and L. Cummings (eds) *Research in organizational behavior*. Greenwich, CT: JAI Press.

Waldrop, M.M. 1992: *Complexity: the emerging science at the edge of order and chaos*. Harmondsworth: Penguin.

Weick, K. 1995: *Sense-making in organizations*. Thousand Oaks, CA: Sage.

Wheatley, M. 1994: *Leadership and the new science: learning about organization from an orderly universe*. San Francisco, CA: Berrett-Koehler.

Wiersema, M. and Bantel, K. 1993: Top management team turnover as an adaptation mechanism: the role of the environment. *Strategic Management Journal*, 14, 485–504.

Wilson, D. and Game, C. 1998: *Local government in the United Kingdom* (2nd edn). Basingstoke: Macmillan.

Yukl, G. 1994: *Leadership in organizations* (3rd edn). Upper Saddle River, NJ: Prentice-Hall.

Part 3
Key Roles in Strategy Implementation

9. From Advice to Execution: Consulting Firms and the Implementation of Strategic Decisions
   Tim Morris

10. The Leadership of Learning: the Core Process of Strategy Implementation
    Dennis Gillen

11. Middle Management Resistance to Strategic Change Initiatives: Saboteurs or Scapegoats?
    Mark Fenton-O'Creevy

12. Constraints on Strategy Implementation: the 'Problem' of Middle Managers
    Philip Stiles

9

From Advice to Execution: Consulting Firms and the Implementation of Strategic Decisions

TIMOTHY MORRIS

Introduction

In the book *Dangerous Company* (O'Shea and Madigan, 1997), the activities of some of the best-known consulting firms are dissected in a relatively unflattering way. A theme is that, although staffed by bright business school graduates, their interventions can be highly disruptive, all too often destroying value rather than creating it. Great at analysis they may be; making it happen is another story. This sort of criticism is not new; it echoes what many managers, on the receiving end of consultants' wisdom, would say. But why do consulting firms have this sort of reputation?

In this chapter I address this question in terms of two related factors: (1) the nature of their interventions and (2) their internal dynamics. I argue that interventions made by consulting firms are usually based on a generalized and over-rationalistic set of assumptions about how organizations work contained in consultants' knowledge bases. Such claims to knowledge are necessary for the consultants' role and status as *expert adviser* but disguise their limited ability to put decisions into practice. Although, as outside experts, they can facilitate strategic change by transferring solutions from other organizations and helping to overcome managerial myopia, they do not have the networks of power and influence necessary to execute change. Yet, it is argued below that there are powerful incentives for consulting firms to make claims to manage the execution of strategies and these are linked to their internal dynamics. Examining these dynamics, I show how they influence the consulting firm's ability to handle strategy execution effectively.

The chapter begins by sketching out how different types of firms appear to be converging on the area of strategy execution. This leads to a more detailed discussion of the roles consulting firms play and the internal dynamics that drive their activities. The chapter concludes by considering the implications for effective strategy execution.

Converging on Strategy Execution

Consulting activities cover a range of intervention methods to provide support for a client (Argyris, 1970). The content of this chapter mainly refers to large consulting firms and their style of intervention.

Involvement in the execution of strategic decisions is a potentially profitable line of business for consulting firms. Executing decisions usually takes time, creating the opportunity for long engagements. Further, if execution is sufficiently important to be classified as strategic by the client, it is likely that the contact with which the consultant works has high authority and access to power and resources, including large budgets. Large budgets can support large projects but this does not inevitably mean that the consultant can exploit the client. Claims have outrun performance in the past and clients have become smarter at contract specification and the use of performance contingent rewards. Further, the spread of knowledge through the popular business literature has placed them under pressure to provide more than elegant solutions on paper.

Various types of consulting firms have converged on the strategy execution and change area because of its value, but each group tends to face a different type of problem in getting there, as figure 9.1 summarizes. Some have traditionally been interested in strategy but less interested in implementation. These strategy houses, such as McKinsey and Booz, Allen & Hamilton developed reputations as analytically oriented firms that worked with chief executives to create superior competitive plans (Bowman, 1984). Indeed, they had deliberately sought to distinguish themselves from other types of consulting firms which had originated from the demand for industrial engineering advice, by not being concerned with operational matters (McKenna 1995; 1998). The strong analytical approach and focus on top-level contacts traditionally precluded close involvement in subsequent phases that were the responsibility of middle management.

A second group of consulting firms working within the implementation arena is composed of systems specialists. These include Andersen Consulting, CSC and other 'Big Six' firms, whose consulting arms are off-shoots of the systems management created in their audit practices. The activities of these firms are largely directed to tightening control of the performance of operating managers by imposing relatively standardized recipes. Latterly, these firms have developed services that are essentially concerned with employment or cost reduction such as Business Process Reengineering. They have also created organizational change models, but these are often built on the back of existing services and largely recombine them rather than being a new approach to consulting. Other more specialist firms are the operations consultants such as A.T. Kearney and A.D. Little. These firms claim to be implementation

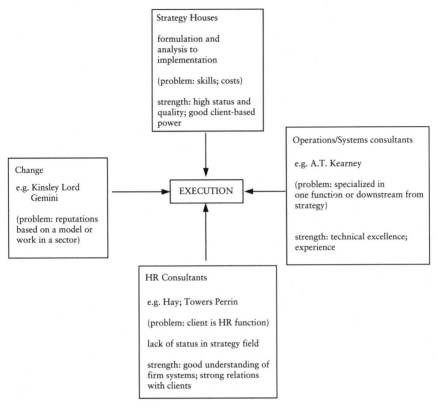

Figure 9.1 Convergence on strategy execution

experts in the sense of concentrating on activities that follow from the strategic plan and are to be staffed by experienced staff recruited from industry, rather than straight from business school. Their expertise tends to bring them into contact with the sorts of managers charged with implementation – namely, middle and senior line managers in operating units. However, the problem for all these firms has been the extent to which they could establish links into the heart of the strategic decision-making process, rather than operate downstream from it.

A third group of firms is composed of technical or functional specialists. These included, for instance, a number of HR firms such as Hay, PA Consulting and Towers Perrin, which are best known for work on compensation, job evaluation, selection and other HR activities. Their clients have traditionally been HR directors through which they regulated the systems in the organization. Their involvement in strategy implementation has been indirect because their clients were not the line managers primarily responsible for making change happen.

In the 1980s, change management emerged as a distinct consulting activity partly to address some of the shortcomings of traditional strategic implementation consulting. Its impact has grown as the rate of change in organizations has accelerated and the nature of change problems has evolved from cost reduction (downsizing) to revenue increasing through new ways of competing ('reinvention'). It has also been a way in which the consulting firms could recombine the issues (and client contacts) of strategy and organizational restructuring which had become segmented under the old division between OD and corporate strategy. Even the strategy houses have moved into this area via models that link strategy with dimensions of organization. Thus, there have been client 'pull' and supplier 'push' reasons for the growing interest in change management.

Specialist change management firms have distinct methods and products. For example, Gemini built the 'transformation' model of major change as its principal product. This involved a radical redefinition of the client organization's purpose, values, strategy and policies. It incorporated a model of the causes and shape of change events inside large organizations, including the politics of making organizational change happen. It also incorporated an emphasis on the process of change management, seeking to leverage momentum among internal champions and redirect sources of resistance. Several large-scale projects made Gemini's reputation, although the sheer scale of the original transformation model reportedly intimidated some potential clients.

A second example is Kinsley Lord. Emerging as a niche firm in the late 1980s, it made its name in the UK public sector which was then being restructured by the separation of central policy-making areas from agencies charged with the delivery of services. This change was accompanied by the development of a new set of management values, enshrined in the term New Public Management. Kinsley Lord developed a strong emphasis on process consulting, working with clients to develop vision and value statements and build understandings of the sorts of behaviours and management practices that went with these issues (Empson and Morris, 1997). It was not a firm with standardized products or methodologies; indeed, it made a virtue of the customized approach to assignments and the emphasis on collaboration with the client in the production of the solution. Its reputation for innovative work in the change area attracted Towers Perrin and Kinsley Lord was acquired in 1996, because of the cross-selling opportunities it could offer.

Yet, while change consulting has become an attractive market for all the large consulting firms, difficulties in developing the appropriate skills and culture have persisted. Traditionally, many of the large firms have focused on highly analytical methods of consulting with relatively low involvement in actual day-to-day management. These have permitted them to leverage the talents of their staff in such activities as data collection, analysis and solution development, based on generic tools that are part of a well-codified knowledge base, but they have not formed the basis for skilled change management. In many, change-consulting specialities have been developed largely on the existing talents and mode of consulting that the firm deploys. Thus, change interventions led by the systems-based firms are typically driven by technology-based initiatives which, by affecting the performance systems, are designed to drive changes in behaviour and organization. The problem is that this is simply seen as old wine in new bottles. In contrast, the change management specialists have typically developed more process-based methods, aiming to become more involved in execution by closer collaboration with the client. The repertoire of skills includes less analytic ones such as coaching and communicating. Without becoming part of the management team, the nature of the intervention has deepened.

Consultant Interventions

While modes of intervention have been classified in several ways (see French and Bell, 1984), one way of understanding them is in terms of the relation with the client and involvement in the client's affairs. The details of the relationship with the client are usually defined contractually at the beginning of the assignment, although the length of the consulting intervention means that the contract is incomplete when agreed. Formally, the professional–client relationship is based on substantial knowledge asymmetry between the parties ('doctor knows best') (Johnson, 1972). This means that the relationship usually starts with a diagnosis defining the problem for the client in terms of the professional's expertise; then, the prescribed solution follows based on the professional's interpretation of the problem and implementation is unproblematic: the client takes the medicine. Management consultants rarely have the power to define the problem so unilaterally. The client can listen to the consultant's description of its expertise and the interpretation of the problem before deciding whether to engage that consultancy or seek another interpretation from another consultant. Further, before the intervention starts, the consultant is likely to try to agree not only the desired outcome but also how it will be reached.

Consultants may therefore be hired to confirm what the client already believes is the solution. As a minimum, their solutions are likely to have to fit with the wishes of the client. The consultant is a 'hired gun' for the principal who is footing the bill. Consultants do not necessarily provide either the optimum solution or impartial advice. They offer the appropriate solution as defined in agreement with the client. Many would be reluctant to go against the wishes of the client to the extent that they lost the engagement, not least because of the internal performance dynamics discussed below.

At one extreme, consultants act as advisers. They simply provide diagnostic advice on the basis of information gathering and analysis about a problem. One such diagnosis involved an analysis of the market and competition to supply mobile telephony in Europe over the medium to long term. This does not go much further than to allow the client (a telecommunications firm thinking of entering this market) to ascertain the status of the problem. It leaves the formation and implementation of the solution in the client's hands. Some consultants – usually economics-based firms – are diagnostic specialists; most will want to go further and provide solutions to problems for the client to implement.

At the other extreme, the consultant is actively involved in the delivery of a service alongside existing staff (see figure 9.2). In effect, the role requires less information gathering and diagnosis as an expert and more the provision of another pair of hands. IT consulting frequently takes this form and this is what makes this functional activity conducive to outsourcing. In between these extremes, diagnosis is mixed with hands-on activity. This requires a range of process consultation activities

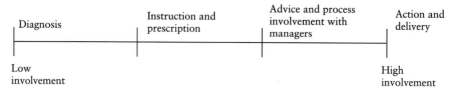

Figure 9.2 The range of consultants' interventions

from problem solving, goal setting, coaching and planning. Here, the consultant acts more prescriptively than if providing pure diagnosis. Some activities require little intervention in the decisions and activities of the client; some involve a closer understanding of the client using techniques that get inside the organization and the way the client thinks. Some, such as strategy execution, require deep involvement because they help to create the appropriate sort of behaviours and attitudes among employees inside the client organization, by example, by training and by benchmarking from outside the firm and by designing incentives for change. This has been the big challenge for all firms trying to enter the strategic change area.

Further, although consultants may therefore shift well beyond diagnosis and limited involvement (Nutt, 1998), it remains difficult for them to substitute for *management* as another pair of hands, precisely because, as other chapters emphasize, the nature of managerial work involves more than technical task completion (Kotter, 1982). One change consultant made the point this way:

> We can build involvement in change. We can educate and what I'd call inform persuasively. . .I cannot force change to happen especially if the management team is not really committed. We can't be part of the networks managers work through day-by-day. . .if I see resistance I can't force people to change . . .I can offer my experience and my toolkit of tricks but it's down to the client . . .to act. (Interview with author, 9/98)

Knowledge and Knowledge Transfer

What, then, are consulting firms doing for their fees? Some have argued that consultants are simply like *shamen*, peddling a form of magic in their rhetoric that is deeply appealing to chief executives, and that their activities are largely symbolic (Clark and Salaman, 1998). One of the problems with this analysis is that it ignores the content of consulting knowledge in focusing on their rhetoric by conflating the role of 'gurus' with other types of consultants.

At the heart of consultants' activities is the application of knowledge in the resolution of a client's problem. When consultants talk of their breadth of experience, some of this is distilled into descriptive models or heuristics ('methodologies') and some is personal and tacit. Their solutions start by seeing the client firm from a wider perspective, as one example of a broader set of problems they have addressed elsewhere. They are less encumbered than the management team by internally focused concerns with politics, heritage or cultural problems which may bias decision making or bound rationality (March and Simon, 1958).

The emphasis on methodologies implies that management is science-like with rules and a means–ends rationality. It is no surprise that the consulting industry emerged out of the scientific management movement and many of the most influential management thinkers operated as consultants, from Frederick Taylor onwards (McKenna, 1995). Some of the most successful consulting firms have been started by business professors, including McKinsey & Co., Arthur D. Little and Monitor, the strategy firm associated with Michael Porter at Harvard. These firms were built on the principle that rigorous analysis of problems using 'objective data' and general principles of decision making could be applied to businesses regardless of sector or origins. The strong analytical approach to managing the organization is reflected in their rationalistic 'methodologies'. These basically include tools for problem identification, information gathering and environment scanning, solution selection and application. However, much of the day-to-day process of consulting involves the reinforcement of credibility in the eyes of the client through symbolic acts, right down to the detailed, highly schematic and well-branded overhead presentation (which, if consultant war stories are to be believed, are invariably put together the night before). The purpose of such symbolic behaviour is important. It serves to suggest that the consultant is the owner of expert knowledge that will be applied in the engagement process (Alvesson, 1993).

The risk is that consulting firms over-generalize their solutions. This occurs partly because the strong sales engines in them lead their members to make claims to clients on which they can sell further work. Over-generalization leads to model development in which cause–effect linkages are likely to be imputed rather than empirically demonstrated, and context specific variables that may have important intervening influences are neglected. For example, the famous BCG matrix of cash cows, stars and dogs quickly became a general model of firm/life cycle and management strategy for clients regardless of industry or political economy. While they generalize and build models, the need to meet client demands drives consulting firms to focus more strongly on the practical application of ideas than other parties that trade in ideas, such as business school academics. Being driven by future sales also makes them concerned to spot developing trends or 'leading edge practice'; in statistical terms, consultants are interested in the tails of population distributions, rather than the mean (Starbuck, 1993).

Interest in 'leading edge practice' provides a clue as to where new knowledge for the consultants comes from and their role in knowledge transfer. There appear to be three sources. First is academic knowledge, particularly that concerned with leading edge activities rather than the mean. Typically, these ideas are reported in practitioner journals such as the *Harvard Business Review*, where they become public knowledge to the extent that it is difficult for them to be patented or declared proprietary. Consider, for example, the Balanced Scorecard, a model disseminated by Kaplan and Norton through the *Harvard Business Review*, on the basis of observations they had made in a number of American firms. This quickly became a widely used tool through its replication in courses in business schools and appropriation by consulting firms, even though the authors had started their own company, Renaissance, to apply the Scorecard model and extract a revenue stream from their work. Indeed, what made this model so appropriable by other firms was the degree to which Kaplan and Norton explicated it in their articles. Most major consulting firms routinely scan academic ideas that can be transferred into products and some have institutionalized this source of knowledge by linking up with business school and university academics to develop their thinking into sources of revenue.

Secondly, consultants develop knowledge from clients. Much of this knowledge comes from those in the operating core of consulting firms who, confronted with particular client problems, find that their existing suite of solutions do not work. Frequently, it is localized and tacit rather than well codified (Morris and Empson, 1998) but it is important because, if it can be codified and redistributed, the knowledge base of the consulting firm is updated. Solutions that work in one client firm are then applied elsewhere so that new knowledge is frequently the recombination of ideas in different contexts (Hargadon and Sutton, 1997). In addition, consultants can appropriate a wider knowledge of the way client firms operate for themselves. Acting as links in a network, they become transmitters of techniques across firms and sectors (Abrahamson, 1991a). Ideally, they will claim to transfer practice from leaders to laggards, but this is dependent on the network of firms they operate within and the quality of knowledge management.

Thirdly, consultants may themselves create knowledge. In most cases, the advances are likely to be highly incremental because of the performance drivers in consulting firms, as discussed below. Some firms are exceptional in this regard: McKinsey, for example, seems to have devoted substantial resources to innovation in recent years, both through consultant time away from the client and creating the appropriate structures for knowledge management. Arguably, its high charges make this investment possible and its competitive position makes it necessary.

Generally, new knowledge is attractive to consulting firms because they can earn higher margins on innovative products and those that have not been widely disseminated. As products get older they invariably become commoditized with the result that the price at which they can be sold moves closer to the marginal cost of delivery. Audit is an example of this. Where a firm perceives sufficient demand for a major product development effort, it will invest in this by drawing on sources of knowledge from outside as well as internally. One consultant from a 'Big Six' firm in America, who had been on such a project, described it as a 'woolly mammoth hunt': the local tribes (i.e. offices across the United States) agreed to pool resources for nearly three months to develop the product, on the basis that all would be able to share the benefits. However, being on the lookout for new products or new combinations of knowledge, consultants tend to run the risk of chasing fashions and fads. Indeed, they are arguably one reason why so many management fashions come and go (Abrahamson, 1991a, 1991b).

The Internal Dynamics of Consulting Firms

Finally, it is worth while considering the internal dynamics of these firms, because of the influence these dynamics have on the way consulting firms actually act and, ultimately, their ability to aid strategy execution. The consulting firm, a classic example of the professional service firm (Maister, 1993) generates profits by leveraging its resources, that is its employees and knowledge base (Morris and Pinnington, 1998). Leveraging staff allows relatively junior employees to be deployed on quite complex assignments by 'lending' them the knowledge based on experience or expertise of more senior staff. This means that the firm can generate profits by charging out staff to clients at rates in excess of their employment costs. Leverage is applied on projects of any size but requires the standardization and routinization of operations to enable juniors to work with relatively little supervision using codified methods.

At times this is entirely appropriate, but where the nature of the problem requires experiential knowledge or a deep understanding of context – that is, tacit know-how as well as formal knowledge – it is not. Effective leverage does not mean the absence of supervision, but permits the experienced manager to co-ordinate activities loosely. Leveraging staff requires a trade-off between experience and cost: experience, generated through work on client projects, is valuable in complex, non-routine assignments but, of course, experienced staff are usually more expensive to employ. Firms therefore have to make strategic choices about the appropriate staff mix, given their market position and the sort of projects they accept. The likelihood that a strategy execution project will, for instance, make considerable demands of the skills and experience of consultants clearly has implications for the extent to which leverage can be achieved.

Firms also have to keep their staff profitably employed. The importance of this is reflected in their key performance measures of billing rate and utilization or time billable to clients. Consultants quickly learn to avoid excess time 'on the beach' – that is, not deployed on client assignments and not charging for their time. They have every incentive to stay utilized, whether this means they are involved in activities where they have real expertise or not. Further, because of the utilization cultures in most firms, off-the-job learning is less legitimate than learning at the client's expense.

Certain risks for clients follow from these powerful performance drivers. For instance, consultants may make unjustifiable claims to knowledge. While this does not mean that consulting firms act unethically, exaggerated claims to expertise may occur in tenders for work. And, because of the credence-based nature of the product, it is difficult for client firms to be able to judge the quality of their purchases until the contract is well underway. Consider, for instance, the comments of one experienced consultant with a 'Big Six' firm in the USA:

> How did we know who had what knowledge? Basically, by what you put on your résumé. The firm's collective knowledge base was very poor because each office was out for itself.
>
> I was put onto a health care sector project as a supposed expert when in reality I had a few days consulting experience there. But my partner-in-charge (boss) needed to show we had expertise in our contract tender. . . . I was pretty worried about this. (Interview 7/1998)

Consultants participate in this game because promotion and pay prospects are so closely driven by utilization figures and the assessment of local partners. Further, partners themselves face demanding sales and profit targets for their practices which drive the required utilization rates. Combined with the need to keep staff utilized this means that firms try to 'cover the field' – that is, to spread themselves widely in order to be able to respond to the maximum number of market opportunities. It also creates in staff the incentive to have, or lay claim to, a range of skills or experience that are like options they can cash in to keep them productively employed on projects. Thus, mode of work acquisition plus the performance dynamics of the professional service firm combine to create breadth rather than depth of client and technical knowledge.

Putting together these performance drivers, one can see that the consulting firm can be caught trying to square opposing forces. It wants leverage by standardizing its knowledge and it also wants innovation for the price premium it can command. It has to balance the routine 'vanilla' favourites with the provision of fancier flavours. It aims to codify and standardize the innovation without over-simplifying.

Implications for Strategy Execution

As other chapters in this volume have shown, making strategies happen is a messy, non-linear process in which persuasion is as important as rational application of finely formulated plans (Quinn, 1978). Execution overlaps with plan formulation. It involves affective as well as rational argument, political activities such as coalition building and power broking and the deployment of incentives and sanctions to encourage waverers or isolate opposition. Symbolic actions are likely to be as important as substantive changes, to bring home messages about the required behaviours, attitudes and values involved in making implementation work.

Strategy execution is, therefore, the sort of complex process in which there is a risk to the client that the consulting firm pursues excessive leverage. By this, I mean that it is unlikely that junior or inexperienced consultants will have the expertise to deal with resistance to change from entrenched groups, to have a sufficiently sophisticated understanding of power or to understand the management networks through which information and decision making proceed. This is not primarily a matter of intelligence but of the skills and experience in handling problems where there is usually no consensus about the desired outcome. In these types of situation the collection of more information, model building and analysis do not necessarily hold the key to success; painstaking attention to detailed operational issues and a good understanding of the firm's heritage or culture are the keys. It also needs to be recognized that consultants are inevitably restricted in the range of interventions they can use because they do not have access to the sort of resources necessary to implement changes themselves. These resources may include rights to reward or punish and access to networks and embedded relationships through which managerial work gets done (Hales, 1993). Consultants may well be able to bring to bear the sort of skills outlined above which can facilitate change in attitude or behaviour, but limits to their authority inevitably restrict their ability to execute – that is, to make things happen.

Furthermore, to be effective in the arena of strategy execution, consultants have to be able to understand how the value chain of an organization is put together. In other words: how do bundles of activities really link with each other through what resource-based theorists would call the routines of the organization? (Peteraf, 1993) In these routines, extensive tacit know-how is likely to be held by the members of the organization and it requires familiarity with these issues if outside observers are really to be able to make successful changes. Such familiarity comes from extended observation, close interaction with working groups and prior experience of similar circumstances; it is experienced-based knowledge. The risks in using consultants, particularly on a one-off basis, are that they either prescribe solutions which do not play to the strengths of the firm, or they eventually contribute to the destruction of strategic assets by, for example, recommending reorganizations that break up routines in which unique knowledge is stored.

I have argued that the performance drivers inside consulting firms may exacerbate these risks for client firms. At the extreme, the standardized recipes and methods necessary to deploy relatively junior staff and achieve leverage mean that there is a failure to appreciate the idiosyncrasies of the client's situation. This can lead to inappropriate solutions which take little account of whether they will work or the degree of resistance to them. Standardization results in satisfying rather than optimal outcomes. It means that the client gets a solution that has worked elsewhere but is unlikely to provide a unique advantage on which to compete. Acting as knowledge transmitters from leaders to laggards, consultants help to establish industry standards. By improving the quality of mediocre firms, this may raise the overall average of economic performance, but it also promotes regression to the mean across firms rather than superiority through difference. At worst, consulting interventions can undermine any inherent advantage the client may have developed on the basis of its own heritage, replacing unique assets with the 'Hallmark card' of the industry.

These risks are most likely where consulting is transaction based and where the consultant puts the client into a relationship of dependency. Where the project is a one-off engagement with the client, insufficient knowledge of the idiosyncrasies of the client makes customization impossible before the assignment starts. Typically, this sort of consulting involves a different form of selling from relationship consulting, being based on tendering for contracts that are highly price sensitive. Where the consultant acts as the expert, offering or providing solutions and advice as he or she thinks fit rather than collaborating with the clients to resolve problems jointly, it is also likely that the clients will get a raw deal. Not only will they be more likely to receive the standard recipe rather than a customized (jointly developed) solution, but they will also be less likely to understand fully the underlying causes of their own problem and therefore the real strengths or weaknesses of their own organization.

To avoid these risks, clients need to insist that their consultants invest in developing more intimate knowledge of the internal organization and the distribution of power in the client organization. This may come through longer term relationships and, of course, consultants have an incentive to construct these. Relationships do not incur repeated set-up costs and are less price-sensitive than one-off transactions. They allow the consulting firm to establish deeper and detailed knowledge of the client's operating routines and to learn from them. From the client firm's point of view, the objective is to avoid the trap of dependency while insisting that the consultants really learn about the business before they move into action. As far as possible, they should also make sure that they are not funding learning that has already taken place in the consulting firm but has not been properly codified or transferred.

Clients should also aim to control excessive delegation of responsibility to juniors while recognizing that leverage is appropriate for some tasks. Simply checking the credentials of those assigned to the project and monitoring compliance with the initial contract can do this. Clients should insist on reviews during the assignment that not only chart progress but also examine what has been learned and how this learning is being captured for the future benefit of the client, as well as the consultant. The consulting engagement should, in effect, transfer knowledge from the consultant to the client in such a way that the client can stand on its own. Even if a longer-term relationship exists, the terms of separation at the end of an assignment always need to be discussed.

Conclusions

Consultants act as conduits through which knowledge flows. They build networks of knowledge from clients, by hiring consultants from other firms and from the practitioner-oriented academic literature. Their role as transmitters of knowledge means that they are always looking for innovations that can be transformed into products before they become commoditized. Transforming ideas and practices into products requires some form of codification. This also helps the firm to standardize its procedures or methodologies as they are called. Standardization allows the consulting firm to achieve leverage, deploying staff of different levels of expertise and experience on jobs using the knowledge encoded in these methodologies, and this is the key to profits. Thus, the consulting firm seeks innovation and standardization simultaneously.

I have argued that these dynamics can be problematic in the area of strategy execution where, frequently, the problem is one of resistance to change from those in the middle of the organization. Change is a political process in which it is very difficult to exert influence as outsiders. None the less, consultants can make effective interventions in the process of change, and are more likely to do so if they work with managers and employees rather than try to impose externally derived blueprints. They are also likely to succeed if, while recognizing the importance of experience, they are prepared to forgo the short-term benefits of high leverage for the longer-term benefits of a strong reputation and sustained client relationships.

References

Abrahamson, E. 1991a: Managerial fads and fashions: the diffusion and rejection of innovations. *Academy of Management Review*, 16, 586–612.

Abrahamson, E. 1991b: Champions of change and strategic shifts: the role of internal and external change advocates. *Journal of Management Studies*, 28, 173–90.

Alvesson, M. 1993: Organisations as rhetoric: knowledge intensive firms and the struggle with ambiguity. *Journal of Management Studies*, 30(6), 997–1015.

Argyris, C. 1970: *Intervention theory and method*. Reading, MA: Addison-Wesley.

Bowman J. 1984: *Booz, Allen and Hamilton: seventy years of client service, 1914–1984*. Chicago: Booz, Allen & Hamilton.

Clark, T. and Salaman, G. 1998: Telling tales: mangement gurus' narratives and the construction of managerial identity. *Journal of Management Studies*, 35(2), 137–61.

Empson, L. and Morris, T. 1997: *Kinsley Lord. London Business School case study*. London, UK.

French, W. and Bell, C. 1984: *Organization Development*. Englewood Cliffs, NJ: Prentice-Hall.

Hales, C. 1993: *Managing through organisation*. London: Routledge.

Hargadon, A. and Sutton, R. 1997: Technology brokering and innovation in a product development firm. *Administrative Science Quarterly*, 42, 716–49.

Johnson, T.J. 1972: *Professions and power*. London: Macmillan.

Kotter, J. 1982: *The general managers*. New York: Free Press.

Maister, D. 1993: *Managing the professional service firm*. Boston, MA: Harvard Business School Press.

March J. and Simon, H. 1958: *Organizations*. New York: Wiley.

McKenna C. 1995: The origins of modern management consulting. *Business and Economic History*, 24, 51–8.

McKenna, C. 1998: Selling corporate culture: codifying and commodifying professionalism at McKinsey and Company, 1940–1980. Paper given at the American Studies Workshop, Pennsylvania State University (November).

Morris T. and Empson, L. 1998: Organization and expertise: an exploration of knowledge management in an accounting firm and a consulting firm. *Accounting, Organizations and Society*, 23(5/6), 604–29.

Morris, T. and Pinnington, A. 1998: Patterns of profit sharing in professional firms. *British Journal of Management*, 9, 23–39.

Nutt, P. 1998: Leverage, resistance and the success of implementation approaches. *Journal of Management Studies*, 35, 213–39.

O'Shea, J. and Madigan, C. 1997: *Dangerous company: the consulting powerhouses and the businesses they save and ruin*. London: Nicholas Brealey.

Peteraf, M. 1993: The cornerstones of competitive advantage: a resource based view. *Strategic Management Journal*, 14, 179–88.

Peters, T. and Waterman, R. 1982: *In search of excellence: lessons from America's best-run companies*. New York: Harper Row.

Price Waterhouse 1995: *Better change: best practices in transforming your organization*. New York: Irwin.

Quinn, J.B. 1978: *Strategies for change: logical incrementalism*. New York: Irwin.

Schein, E. 1969: *Process consultation: its role in organization development*. Reading, MA: Addison-Wesley.

Starbuck, W. 1993: Keeping a butterfly and an elephant in a house of cards: the elements of exceptional success. *Journal of Management Studies*, 30, 885–921.

10

The Leadership of Learning: the Core Process of Strategy Implementation

Dennis Gillen

Introduction: Leadership and Learning

Cyert and March, in introducing the concept of organizational learning, were among the first theorists to address crucial questions associated with the emergence of knowledge workers. In the early 1960s they stated:

> Organizations learn: to assume that organizations go through the same processes of learning as do individual human beings seems unnecessarily naïve, but organizations exhibit (as do other social institutions) adaptive behaviour over time. (Cyert and March, 1963: 123)

A growing number of organization scholars have now begun to link leaders with the learning process of an organization. For example, Peter Senge (1990: 340) stated:

> The new view of leadership in learning organizations centers on subtler and more important tasks. In a learning organization, leaders are designers, stewards and teachers. They are responsible for building organizations where people continually expand their capabilities to understand complexity, clarify vision and improve shared mental models.

Of course, many practising leaders and managers have recognized what Senge observed, and have actively practised this role of leadership. George D. Smith, the former chairman and CEO of UPS, once put it this way: 'Managing is: to teach, to coach, to be taught, to learn.'

Frank Friedlander (1983: 220), one of the pioneers of organizational learning theory, first described this direct relationship between leadership and learning:

> The executive function is also to lead the organization in its reconstructive learning. This means to encourage exploration and confrontation of differing viewpoints, to foster structures within the organization that encourage contact between differing subsystems in which power balance as well as trust and valuing occur. The executive role is to foster a structure and a climate for planned transition in which the organization's knowledge resources are fully utilized.

Organizational learning is a critical process in the implementation of strategy which is often overlooked in organizational change programmes. It is an essential component in the success of major strategic initiatives that firms are attempting to implement in today's competitive business environment. Whether it is a merger between Chrysler and Daimler-Benz, a product launch by Intel, or the globalization strategy of Dell computer, employee learning requirements have proved to be very extensive and often underestimated.

$$\begin{bmatrix} \text{Strategic} \\ \text{Change} \end{bmatrix} \longrightarrow \begin{bmatrix} \text{Leadership} \\ \text{(Organizational Learning)} \end{bmatrix} \longrightarrow \begin{bmatrix} \text{Strategy} \\ \text{Implementation} \end{bmatrix}$$

The underlying assumption of this model is that learning in an organization must be effectively led in order for a strategy to be implemented successfully. Under this model the definition of a leader is someone who guides and inspires the learning process throughout the organization in order to create and motivate the thoughts and actions required to implement the key strategies of the organization based on the overall strategic mission and vision. The role of the leader as a manager of learning will be discussed, citing the writings of Michael Porter, Peter Senge, Frank Friedlander, Edgar H. Schein and others as appropriate. The chapter will also draw upon some of the author's conceptual models concerning organizational learning and some 'real-life' examples of organizational learning from the author's consulting experiences.

Leadership and Learning: Some Critical Capabilities

The leadership of organizational learning is obviously a very complex subject with many facets to it. However, given the space limitations, in this chapter I will focus on only some of what I feel are the most critical leadership requirements associated with organizational learning and strategy implementation. Given this focus, I feel that the leader should possess each of the following five organizational learning capabilities to assure the successful implementation of organizational strategy:

1. The ability to help to create a vision and core values that focus employees' learning on corporate priorities and strategies, while eliminating the waste associated with non-essential learning.

The ability to transform a vision of the future into needed explicit knowledge. The ability to lead key individuals and groups to develop both the specialized and the convergent knowledge needed to ensure the successful implementation of strategy.

✓ 4. The ability to adjust the learning rate to the degree of competitiveness required.

✓ 5. The ability to encourage employees to use imagination to see and understand situations in new ways in their learning activities.

I see these abilities as translated into behaviours as essential for all managers in the changing organization not just those at the highest levels. I also see that they involve unrelenting constant interpersonal actions from all managers especially as strategies and/or tactics constantly change over time. The realities of the manager's role indicate that they involve a very dynamic process. As Carroll and Gillen (1987: 76) point out:

> It appears that managers, especially top managers, work from a 'goal agenda' which is a set of desired future states that they are trying to move towards, and they only have tentative plans about how to get to these states, which are constantly changing as new information is received and new opportunities to make progress arise. Detailed planning is difficult to do because of the many interdependencies and restraints faced by managers at all levels. Progress toward such goals is often slow perhaps interrupted by movement backwards from time to time.

Vision, Mission and Core Values

As I have indicated, leaders must possess certain abilities to effectively direct and inspire the necessary learning processes in their organizations. The first is the ability to help create a vision and a set of core values that help to focus employees attention to and understanding of current corporate priorities and strategies and thus direct learning efforts.

Vision, mission and core values are critical to the leadership of learning. Peter Senge (1990: 206) in *The Fifth Discipline* states: 'A shared vision is not an idea. Rather it is a force in people's hearts, a sense of purpose which provides energy and focus for learning.' The leader of an organization is primarily responsible for developing this vision and the culture that supports it. 'The most intriguing leadership role in culture management is one in which the leader attempts to develop a learning organization that will be able to make its own perpetual diagnosis and self-manage whatever transformations are needed as the environment changes' (Schein, 1992: 363). Again, this new corporate environment not only calls for a CEO to lead the learning process, but also for managers and employees to become leaders of learning.

Leadership is a process that can transform the thoughts, learning approaches and behaviours of employees to create a culture that enhances the daily experiences of both employees and customers. A clear vision and mission provide the opportunity for current and future employees to understand the purpose and direction of their work and adapt their behaviours to achieve both vertical and horizontal alignment.

Jack Welch (Tichy and Sherman, 1993: 246) stressed the vital role of organizational values as follows:

> Every organization needs values, but a lean organization needs them even more. When you strip away the support systems of staffs and layers, people have to change their habits and expectations; or else the stress will just overwhelm them. We're all working harder and faster, but unless we're also having more fun, the transformation doesn't work. Values are what enable people to guide themselves through this kind of change.

The learning process in an organization is given structure and direction by both its core values and the vision. According to Collins and Porras (1994: 220–1) authors of *Built to Last*:

> A well-conceived vision centers around two major components: core ideology and an envisioned future. A vision builds on the interplay between these two complementary forces that define 'what we stand for and why we exist' and 'what we aspire to become, to achieve, to create' that will require significant change and progress to attain. Without established core values and vision, employees will not have the ability to focus their learning on the behaviors/actions that are aligned with the strategic intent of the organization.

Senior management cannot make every decision, but by encouraging learning they can help to foster the climate for the distributed decision making necessary for strategy implementation throughout the organization. In short, they must be the catalysts for learning. According to Fry and Pasmore (1983: 292):

> The ultimate contribution of the executive mind, we believe, lies in the ability to rise above the immediate situation, go beyond current definitions of problems, and think past current solutions towards a new vision, new conception of issues and new questions. More precisely, both the rate and the eventual level of learning achieved will be a function of the executive's ability to enter, develop relationships within, and manage groups of significant others.

This dynamic process of leaders involves encouraging employees to take ownership of the core corporate values and vision and to motivate and guide the learning that is essential to successful strategy implementation.

The reason strategy implementation is more difficult than strategy formulation is that, to be completed, it involves so many more people. According to Hunger and Wheelen (1997: 124):

> Depending on how the corporation is organized, those who implement strategy will probably be a much more diverse group of people than those who formulate it. In most large multi-industry corporations, the implementers will include everyone in the organization. Most of the people in the organization who are critical to successful strategy implementation probably had little, if anything, to do with the development of the corporate and even business strategy. Unless changes in mission, objectives, strategies and policies and their importance to the company are communicated clearly to all operators and managers, resistance and foot-dragging are likely to result.

Vision to Explicit Knowledge

The problem with most strategies is that they are never fully implemented, because the learning required to implement the strategy never occurs. The tactical knowledge of the strategy leaders never becomes explicit knowledge that the employees can use to implement the strategy. 'Tactical knowledge is what we know implicitly inside, while explicit knowledge is what we know formally' (Nonaka and Takeuchi, 1995: 111–12).

The nature of knowledge requires that it be made usable. This is really the heart of strategy formulation and implementation. According to Harland Cleveland (1985: 23):

> Most knowledge is expertive – in a field, a subject, a science, a technology, a system of values, a form of social organization and authority. Wisdom is integrated knowledge; information made superuselful by theory, which relates bits and fields of knowledge to each other, which in turn enables one to use knowledge to do something. That's why wisdom is bound to cross the disciplinary barriers we set up to make the fields of knowledge manageable.

Excellent theory quickly becomes successful practice and weak or mediocre theory just lasts for ever, confusing everyone. This is why good leaders have a teachable point of view. According to Charan and Tichy (1998: 13), 'Real leaders at any level in an organization control their own destiny. They use their teachable points of view to challenge the system.'

Leading the Development of Needed Specialized and Convergent Knowledge

Organizations in the new information age learn by expanding their knowledge base and then converging what they have learned into a new synthesis with what they already know. This requires sorting through the critical connections between the new and the old. Convergent knowledge based on linking specialized knowledge and the ability to synthesize diverse sources of expertise is as critical to organizational success as specialized knowledge. In this era of mergers, buy-outs, alliances and new product development, the ability to expand an organization's knowledge is critical. In order to merge, two organizations must expand their knowledge of each other at an extremely wide band in order to converge what is important to them. Convergence is the process of combining diverse organizational competencies and knowledge into collaborative efforts that solve problems and take advantage of opportunities (Gillen and Fitzgerald, 1991). Many organizations throughout the 1980s and 1990s have unbundled their specialized knowledge and created new forms of convergent knowledge structures (see figure 10.1).

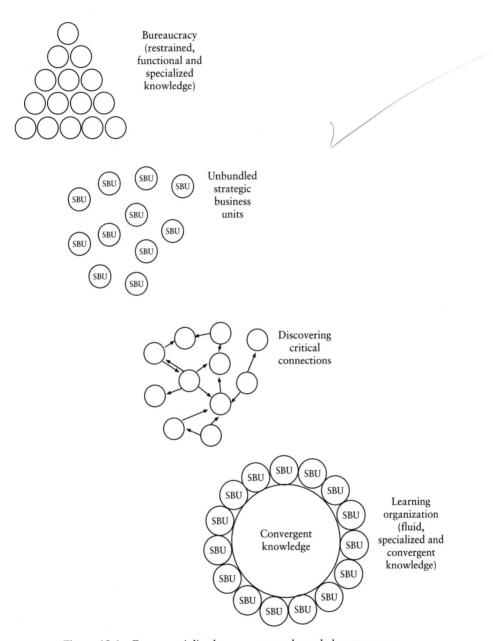

Figure 10.1   From specialized to convergent knowledge structures

Figure 10.1 describes how organizations have moved away from an era where knowledge was mostly functional and specialized, trapped in silos and converged at the highest levels of the organization in what might be described as a very political environment. Organizations have since been led to more decentralized organizational designs and have unbundled their specialized knowledge assets. These strategic business units (SBUs) are very self-contained and can mobilize knowledge to where it is needed to deal with problems and take advantage of opportunities more quickly. This unbundling has made companies faster, while making it easier for SBUs to become isolated and disconnected from other SBUs in the organization. When this happens new knowledge linkages must be created in order to share critical information and create valuable convergent knowledge. These networks or linkages – described by Fry and Pasmore (1983) as frame-linking and frame-sharing, and later by Badaracco (1991) as knowledge links – allow units to create convergent knowledge about technology, customers, markets, practices, personnel, processes and any number of valuable sources of knowledge without incurring the costs associated with the old-line bureaucracies. This new way of relating organizations and organizational units requires new forms of learning and has made the decisions involving connections of knowledge critical for leaders.

According to Nahapiet and Ghoshal (1998), social capital is needed to develop intellectual capital, while intellectual capital aids in the development of social capital. According to the authors, this dynamic interplay of social and intellectual capital in the modern organization may lead to organizational advantage. The leadership of learning is much more critical in today's evolving organizational structures for the implementation of strategies than it was in yesterday's bureaucracies. The convergent knowledge developed among the SBUs becomes a very valuable resource over time. General Electric's sharing of knowledge, through the use of its Crotonville training centre, has helped all of its businesses share the GE philosophy and best practices. They have also used this major resource to leverage their service businesses by offering to their customers much of the knowledge developed at Crotonville.

Successful athletics teams develop convergent knowledge by practising and playing together. Each specialized position learns how different multiple interactions can lead to success or failure. This shared knowledge becomes a resource for the group or team. It is a pity that most executive teams do not practise as hard as successful athletics teams.

In regard to structure, organizations operating in the informational age are not only converging knowledge among the SBUs and many internal functions, but also are in a continual process of expanding by forming interactive networks of relationships outside the organization. Frequent communication, co-operation and information exchanges made possible by the information revolution create a vision of a boundaryless organization, as this picture of the information-based organization by Tom Peters (1990: 75) suggests:

> We can no longer think productively or profitably about 'the company' alone. All models of 'the firm' must include seamless global connections with vendors, vendors' vendors, middlepersons, customer, and customers' customers.

These stakeholders of the convergent knowledge network are all critical for strategy implementation.

Competitiveness and the Learning Rate

Business organizations operate in a competitive arena where Darwin-like forces can eliminate them if they do not also focus on competitive strategy. Winners are invested in through the financial markets and losers are cut-off from financial resources, allowing the best to prosper and the failures to disappear. Leaders of learning must understand the use of the relationship between competition and learning to direct strategy implementation.

Competition and the learning rate have a complex relationship – at times conflicting and at times complementing each other. A balance must be struck between competitiveness and learning. At times, learning may be disrupting to the progression of the organization. According to Frank Friedlander (1983: 195), 'the chaos of learning is frequently incompatible with being productive, at both the individual and organizational levels'. There are times to learn and times to produce, as figure 10.2 indicates. The competitive learning model displays this in the upper left-hand quadrant. Organizations faced with urgent or life-threatening learning requirements can start to grasp at everything now to learn at once. Also, organizations that ignore the opportunity costs of learning can develop the grasping mode. This grasping mode represents firms that are not focused on competition. Organizations that avoid major and sometimes disruptive learning may become complacent to discontinuous changes and end up highly successful at yesterday's market rules. These firms would be placed in the model's complacent mode.

Companies that do not allow for what Friedlander terms 'reconstructive learning' can find themselves non-competitive over time. According to Hamel and Prahalad (1994: 6), 'few companies that began the 1980s as industry leaders ended the decade with leadership intact and undiminished'. The reason for this is that learning allows an organization to participate in the development of the new rules of the marketplace and be a trendsetter rather than a follower. We are beginning to realize that learning and competition are neither strictly opposing nor complementary forces, but are part of a complex synthesis of critical connections with many multiple variables that must be learned, understood and led.

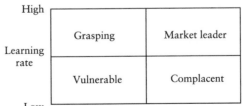

Figure 10.2   Organizational learning and competitiveness

What organizations must do is manage a high rate of learning and competitiveness. An organization must find the critical connections between competition and learning. Competition can bring structure and discipline to an organization's learning process by focusing it on learning activities that will result in market success. It also makes employees aware of the opportunity costs of different learning options. Successful CEOs demonstrate this focus by paying strict attention to the bottom line. Bernie Ebbers, CEO of MCI Worldcom, says: 'I look at every single line item in the budget for the company. I think the MCI people are pretty amazed about the level of detail I get into.'

Michael Porter (1980), in his groundbreaking book *Competitive Strategy*, provides techniques for analysing industries and competitiveness. This book is about learning more about competitors and the industry in which one's organization competes. Many leaders have used Porter's five fundamental forces of competition and industry as a structural framework for leading the learning of their organizations.

Organizational leaders must balance the paradox of competition and learning by realizing at times that switching learning frameworks and disrupting current competitive practices can lead to future success. According to Hamel and Prahalad (1994: 6), the real competition problem is:

> ... laggards versus challengers, incumbents versus innovators, the imitative and emulative versus the imaginative. Challengers typically invent more efficient solutions to customer problems. They discover the new solutions because they are willing to look far beyond the old.

The learning–competitiveness model shows that organizations which concentrate on competitive factors can become bottom-line obsessive to the point of being myopic, complacent and 'missing the future'. The opposite problem would be one of constantly learning and encouraging change to the point where the organization was in constant disruption, not allowing for competitive advantage to be employed (upper-left quadrant). Order is necessary for most competitive factors to be employed, but order that becomes rigid will inhibit the learning required to adapt to the competitive challenges in the future. An organization must emphasize both learning and competition at high levels and understand the critical connection between these forces to be a market leader.

Imagination and Strategy Implementation

Imagination is about improving our abilities to see and understand situations in new ways (Morgan, 1997: 2). A leader of learning must encourage employees' implementing strategies to see and understand situations in new ways. This ability to imagine allows employees to change the old practices of bureaucratic organizations and produce new self-organizing systems. Jack Welch (Slater, 1994: 13) described the freedom necessary to get individuals to succeed in the new organization as follows:

The old organization was built on control, but the world has changed. The world is moving at such a pace that control has become a limitation. It slows you down. You've got to balance freedom with some control, but you've got to have more freedom than you ever dreamed of.

This freedom is necessary for employees to explore their imaginations. Gareth Morgan (1997: xxiv), in his book entitled *Imaginization*, describes the many uses of imagination in today's organizations:

Imagination is a way of thinking. It's a way of organizing. It's a key managerial skill. It provides a way of helping people understand and develop their creative potential. It offers a means of finding innovative solutions to difficult problems. And, last but not least, it provides a means of empowering people to trust themselves and fine a new role in a world characterized by flux and change.

Mackenzie-Childs is an example of a company that thrives on imagination. Mackenzie-Childs creates hand-crafted painted pottery and other home furnishings, and has developed an international customer base. Its products are sold through Neiman Marcus and specialty retailers. The company store on Madison Avenue in New York City does a brisk business despite the very steep price tags. Richard and Victoria have built a company based upon their desire to share the ideals of freedom, jubilance and purity. One afternoon, while sipping tea with Richard Mackenzie-Childs during an interview about the culture of their rising company, it occurred to me how philosophically and emotionally involved the employees and customers were with the lives of the owners and the overall goal of the organization to spread freedom, purity and joy. They all seem to know about Richard and Victoria's epic journey to their present-day success as leaders of the craft industry and premier designers of spirited home furnishings, dinnerware, glassware, linen and special accessories. Their headquarters, a former dairy farm, has been turned into what resembles the Land of Oz and attracts busloads of followers in hot pursuit of the latest pottery designs and breaking details about Richard and Victoria's lives. The reputation of the company is a great example of the strong integration of culture and vision development. One might say they have created a land where freedom, jubilance and purity reign for customers and employees. Imagination is not a part of their business, it is their business!

The following two organizations, with which the author has been involved in a long-term consulting relationship, demonstrate many of the concepts about the leadership of learning that we have discussed. They show how two different organizations have obtained the same results by leading the learning required to implement their strategies. Each of these organizations demonstrates the seven abilities that leaders need to lead the learning requirements for strategy implementation.

New Venture Gear

New Venture Gear officially came into being on 1 January 1990. In the joint venture, Chrysler assumed 66 per cent equity and General Motors assumed 34 per cent. This joint venture represented the first effort among the Big Three in the US automobile industry to form a joint supplier venture. Two plants, one in Muncie, Indiana, and the other in Syracuse, New York, comprise the joint venture, in addition to a headquarters unit which was formed at the time the joint venture started, staffed by executives from both Chrysler and GM and located in Troy, Michigan. The Troy headquarters was created to serve as a senior umbrella management for the entire joint venture.

New Venture Gear refers to itself as the 'world's premier driveline supplier': because it is the largest manufacturer of manual transmissions, manual transaxles, viscous couplings, and overdrive compounders in the US auto industry. The three major objectives in forming the joint venture were: (1) lowering costs by increasing economies of scale; (2) increasing capacity at the lowest possible cost by using the excess capacity at Muncie; and (3) increasing the independence of both plants from the parents by creating incentives to solicit other customers in the global market-place. One of the conditions of the joint venture agreement is that GM and Chrysler are not obligated to buy components from New Venture Gear if the components are not competitive in price to other global suppliers. This arrangement has the intention of making sure that New Venture Gear is not insulated from global market pressures to lower costs and increase quality, and also frees New Venture Gear's management to seek out additional customers around the globe.

At the start of 1990, many uncertainties, both external and internal, combined to create a sense of urgency and pressure in addition to the pressure to form a new organization. Externally, Japanese manufacturers were creating indirect pressure on New Venture Gear. Because of the tremendous improvements the Japanese companies achieved in product quality during the 1980s, standards became increasingly stringent for what constitutes world-class quality in global automobile components markets.

The struggle to increase quality and productivity while creating a new organizational infrastructure put incredible pressure on New Venture Gear's plant managers. During its initial years, the plant managers seemed to sense that competitive products could only be produced by organizations that possess world-class processes and practices, and that products reflect the competitiveness of organizational structures. The learning requirements for this joint venture were tremendous and the organizations leaders rose to the challenge of leading the learning of their employees.

Progressive centralization of values and objectives through a process of functional convergence and organization learning requires functions to relinquish sovereignty (Gillen and Fitzgerald, 1991: 21). Before the joint venture was formed, most power and authority for decision making rested in the 'fiefdoms' or individual territories of the different functional areas in the plants. Both plants found themselves suffering because expertise and knowledge was locked up in the functions, as opposed to being shared. This lack of cross-functional integration had a detrimental impact on decision making, as levels of organizational learning were low. Plant managers found it difficult to converge interests and objectives across functions, and could not utilize potentially high levels of learning that could be produced if functional knowledge converged. The joint venture, however, provided both plants with this opportunity. Much higher levels of organizational learning, including the entire joint venture, occurred when the managers and engineers of both plants were brought together in cross-functional teams for new product planning and development, the design of new training programmes, and strategic planning projects. This leading of the learning processes to implement New Venture Gear's strategy was called 'Smart Enterprise'. Since this initial leadership of learning, many projects have been developed to encourage the expansion convergence process and balance learning with competitiveness. The development of its centre for learning in 1992 has acted as an engine in driving the learning process. All employees and their families have access to the centre, which is open 24 hours each day.

Perhaps the most critical agreement made between the management and the union of New Venture Gear was a complete commitment to learning. The management agreed to learn to think and act like entrepreneurs and capture new businesses in exchange for union members abandoning old jobs and learning new skills and behaviours. Both groups use the realities of external competitors to channel and focus their learning. This led to the creation of new contracts with Chrysler Corporation and General Motors. It also led to entirely new business contracts with Ford, BMW and Diamond Star Motors. Union members learned an array of new skills and practices and the cycle of job depletion was eliminated where union members try to hold on to antiquated jobs and management just trims cost from existing business. This major commitment to learning has had great results. New Venture Gear has continued to expand rapidly in capturing more than 70 per cent of the world's four-wheel drive market and tripled sales in eight years; it has expanded its learning on a continuous basis and converged all the critical connections to avoid complacency and disruption. It has found a synthesis between learning and competing.

Agway

One of the most important leadership roles an organization can perform is seeing that all senior managers and board directors are involved on a personal basis in organizational learning. An example of this would be the efforts Agway, a co-operative of 80,000 dairy farmers in the north-east United States, has made to instill the learning process through its fifteen farmer directors. In 1995, Agway was an organization that was on the brink of insolvency and needed to do something drastic. The newly appointed CEO and the chairman of the board of directors made a commitment to foster learning throughout the co-operative. The results have been significant, as the co-operative has moved from a loss of $15 million to a profit of $41 million on yearly sales of 1.6 billion in three years. Learning is spreading rapidly throughout the organization and the board itself is at the centre of the learning process. Boards nationwide are increasingly being asked to make decisions on very challenging issues and transitions with very little lead times. They cannot wait to educate themselves in order to make decisions when they arise; therefore, they must constantly be learning.

At the August 1997 meeting, members of Agway's board of directors learned how today's competitive environment is increasing the activity of boards of directors nation-wide in the following ways:

- independence and empowerment are increasing among board members to make organizations quicker and more flexible;
- board members are expected to become familiar with the competitive environment of their organizations;
- the time commitment required of directors outside of meetings is increasing;
- meeting time is decreasing;
- boards are increasingly composed of individuals with diverse sets of skills and backgrounds;
- an increasing number of organizations are having board compensation based on organizational performance;
- boards are being held accountable for their decision and actions.

All of these trends point to the fact that a board with a strong learning culture will be a real competitive advantage for strategy implementation. Through their governance they will be able to lead the learning of the organization to implement the strategies they help to develop.

An example of the use of imaginative learning at Agway would be their efforts to see themselves as more than a north-east, supply-side co-operative of 80,000 dairy farmers. This 'breaking out of the box' has led to several profitable new business ventures. The board and management, while pushing for imagination competencies throughout the organization, have also worked hard through benchmarking and learning to increase implementation skills through the training of business basics and baseline financial practices. This combination of imagination and implementation has attracted the close attention of other companies in the industry.

This type of commitment to learning that connects leadership to the learning process and the learning process to strategy implementation has resulted in spectacular market results, not only at Agway and New Venture Gear but also at a wide variety of businesses. As both a consultant and researcher, the author has seen these same results in a wide variety of industries and has also observed the importance of the capabilities concerning the leadership of learning outlined in the opening paragraphs.

Summary

Strategy implementation is too important to be just managed, it must also be led and a major part of this leading involves the inspiring and directing of the learning needed to implement the strategies in a turbulent world of change. The leaders of this learning at every organizational level must use the vision and core values to focus the learning, thus creating explicit knowledge for those implementing the strategy.

Competitiveness must be used to structure and focus the learning while it redefines the rules of competitiveness. Imagination and action must be used to stimulate bold new ways of doing things derived from radical learning. Every leader has a strategy, but only those who implement are remembered as leaders of learning.

References

Badaracco, J.L. 1991: *The knowledge link: how firms compete through strategic alliances.* Boston, MA: Harvard Business School Press.

Carroll, S.J. and Gillen, D.J. 1987: Are the classical management functions useful in describing managerial work. *Management and organizational behavior classics.* Homewood, IL: Irwin.

Charan, R. and Tichy, N.M. 1998: *Every business is a growth business.* New York: Times Books.

Cleveland, H. 1985: *The knowledge executive.* New York: E.P. Dutton.

Collins, J. and Porras, J.I. 1994: *Built to last.* New York: Harper Collins.

Cyert, R.M. and March, J.G. 1963: *A behavioral theory of the firm.* Engelwood Cliffs, NJ: Prentice-Hall.

Friedlander, F. 1983. Patterns of individual and organizational learning. *Executive mind.* San Francisco: Jossey-Bass.

Fry, R. and Pasmore, W. 1983: Strengthening management education. *Executive mind.* San Francisco: Jossey-Bass.

Gillen, D. and Fitzgerald, E. 1991: Expanding knowledge and converging functions. *Concurrent Engineering*, 111(3), 20–8.

Hamel, G. and Prahalad, C.K. 1994: *Cometing for the future.* Boston: Harvard Business School Press.

Hunger, J.D. and Wheelen, T.L. 1997: *Essentials of strategic management.* New York: Addison-Wesley.

Morgan, G. 1997: *Imaginization: new mindsets for seeing, organizing and managing.* New York: Sage.

Nahapiet, J. and Ghoshal, S. 1998: Social capital, intellectual capital and the organizational advantage. *Academy of Management Review*, 23(2), 242–66.

Nonaka, I. and Takeuchi, H. 1995: *The knowledge-creating company: how Japanese companies create the dynamics of innovation.* New York: Oxford University Press.

Peters, T. 1987: Trometheus barely unbound. *Academy of Management Executive*, 4, 70–85.

Porter, M. 1980: *Competitive strategy.* New York: Free Press.

Senge, P. 1990: *The fifth discipline.* New York: Doubleday.

Schein, E. 1992: *Organizational culture and leadership.* San Francisco: Jossey-Bass.

Slater, R. 1994: *Get better or get beaten.* New York and Homewood, IL: Irwin.

Tichy, N.M and Sherman, S. 1993: *Control your destiny or someone will*, New York: Doubleday.

11

Middle Management Resistance to Strategic Change Initiatives: Saboteurs or Scapegoats?

MARK FENTON-O'CREEVY

In recent writings on strategy there has been a trend away from the view of strategy as a rational plan devised by the senior team. Many researchers and theorists in the field of strategic decision making now emphasize the processes by which strategic responses emerge, often in a relatively complex and incoherent fashion in response to internal and external events. Mintzberg in particular has described the ways in which strategies may emerge over time as a series of incremental trials which often only develop a clear rationale in hindsight (Mintzberg, 1990, 1994). Such process-oriented accounts of strategy move the spotlight from the formal decision-making processes of a core group of senior managers to a much wider set of decisions taken by managers at middle as well as senior levels. Furthermore, such accounts of strategic processes blur the distinction between strategy formulation and implementation. To a very great extent, the tactics are the strategy. As we move into the arena of strategic process as opposed to strategic planning, new issues move centre-stage. It becomes increasingly important to understand the role of political process, emotion, decision-making structures and the nature of communication.

This chapter considers the role played by middle level managers in implementing, and to some extent developing, organizational strategies. Particular attention is paid to the often-stated claim that many attempts at strategic change fail or are less successful because of middle management resistance. The central argument of this chapter is that, in many cases, middle managers are scapegoats for wider organizational failings. That is not to say that middle management resistance to strategic change does not occur, but what senior managers perceive as 'bloody-minded resistance to change'[1] is often a function of the conflicting signals about goals

---

[1] Quote from a senior manager in an interview with the author.

and priorities received by middle managers and, in some cases, a function of different perceptions of strategic priorities. First, we need to understand better how the nature of the middle management role has changed and is continuing to change.

The Changing Role of Middle Management

There is evidence that middle management roles have been undergoing significant changes, including intensified competition and an increase in environmental turbulence (Dopson and Stewart, 1990). The need for increased speed of response to market signals has created a need for more lateral co-ordination at middle management levels. As a consequence, greater emphasis is placed on the need for 'people management' and 'integrating' skills.

There is also a trend towards more complex and sophisticated management systems for the measurement and control of performance (Thurley and Peccei, 1988; Dopson and Stewart, 1990). In many organizations large-scale strategic change initiatives have involved both job losses and delayering for those in the middle levels. Not only has job security been reduced, but also opportunities for frequent incremental promotion have been removed.

There is some evidence of a recent trend away from large, vertically integrated firms towards networks of firms in close partnership to manage flows of goods and services across an entire value chain (Johnson and Lawrence, 1991). This is particularly true of the high-tech sectors such as information technology and biotechnology, and has led to an increased pace and complexity of work for middle managers as well as difficulties for some managers with the resulting lack of clear structure (Ferlie and Pettigrew, 1996).

Middle Management and Strategy

An important recent debate about the role of middle managers concerns the extent to which they are involved in strategic decision making. A number of writers and researchers have characterized the modern middle management role as crucially involving innovation and strategic entrepreneurship. With an increasing emphasis on 'emergent strategy' in the last decade, attention has shifted to the role played by middle managers in helping to shape strategy. Floyd and Wooldridge (1997) suggest the following ways in which middle managers may influence the development and implementation of strategy.

Upward
Synthesizing information:
• Gather information on the feasibility of new programmes

- Communicate the activities of competitors, suppliers, etc.
- Assess changes in the external environment

Championing:
- Justify and define new programmes
- Evaluate the merits of new proposals
- Search for new opportunities
- Propose programmes or projects to higher level managers

Downward
Facilitating adaptability:
- Relax regulations to get new projects started
- 'Buy time' for experimental programmes
- Locate and provide resources for trial projects
- Provide a safe haven for experimental programmes
- Encourage informal discussion and information sharing

Implementing deliberate strategy:
- Monitor activities to support top management objectives
- Translate goals into action plans
- Translate goals into individual objectives
- Sell top management initiatives to subordinates

(Source: Floyd and Wooldridge, 1997: 46)

Burgelman (1994) carried out an in-depth case study of Intel's withdrawal from the memory chip (DRAM) market. His findings emphasized the role of middle managers in making decisions in response to external market conditions that effectively determined Intel's strategic direction.

> While Intel is widely regarded as one of the most innovative and adroitly managed high-technology firms, the DRAM exit story suggests that even extraordinarily capable and technically sophisticated top managers, such as Gordon Moore and Andy Grove, do not always have the foresight of the mythical Olympian CEO making strategy... [This study] confirms that strategic actions often diverge from statements of strategy, that resource allocation and official strategy are not necessarily tightly linked, and that strategic actions of complex firms involve multiple levels of management simultaneously. (Burgelman, 1994: 48–9)

Other writers have cast doubt on this picture of entrepreneurial middle managers engaged in decisions and actions that have significant bearing on the strategic direction of the firm. In a study of middle managers in a UK financial services organization, Redman et al. (1997) suggested that for many managers the trend was in fact towards less autonomy and less opportunity for involvement in strategic decision making.

> In our case study... managers were under considerable pressure of change, with the proliferation of new products along with the emphasis on cost containment. However,

contrary to the suggestion in the optimist literature that middle management jobs are becoming more entrepreneurial, we found no evidence of this. Indeed, particularly amongst branch managers, there was a sense in which the pressures of new product development limited their autonomy, by increasing the emphasis on staff training and administration, and limiting the scope for business development work outside the office. The feeling from our interviews was that managers felt themselves to be the 'victims' rather than the 'architects' of change. This is hardly consistent with a view of middle managers as empowered entrepreneurs.   (Redman et al., 1997: 111–12)

It is likely that these different findings represent, in part, differences between organizations in the roles played by middle managers. However, they also point to another theme, the tension between the role played by middle managers in influencing or implementing strategy and the situation of managers as recipients of change brought about by senior managers' strategic decisions. Box 11.1 gives one, extreme but real, example of this role tension.

Box 11.1   Middle managers' dual role as targets and implementers of change: an example

In one large (blue chip) UK company during the early 1990s, department heads were summoned to a meeting with the personnel director.

He explained that in common with many other companies they faced strong pressures for improved cost performance. He went into some detail about the nature of the economic and competitive climate. He then told them that in conjunction with consultants the senior team had examined options for performance improvement and had decided the way forward was to 'do more with less'. The company was to be 'right-sized'. In consequence, a detailed plan had been drawn up for workforce reductions. Each department was to lose staff. Additionally, all other staff were to be invited to sign new contracts, designed to increase internal flexibility.

The immediate task of the department managers was to draw up plans to resource departmental objectives with their reduced staffing complements. They would of course need to inform employees immediately that were being made redundant.

As the personnel director drew the meeting to a close he explained that at the back of the room, on their way out they would find boxes of envelopes labelled with the names of staff in their departments. The white envelopes, he explained, were redundancy notices. The brown envelopes were invitations to sign the new contract *and the top envelope in the box was their own: it might be either brown or white.*

Middle Management Resistance

The idea of middle management resistance to new initiatives is common in accounts of change processes. Such resistance is not a new phenomenon. Buhl (1974)

describes the resistance among officers in the US Navy to the introduction of steam ships after the civil war. He attributes the underlying cause of resistance to the disruptions to rank, status and authority caused by the rise of a professional cadre of engineers.

A wide range of research studies point to the role of middle management resistance in disrupting strategic change initiatives. Research findings include:

- Active resistance by middle managers to strategic decisions which threatened their own self-interest (Guth and MacMillan, 1986).
- Middle managers' resistance to playing an active role in the market-driven changes in which their companies were engaged (Nilakant, 1991).
- A study of TQM in UK firms found that 50 per cent of the firms saw middle management resistance as a barrier to effective implementation (Develin & Partners, 1989).
- Concern among middle managers and supervisors about the loss of authority and increasing workload that they associated with TQM led to resistance to programme implementation (Wilkinson et al., 1992).
- Middle managers subverted the aims of quality circle programmes (Baloff and Doherty, 1989; Connors and Romberg, 1991).
- Middle management resisted the introduction of self-managing work teams (Verespej, 1990; Buchanan and Preston, 1991).

Box 11.2   Middle management resistance to change in Shell

Major companies undergoing change programmes frequently identify middle-level managers as an obstacle. Shell is a recent example, as the following extract from a feature in the *Financial Times* illustrates:

'We have seen the enemy and he is us.' That, in a nutshell, is the biggest threat to Shell's corporate transformation programme . . .

Although top managers say the message that Shell must undergo a profound cultural and behavioural change is filtering to the lower levels, it is also clear that there is still substantial resistance to change. 'I can see the terror in the eyes of the local management team,' says Phil Watts, head of global exploration and production. 'People hate giving up predictability, order and stability.' Concern among top managers that the message may not get through prompted Shell to put together in five weeks one of the world's biggest corporate satellite television networks. The aim was to get the message across to lower-level staff that it was okay to do things differently, in spite of what some mid-level managers might say. (Corzine, 1998)

The Meaning and Provenance of Resistance

Theoretical accounts and explanations of resistance to change fall into three major categories: individual level explanations; systems explanations; and radical/critical.

Individual level explanations of resistance

One account views resistance to change as a form of 'inertia'. Watson (1971) has argued (from empirical evidence) that the way in which a person first copes with a situation tends to set in a pattern of adaptation that is highly resistant to change. There is some evidence that certain components of individual resistance to change may be related to personality. Inertia may also arise out of the formation of shared normative beliefs that serve to preserve the status quo. Other accounts see resistance as an expression of rational self-interest. Individuals or groups fear they will be the losers in planned change and mobilize resources to prevent change or to dilute its impact.

Middle managers see their interests threatened by change in a number of ways. A frequent concern of middle managers is that they will suffer a loss of control, that their perceived low levels of authority and status will be significantly eroded. There is ample evidence that many middle managers feel relatively powerless with insufficient access to what Kanter calls 'power tools': information, control of resources and influence in the organization. Given the pyramidal nature of organizations, in the absence of organizational expansion, a significant proportion of middle managers find their upward career paths blocked (Nicholson, 1993). Kanter found career-plateaued managers to be particularly preoccupied with issues of power and control (Kanter, 1977). Kanter argues that those who have little hope of upward mobility have a greater tendency to be authoritarian and rule-minded. On the principle that upward mobility brings power, and in the absence of upward mobility, plateaued managers may see tight control and reliance on rules as their only source of power. Additionally, those who resent their situation and feel passed over by senior management may be predisposed to resist initiatives from senior management. As many organizations are restructuring to remove layers of middle management, the impact on middle managers is not only to affect job security for those remaining, but also to alter dramatically the nature of their work, not least because of increased spans of control. More recently, many firms have recognized that the stripping out of middle-management posts may have gone too far. Indeed, some research suggests that the gains to many firms from downsizing and delayering have been at best marginal (Henkoff, 1990).

Systems explanations of resistance

Systemic accounts focus on resistance to change as a system property of organizations. In their discussion of organizational change from a systems perspective, Katz and Kahn note that:

> Enduring systems are over determined, in that they have more than one mechanism to produce stability. For example they select personnel to fill role requirements, train them to fill specific roles and socialise them with sanctions and rewards. (Katz and Kahn, 1978: 713)

In this context, they point out, strategies to bring about change which act only on individuals or groups often fail. The larger system nullifies local changes. For example, there is little point in sending managers on a customer service training programme if resource allocation systems, promotion decisions, appraisals and rewards all stress priorities other than customer service.

Some accounts of middle management resistance suggest that this resistance may be a consequence of a lack of congruence between organization subsystems, signalled priorities and the goals of change. For example, pay systems, promotion decisions, performance measures and the allocation of resources may all signal different priorities to the publicly voiced commitment of senior managers to a new initiative.

A number of these accounts suggest that the people expected to implement new initiatives see themselves as placed in a double bind. The concept of double bind comes from work on the familial roots of dysfunctional and self-destructive behaviour. In many dysfunctional families, family members find themselves faced with conflicting unspoken and spoken demands on their behaviour. The consequences are psychologically damaging where family members feel unable to articulate or discuss these conflicting demands. Management researchers have applied this idea to the circumstances faced by middle managers (Dopson et al., 1997). In a discussion of their case study-based research on changing middle management roles, Dopson and colleagues noted that managers in mid to late career were far more vulnerable to double-bind situations. These managers perceived the fewest alternatives to their current job and felt most insecure about initiating discussion of the apparently conflicting demands they experienced. In response they often adopted a pattern of passive resistance. Conflicting signals about priorities are common in organizations. At the same time, where middle managers do seek to raise issues concerning apparently conflicting signals about priorities, they risk being labelled as resistant to change or as troublemakers. Often managers are required to implement new ways of working but their own performance is still measured in the same narrow fashion or by unchanged output criteria. It is unusual, for example, for reward systems for supervisors and middle managers to be aligned with the goals of a total quality management or employee involvement programme (Bradley and Hill, 1987; Brennan, 1991). In many cases, middle managers remain unconvinced of top management commitment to initiatives (Bushe, 1983; Connors and Romberg, 1991) and often believe that 'this is just another fad' that will be very short term. This impression may be reinforced by dissension among the top management teams concerning the value of the initiatives or how they should be implemented.

Failures of training and development systems are also implicated by a number of accounts. Many middle managers perceive themselves as lacking in more general management skills as opposed to technical or function-specific skills (e.g. interpersonal management skills – see Scase and Goffee, 1989). In many organizations, levels of non-technical training are very low, and the introduction of new strategic initiatives that imply changes in middle management roles are often accompanied by, at best, cursory training for the managers expected to implement them (Buchanan and Preston, 1991).

Radical/critical explanations of resistance

The radical perspective has typically focused on resistance by blue-collar workers. In this view, resistance arises out of class conflict as an inevitable consequence of capitalist social structures, which serve to embed the exploitation of workers by the owners of capital in the functioning of society. Resistance is thus seen as a rational defence of individual and class interest. Radical/critical writings have less to say on the subject of *managerial* resistance to change. However, Giddens's work has more relevance to managerial behaviour. Giddens stresses the reflexive nature of social/organizational systems – that is, social structures constrain us but we are also able to act to change them. Secondly, he stresses the contradictory and overlapping nature of such structures. Whittington (1992: 705-6), building on this perspective, suggests:

> Managers . . . are faced with a variety of conflicting rules of conduct, all legitimate and plausible, but, often none with obvious superiority. Choice is possible, even mandatory, because more than one course of action has systemic legitimacy . . . Managers and managed alike are also people, who as full members of society, operate in a diversity of systems, and are therefore able to draw upon and respond to a multiplicity of rules and resources.

Within this framework of managers making choices between the demands of competing legitimate structures, systems and goals, managers might be seen from one perspective as engaging in resistance to legitimate organizational initiatives, but from another, as engaging in the pursuit of legitimate goals. For example, a manager may be faced with the choice between (1) spending time developing subordinates and encouraging their participation in decision making and (2) spending time in the pursuit of short-term production targets. Both may be formally sanctioned organizational goals. From one perspective, the manager who focuses on short-term production targets can be seen as resisting an initiative; from another, he or she may be seen as diligently pursuing a key organizational goal.

Based on a study of 120 'resistance episodes', Brower and Abolafia (1995) concluded that resistance to change is often less a signal of unwillingness to support organizational goals than a symptom of different interpretations of information or conflicting pressures from internal and external stakeholders. Alternatively they suggest that such resistance may arise out of quite different understandings of organizational policies and goals. For Brower and Abolafia, resistance is 'structurally embedded'; by this they mean that behind the superficial causes of conflict lie structural conditions which create inherent procedural or policy conflicts. The conflicts that emerge may be caused as often by inherent contradictions in the way an organization is structured as by individual self-interest. It is common, for example, to see conflict between marketing and sales groups produced by their different perspectives on the business.

This theme of structurally embedded resistance was clearly illustrated in a company in which the author carried out research.

ALPHA MOTORS   Alpha Motors[2] is a vehicle retail business with fifteen dealership companies. The companies within the group have traditionally been run in an autonomous manner. For all staff in the dealerships, a substantial proportion of their pay is based on sales performance. Out of a concern with market positioning and product liability issues, the directors of Alpha Motors began to consider how total quality management could be implemented in their business and decided to work towards BS 5750 (the then British Standard on quality procedures). A quality co-ordinator was appointed in each dealership, and a quality committee was set up across all departments in the dealership with one manager and one non-manager per department. The quality co-ordinators reported to both the manager of their dealership and to the Alpha Motors quality manager.

The process of establishing quality procedures met considerable resistance from dealerships and departmental managers. They resented the time taken by the process of writing quality procedures and frequently insisted (despite evidence to the contrary) that existing procedures were already adhered to in the majority of cases. Very little co-operation was given to the quality controllers. Many managers saw the passing of responsibility to their employees in this way as reducing their own profile in the organization. Additionally there was poor co-operation between departmental managers in dealerships.

Two crucial factors were the nature of the management reward systems and the level of autonomy of the dealership managers. First, a significant proportion of managers' remuneration was contingent on monthly sales performance. A number of other factors were taken into account in calculating bonus payments but, crucially, quality measures played no part in the calculation. Secondly, dealership managers had previously been given a great deal of autonomy in how they ran their dealerships. They were unaccustomed to such detailed interventions by head office in how they ran these businesses.

After three years, BS 5750 had not been achieved. Although some progress had been made on establishing and implementing quality procedures, conformance was still not high. The quality programme only began to make progress once a group of dealership managers was brought together to help design the quality programme and (at their suggestion) bonus payments incorporated quality targets.

CONCLUSION   The above example illustrates a number of points. First, the dealerships managers were not involved in developing the quality policies. The decision to put total quality management processes in place was imposed from the top of the organization. There was no ownership of this strategic direction among this crucial middle layer of managers. Further, this was a group of managers used to a wide degree of discretion in managing their dealerships in their local markets. Secondly, in this (sales-driven) organization the bonus system was the central mechanism for signalling organizational priorities. In a sense, if a goal was not mentioned in the bonus criteria it didn't exist. Thirdly, the quality co-ordinators had

---

[2] Some details have been modified to disguise the identity of the company.

been given a difficult goal to achieve without access to the resources they needed to achieve that goal. Kanter suggests that, to be successful, managers need access to three key 'power tools': access to information; access to resources; and access to influence. None of these was effectively available to the quality co-ordinators. The dealership managers, who had little commitment to the quality co-ordinators' goals, effectively controlled information and resources. Indeed, they saw the co-ordinators as an imposition to be endured. While in theory the quality co-ordinators had access to influence via their reporting relationship with the head office quality manager, in practice this counted for very little in their isolated positions within the dealership.

It might be tempting to see this as a simple case of obstinate middle managers resisting a change in strategic direction at the expense of the best interests of the company. However, we might also view this as an example of 'structurally embedded' resistance – that is, arising out of the structure and systems of the organizations and from different perspectives held by senior and middle managers on the 'best interests' of the organization. In the dealership managers' terms their behaviour was not 'resistant' but simply a matter of giving priority to what they saw as the prime goal – monthly sales figures.

The lack of congruence between organization subsystems (in particular, pay and performance measurement) and strategic goals reinforced this difference of perspective. Not for the first time, a group of senior managers had the experience of pulling levers only to discover that they were not connected to anything.

A Study of Resistance to Change

It is important to understand that resistance to strategic initiatives may have multiple causes, and each of the explanations considered in the previous section may be important. We turn now to consider some empirical evidence of the multiple causes of resistance. This section gives a brief overview of two studies the author carried out of middle management resistance to the introduction of employee involvement initiatives, such as self-managing teams and quality circles.

Study 1

In the first study (described in full in Fenton-O'Creevy, 1998) a sample of organizations was chosen randomly from five industry sectors: public utility organizations; automotive manufacturers; pharmaceutical companies; soap and cosmetics manufacturers; and retail organizations. These sectors were chosen to provide sufficient diversity that results could be generalized beyond industry-specific effects. Companies with less than 100 employees were excluded. A total of 465 organizations were asked to complete the questionnaire. In each case the human resources director, managing director or nearest equivalent completed the questionnaire. Follow-up letters and phone calls were used to achieve a final sample of 155 companies, representing a response rate of 33 per cent. Of these, 114 claimed to be making 'significant use' of employee involvement practices (team briefing, task forces, consultative committees, self-managing teams, small business units, attitude surveys, quality circles, suggestion schemes, or participative job redesign).

Questionnaire respondents were asked to what extent they believed these employee involvement practices had resulted in seven different outcomes: (1) quality improvements, (2) cost improvements, (3) improved responsiveness to customers, (4) improved responsiveness to change, (5) improved productivity, (6) greater job satisfaction or commitment among employees, and (7) a greater sense of responsibility for business success among employees. They were asked a series of questions about the nature of middle management attitudes and behaviour. Answers to these questions were combined into a single measure of middle management resistance. Examples of these questions include: 'Many middle managers show anxiety about the impact of greater employee involvement on their own roles' (scored on a 5 point scale from 'strongly disagree' to 'strongly agree'); 'To what extent are the following barriers to the implementation of greater levels of employee involvement in your organization? ... Middle management resistance' (scored on a 3-point scale: little or no extent; moderate extent; great extent).

Of the 114 organizations making significant use of employee involvement practices, middle management resistance was said to have been a barrier to the introduction of employee involvement to a 'moderate extent' by 49 per cent and to a 'great extent' by 14 per cent. Most claimed some benefit from these practices.

The study found that middle management resistance was a significant factor in the success or failure of these initiatives. Analysis of the responses (using regression analysis) showed, as expected, a significant relationship between the level of use of employee involvement practices and all seven reported positive outcomes. However, organizations that reported higher levels of middle management resistance to the initiatives also reported less favourable outcomes. In other words, the study supported the view that middle management support for resistance to these initiatives was a significant factor in their success or failure.

Further analysis suggested that this resistance from middle managers was a symptom of a wider failure to set up employee involvement initiatives effectively. The analysis of middle management resistance to employee involvement revealed a high proportion of variance in the extent of reported middle management resistance to be explained by the extent to which the organization had supported the initiatives with wider systemic change.

Middle management resistance was lowest in those organizations that had:

- strong senior management support for the employee involvement initiative;
- adapted performance measurement and reward systems to support the goals of employee involvement;
- made improvements to communications systems;
- decentralized resource control;
- lower levels of short-term performance pressure and 'change fatigue'; and
- less job loss, delayering, and loss of promotion opportunities associated with the introduction of employee involvement initiatives.

In other words, in the more successful companies, implementation of this new strategic initiative did not simply consist of a series of instructions to middle managers but rather involved careful realignment of internal systems and controls to support the goals of the initiative. Finally, we should note that middle managers' support for employee involvement also varies with the extent to which it affects their own interests.

Study 2

In an extension to study 1 (described in full in Fenton-O'Creevy, 1996) questionnaires were distributed to middle managers within companies drawn from the first sample (27 companies). A total of 975 questionnaires were distributed and 482 were returned: an overall response rate of 49 per cent.

Perhaps the most important finding of this study was that there was no significant difference in support/resistance by management level. Middle managers were no more resistant to employee involvement initiatives than their senior management colleagues.

The key factors associated with less favourable management attitudes to employee involvement initiatives were:

- *Existing levels of employee involvement* Managers in organizations that had low levels of employee involvement were less supportive of employee involvement initiatives. This is consistent with Watson's 'inertia' explanation of resistance: people tend to support the status quo.
- *The extent of common purpose* Managers in organizations with low levels of conflict and high levels of agreement about goals were more supportive of employee involvement initiatives.
- *Senior management support* Management attitudes were more favourable in organizations where senior managers communicated unambiguous and undivided support for initiatives.
- *Own experience of employee involvement* Managers' attitudes were more favourable in organizations with managers who had higher levels of experience of employee involvement. This applied not only to the experienced managers but also to their less experienced colleagues. There was clear evidence that managers with experience of these initiatives were able to influence positively the attitudes of others in the organization.

It is clear from the studies noted above that senior managers in a significant proportion of companies (about 50 per cent) perceive middle management resistance as a barrier to the successful introduction of employee involvement initiatives. However, study 2 revealed only a weak link between senior management perceptions of middle management resistance to employee involvement and managers' self-reported support for employee involvement. To understand this we can draw on the picture of *structurally embedded* resistance to change, drawn by Brower and Abolfia. As they point out (1995: 161):

... resistance also often signals the clash of conflicting routines, disparate interpretations of organizational events, conflicting demands from customers and other stakeholders, or even fundamental differences over organization norms, policies and goals.

Middle managers operate within the constraints of their organization systems and
structures. They also receive multiple and often conflicting signals about the
goals and policies they should pursue and the relative priority of those goals. Such
signals include how performance is measured, who gets promoted, which achievements receive most recognition, the operation of pay systems, communication with
peers and communication with senior managers.

It is likely that senior managers find it difficult to distinguish between on the one
hand, middle management failure to act in support of initiatives because of systemic
constraints and conflicting signals about organizational priorities and, on the other,
resistance arising out of negative attitudes towards the initiatives. Indeed in study 1,
the extent of middle management resistance reported by senior managers was
strongly related to lack of organizational subsystem congruence with the goals of
employee involvement initiatives. It is also clear that middle management support
for initiatives is strongly related to the extent of unambiguous support shown by
senior management.

In short, there is little evidence that middle managers, as a distinct group, are a
barrier to successful employee involvement. Rather, it seems likely that senior
management perceptions of middle management resistance to employee involvement
largely arise out of middle managers' behaviour in response to the constraints of the
systems within which they operate and out of mixed signals from senior managers
and organization systems about goals and priorities.

Conclusions

Resistance to change may sometimes be founded in individual conservatism or
inertia. However, the evidence suggests that what is often interpreted as obstinate
resistance to change is a consequence of organizational constraints and conflicting
signals. Success requires that these constraints be addressed. Change sufficient to
have strategic impact generally requires the transformation of the core organization.
Nothing less than the complete restructuring of pay systems, career systems,
resource control, information flows, training, and communication will suffice to
really embed change in the daily life of an organization.

Empirical evidence suggests that many senior managers not only fail to recognize
the range of issues that must be addressed to embed strategic change successfully, but
are also often complacent about the success of change efforts in their organizations. I
have seen from the work of Burgelman and others that middle managers may play an
important role in developing emergent strategies in response to changes in the
environment faced by the organization. Further, it is often the case that middle
management actions (especially in prioritizing and allocating resources) precede
formal statements of strategy rather than the other way around. In some cases it is
likely that what is experienced as resistance to the strategic direction defined by

senior managers simply reflects a different understanding of the environmental contingencies faced by the organization. A useful response may be dialogue rather than a simple demand for compliance.

Such dialogue also opens up another possibility. As well as the possibility of mutual learning, effective dialogue is likely to lead to greater middle management commitment to implementing new strategies and a more thinking and adaptive response to the inevitable difficulties of implementation.

At the same time such a dialogue is only one channel through which middle managers receive signals about organizational goals and priorities. Attention needs to be paid to other organizational systems. For example, it makes little sense to protest the importance of developing long-term customer relationships while at the same time promoting only managers who maximize short-term sales at the expense of such relationships. Equally, as we have seen in the case of Alpha Motors, there is little hope of persuading managers to give high priority to achieving quality object-ives if key organizational systems (such as pay) signal that these objectives are unimportant.

In summary, several key recommendations for avoiding middle management resistance and maximizing their contribution to strategy implementation arise from this chapter:

1. Recognize the role that may be played by middle managers in strategy formulation and engage them in real dialogue. This will not only enrich the process of strategy formulation but will also generate greater commitment to implementing change.
2. Recognize that middle managers are the targets as well as implementers of change processes and provide them with appropriate support. This needs to be more than just a 'sheep dip' training course. Long-term management development, allocation of resources, and senior management actions (*inter alia*) all need to support new strategic priorities.
3. Audit the extent to which messages from top management about strategic priorities are supported by or in conflict with other signals from top manage-ment and key organizational systems (performance measurement, promotion practices, resource allocation, pay, training and development, etc.).
4. Provide a forum in which managers are encouraged to discuss apparently conflicting priorities and the trade-offs that may be necessary to achieve strategic objectives. By acknowledging the conflicting demands on middle managers, it becomes possible to avoid double binds.

Certainly middle management resistance to strategic change exists and can have serious consequences for organizations. However, to assume that failure to imple-ment senior management-designed strategies is simply a matter of 'bloody-minded resistance to change' on the part of middle managers would be a serious error. Senior managers who take the simple route of scapegoating middle managers for strategy failures do their organizations a great disservice. A much more sophisticated analysis is required. All too often diagnosis of strategic failure stops with the symptom (middle management resistance). Frequently the root of the underlying disease is the failure of senior management to understand either the crucial role of middle managers or the radical transformation of systems and structures required to support strategic change.

References

Baloff, N. and Doherty, E. M. 1989: Potential pitfalls in employee participation. *Organizational Dynamics*, 18(2), 51–62.

Bradley, K. and Hill, S. 1987: Quality circles and managerial interests. *Industrial Relations*, 26, 68–82.

Brennan, M. 1991: Mismanagement and quality circles: how middle managers influence direct participation. *Employee Relations*, 5, 22–32.

Brower, R.S. and Abolafia, M.Y. 1995: The structural embeddedness of resistance among public sector managers. *Group and Organisation Management*, 20(2), 149–66.

Buchanan, D. and Preston, D. 1991: Life in the cell: supervision and teamwork in a 'manufacturing systems engineering'. *Human Resource Management Journal*, 2, 55–76.

Buhl, L.C. 1974: Mariners and machines: resistance to technological change in the American navy, 1865–1869. *Journal of American History*, 61, 703–27.

Burgelman, R.A. 1994: Fading memories – a process theory of strategic business exit. *Administrative Science Quarterly*, 39(1), 24–56.

Bushe, G.R. 1983: *Overcoming managerial resistance to worker problem–solving groups: A comparative study*. PhD thesis. Case Western Reserve University, p. 226.

Connors, J.L. and Romberg, T.A. 1991: Middle management and quality control: strategies for obstructionism. *Human Organisation*, 50, 61–5.

Corzine, R. 1998: Inside track. Shell gets its own TV shows: communicating the message. *Financial Times*, London, p. 12.

Develin & Partners 1989: *The effectiveness of quality improvement programmes in British business*. London: Develin.

Dopson, S., Neumann, J. and Newell, H. 1997: The changing psychological contracts of middle managers in Great Britain. In Y.-F. Livian and J.G. Burgoyne (eds) *Middle managers in Europe*. London: Routledge.

Dopson, S. and Stewart, R. 1990: What is happening to middle management? *British Journal of Management*, 1, 3–16.

Fenton-O'Creevy, M.P. 1996: *Employee involvement and the middle manager: a multi-level, cross-company study of their role in the effectiveness of employee involvement initiatives*. PhD Thesis. London Business School, London University, p. 312.

Fenton-O'Creevy, M. 1998: Employee involvement and the middle manager – evidence from a survey of organisations. *Journal of Organizational Behavior*, 19(1), 67–84.

Ferlie, E. and Pettigrew, A. 1996: Managing through networks. *British Journal of Management*, 7, 581–99.

Floyd, S.W. and Wooldridge, B. 1997: Middle management's strategic influence and organizational. *Journal of Management Studies*, 34(3), 465–85.

Guth, W.D. and MacMillan, I.C. 1986: Strategy implementation versus middle management self-interest. *Strategic Management Journal*, 7, 313–27.

Henkoff, R. 1990: Cost cutting: how to do it right. *Fortune*, 9 April.

Johnson, R. and Lawrence, P. 1991: Beyond vertical integration: the rise of the value adding partnership. In G. Thompson, J. Frances, R. Levacic and J. Mitchell (eds) *Markets, hierarchies and networks*. London: Sage.

Kanter, R.M. 1977: *Men and women of the corporation*. New York: Basic Books.

Katz, D. and Kahn, R.L. 1978: *The social psychology of organizations*. New York: Wiley.

Mintzberg, H. 1990: The design school: reconsidering the basic premises of strategic management. *Strategic Management Journal*, 11, 171–95.

Mintzberg, H. 1994: The rise and fall of strategic planning. *Harvard Business Review*, January/February.

Nicholson, N. 1993: Purgatory or place of safety? The managerial plateau and organisational agegrading. *Human Relations*, 46(12).

Nilakant, V. 1991: Dynamics of middle managerial roles. *Journal of Managerial Psychology*, 6, 17–24.

Redman, T., Wilkinson, A. and Snape, E. 1997: Stuck in the middle? Managers in building societies. *Work Employment and Society*, 11(1), 101–14.

Scase, R. and Goffee, R. 1989: *Reluctant managers: their work and lifestyles*. London: Unwin Hyman.

Thurley, K. and Peccei, R. 1988: *Changing functions of lower and middle management: Phase 1, consolidated report*. Dublin: European Foundation for the Improvement of Living and Working Conditions.

Verespej, M.A. 1990: When you put the team in charge. *Industry Week*, 239, 29–32.

Watson, G. 1971: Resistance to change. *American Behavioral Scientist*, 14(5), 745–66.

Whittington, R. 1992: Putting Giddens into action: social systems and managerial agency. *Journal of Management*, 26(6), 693–712.

Wilkinson, A., Marchington, M., Ackers, P. and Goodman, J. 1992: Total quality management and employee involvement. *Human Resource Management Journal*, 2(4), 1–20.

12

Constraints on Strategy Implementation: the 'Problem' of the Middle Manager

Philip Stiles

In the waves of large-scale change which accompanied the recession in the early 1990s, organizations followed broadly similar paths in reacting to the new competitive conditions: restructuring, downsizing, outsourcing, and refocusing on core businesses, divesting others. In the delayering and mass redundancies which followed, no group was harder hit than middle managers. Perceived by organizations as adding to bureaucracy, slowing down decision-making and seated too far from the customer front-line, middle managers became an endangered breed and were in many companies, dispatched with a ruthless zeal.

Other issues have hastened this trend. Middle managers have been squeezed by: (1) the rapid rise of information technology, which has replaced many of the information-processing functions middle managers have carried out; (2) the reduction in traditional career paths, leading to lowering of job satisfaction and psychological disengagement from work; and (3) a general intensification of competitive activity. Many middle managers have been discarded, while, for those that remain, larger spans of control, increasing workloads and the need to embrace fast-changing skill requirements have dramatically altered job roles.

But the picture of the middle manager as being in some senses, a barrier to effective organizational running, was simplistic and only led to further problems. Far from creating greater effectiveness and efficiency, the slash-and-burn tactics of many companies resulted in the loss of a large degree of embedded knowledge and tacit routines which enabled the organization to run smoothly and were, in a strong sense, unique to the firm. There is a growing awareness that middle managers have been unfairly maligned and the 'lost citizen' of the early 1990s is experiencing a reassessment as the result of several factors: (i) the co-ordinating function of the middle manager is crucial, particularly in large diverse organizations; and (ii) middle managers have a strong grasp of the organizational memory and hold a clear notion of the identity of the firm. This makes middle managers significant communicators, both formally and symbolically, for organizational norms and values.

The reassessment of middle managers has gone hand-in-hand with the attempt by organizations to move beyond more productivity growth to secure long-term growth based on creativity and innovation. Firms looking to unlock their human capital have begun to give managers a 'voice' in a range of organizational initiatives, from strategic decision making and implementation to the design of human resource practices.

However, in most models of strategy implementation, middle managers are accorded at best a support role. They have traditionally been seen as suppliers of information and recipients of decisions made by top management. What we explore in this chapter is the extent to which middle managers enable or constrain strategy implementation initiatives.

Human Resource Management: Manufacturing Consent

Westley (1990: 337) argues that:

> the daily life of organizations is patterned around communication events or habits; the quality of life often informed by how those communication events are experienced by the actors themselves...at the micro level it involves the procurement, production, synthesis, manipulation and diffusion of information in such a way as to give meaning, purpose and direction to an organization.

Within organizations, such events, including crucially strategic change events, occur across hierarchical levels. Viewing organizations as hierarchical systems has been commonplace in organization theory and there has been broad agreement over the classification of levels: (1) *institutional* – the level which determines strategic direction and engages in boundary spanning activity with external constituencies; (2) *managerial* – the level which controls the work of technical staff; and (3) *technical* (or operating core) – the level that actually delivers or processes the firm's offerings (Bacharach et al., 1996; Mintzberg, 1979). What concerns us in this chapter is the position of middle managers in the hierarchy and their capacity to enable or constrain strategy implementation. Early writings of labour process theory espoused an inevitable tension and antagonism between the private ownership of production and human labour. The intensification of labour, rigorous technologies of control and de-skilling brought theoretical attention to the issues of labour degradation, subordination and alienation. Development of these issues embraced the concept of employee resistance, and sophisticated analyses have sought to understand 'how concrete local situations interact with the subjectivity of agents involved in complex power resistance relations' (Jermier et al., 1994: 21). In recent years, however, the growth of human resource management (HRM) has called into question the nature of conflict and resistance practices. The so-called 'new' practices of HRM have been seen as largely effective in generating employee consent and commitment. In this chapter, I argue that this is over-optimistic, and that middle manager resistance and so-called 'guerrilla tactics' are still in evidence in firms which show strong adherence to HRM practices

Research Design

This chapter draws on evidence from eight large UK organizations (seven private sector, one public sector) which were examined, in part, to understand how organizations were attempting large-scale change programmes and what were the enabling and constraining influences on their effective implementation. These organizations – BT Payphones, Citibank, Glaxo, Hewlett-Packard, Kraft Jacobs Suchard, Lloyds Bank, NHS, and WH Smith News – are members of the Leading Edge Forum, a consortium-based research project begun in 1992 at London Business School to examine the organizational links between strategic management and human resource management. The sample of organizations was therefore self-selected in that the HR director of each organization was a member of the Leading Edge Forum who sponsored the research. Although the sample was self-selected, the research team had full methodological independence. The self-selection suggests that these organizations pride themselves on being at the 'leading edge' of human resource practices and initiatives. The sample allows me to provide a detailed investigation of practices among major 'blue chip' private sector firms and a public sector organization. All the private sector firms were in the top five in their market with regard to profit. The sample also provides a wide range of business sectors. While this means I am unable to provide generalizations for each of the sectors/industries from which my cases are drawn, I can contribute to theory building through an intensive multiple-case research strategy which allows for some comparative analysis (Eisenhardt, 1989). Case studies are also suited to the study of HRM because they allow for intensive research of ongoing social processes.

The research is based on empirical evidence drawn from focus groups conducted with HR staff and semi-structured interviews through all levels of management and operating core staff. In addition, a rules-based methodology – 'The Unwritten Rules of the Game' – developed by ADL Consultants, examined the actual incentives provided within different organizational cultures for line managers to implement consistent HRM practices. This consisted of twelve interviews per company with functional managers (see McGovern, 1995, for full review and discussion). This gave a total of 287 hour-long interviews. Questionnaires were also distributed to and collected from all participating companies. Employees from line manager level and below were included, yielding a total sample of 2,200. The return rate for questionnaires was 52 per cent. Accounts of company history, internal reports, strategy and personnel documentation, and external data derived from press and (where available) analysts' reports were gathered and analysed. Feedback was provided to the firms through workshops and reports.

Strategy Implementation: 'Connecting with Middle Managers'

In strategy implementation, there are two broad causes of problems: one is simple, one is more complex. The simple cause is through bad decision making, either at the level of strategy making itself, in terms of poor design or unrealistic aims, or through choosing inappropriate communication media with which to transfer the plans or processes through the organizational hierarchy. The complex (and less readily rectifiable) cause lies in the interpretations that middle managers make about the strategy to be implemented. Employees use framing – cognitive sense making of events and actions – in order to interpret information, to determine how previous information is remembered and to determine how inferences are drawn from past events and at times when information is missing (Reger et al., 1994). This plurality of interpretations obviously throws up considerable problems for organizations attempting to implement strategy. The importance of this assumption is that, in analysing the nature of organizations and, in particular, the nature of strategic change events, a clear understanding of the interpretative process is critical.

In a strategy implementation event, we found that transferring organizational intentions through the hierarchy of the firm depended on four factors: the characteristics of (a) the knowledge transferred, (b) the source, (c) the recipient and (d) the context in which the transfer takes place. Middle management interpretation of each of these stages can give rise to resistance or acceptance. In the first instance, we shall examine these four factors in more detail, highlighting some of the tactics of resistance that middle managers use to thwart implementation initiatives. We shall then turn to more general issues of strategy implementation, identify three types of problem, and pick out various remedies.

Legitimacy of top management

When the source of the organizational change initiative was expert and trustworthy, it was likely that the message would be accepted by managers. This also concerns the concept of legitimacy ('legitimation is the process whereby an organization justifies to a peer or subordinate system its right to exist' – Maurer, 1971: 361). The legitimacy of the senior management team affected the degree to which the message was received and accepted. At Glaxo Wellcome, the internal merger of Allen & Hanbury's and Glaxo Laboratories, and the restructuring of the entire GWUK operations necessitated a change of senior managers. One manager said: 'When the new top team came in they were seen as experimenting. Why did we need to change? Some people took a lot of convincing.' At Lloyds Bank, dissatisfaction with the change process was tempered by the fact that, in Sir Brian Pitman, the bank had at that time a highly respected chief executive who inspired confidence among employees.

Relationship between senior management and middle managers

Responsibility for strategic decision making and for setting the organizational context in these companies rested with top management. This tight control was a feature not only of bureaucratic organizations, but also of innovative ones. The degree to which lower level managers were excluded from the decision-making process increased resentment about the process and increased their sense of powerlessness, with the result that some lower level managers impeded or ignored the organizational initiatives. Companies with a tradition of paternalism and bureaucracy were prone to the dangers of a rather strained relationship with top management. At BT Payphones, staff perceptions of BT Group top management were frosty, particularly in light of large-scale job cuts: 'They treat us as a number, that's all. It doesn't inspire you.' At Lloyds Bank, branch managers called Retail Bank HQ 'planet Bristol', for their remoteness.

Characteristics of Implementation Content

Ambiguity

The content of the change event had considerable influence on how the initiative was received by managers. The extent to which the organizational information was complex and ambiguous affected how the information was received and implemented. There were two main strands to this point. First, if managers have to make sense of a large amount of information, it is probable that they will not retain it all, or will deliberately overlook some of it in order to simplify their information processing. Secondly, ambiguous messages will be construed differently by different employees, thus diminishing the impact of the initiatives. For example, at BT Payphones, one manager said: 'We get so much information from the company, we are deluged by it. It's hard to keep on top of it all, or know what is really important.'

Routine/non-routine

The degree to which the initiative is routine or non-routine may impact the degree to which employees accept the content and absorb it. If the message concerns an issue which is non-routine, which may necessitate new ways of working or the disruption of existing power structures, it may be difficult for this to gain legitimacy and be perceived as useful, so hindering buy-in. Connecting with existing structures and conforming to existing organizational norms may reduce cognitive dissonance and not violate interpretations of organizational identity. In our sample, downswing was implemented across the board, a process in the case of BT, Lloyds and WH Smith which seemed to tear up the former identity of the organization, previously reputed to be a highly secure employer. Though the passage of time has ensured that downsizing is now seen as a useful, even necessary, initiative (though by definition, we asked only survivors of the workforce reduction) the method of the downsizing process is still questioned. This brings up a crucial point. The downsizing was most certainly seen as a threat, which brought about distinctive threat-rigidity behaviour (Staw et al., 1981). When changes were perceived by managers as *opportunities* – such as enhancing work-life balance at Hewlett Packard, or reducing bureaucracy at Kraft Jacobs Suchard – acceptance by managers was much more forthcoming.

Saliency

The degree to which the organizational change initiative is tailored to meet the interests of managers will influence its absorption. Spreitzer (1996: 486) cites Comstock and Scott's (1977: 178) assertion that:

> Most research rests on an implicit assumption of homogeneity, positing uniformity of work and structural forms across participants and departments, although we know that differentiation is characteristic of complex organizations.

The diversity within complex organizations can mean that employees view initiatives from the point of view of their own department rather than the business as a whole. If the change initiative is not seen as appropriate to this level of meaning, then it may be ignored or changed. At BT Payphones, for example, 'they [BT top management] are always issuing edicts or change initiatives. But they only last a few months until the next change comes along. We just try to sit each one out. Nothing ever really affects us here.'

Characteristics of Middle Managers

Selective perception

Managers usually only attend to the information in a situation which relates specifically to the activities of their department. Such practice is a suboptimal information-processing strategy and militates against organization-wide initiatives. Concerning the type of organization, the nature of bureaucracy in the firm – the degree of formalization, whether it is coercive or enabling in its orientation – may also affect the readiness of employees to accept organizational initiatives without distortion or resistance (Walsh, 1988).

The role of identity schemas has also been invoked to examine why change efforts do not succeed (Reger et al., 1994). Organizational identity 'is the set of constructs individuals use to describe what is central, distinctive and enduring about their organization' (Reger et al., 1994: 568) and suggests that resistance to organizational initiatives occurs because beliefs about the organization's identity constrains understanding and creates cognitive opposition to radical moves.

The handling of the downsizing programmes – which brought considerable anxiety and ambiguity to the organization – prompted interpretations of hidden agendas, covert threats to particular labour groups, marginalization of the unions and the increased use of contractors and other outsourcing tactics. The most common response in terms of framing was to simplify the whole process into the question 'Will I lose my job?'. Despite the rhetoric of voluntary redundancies only, both managers and technical staff asked 'Will I be next?' or 'Can I survive here past 50?'.

At the managerial level, the restructuring which accompanied the downsizing programmes meant considerable shifts in power, with consequent winners and losers. Managers were concerned not with the effects of the workforce reductions on BT profitability and growth, but with the consequences for their unit or department. A heavy emphasis was placed on managers to meet workforce reduction targets each year and so a major part of managerial work became achieving the all-important headcount numbers to satisfy cost-reduction goals.

Political activity

Political behaviour within and among groups may also affect interpretation of organizational initiatives. According to Cyert and March (1992), organizations represent environments where individual and coalitions seek to impose their views on organizational issues and to effect control on decision making. As a result, various factions or individuals may attempt to distort information in order to protect their self-interest (Thomas et al., 1994). At Lloyds Bank, branch managers sought to protect their staff by filtering out information on change initiatives in order to preserve morale and motivation. At WH Smith News, the warehouse managers, who held considerable power in the organization, resisted changes in working practices and the demand from Group to encourage employee involvement because of the threat to their traditional power base. Co-operation over organizational goals may not therefore be as straightforward as suggested by the normative literature. (According to Adler and Borys, 1996, the goal of congruence or alignment between organizational rhetoric and the reality as experienced by employees may be said to be illusory, in light of Marxist or neo-Marxist claims on the inherent antagonistic nature of class interests. Employees may believe that organizational initiatives are by their nature coercive and may represent a negation of their individual autonomy rather than a valuable means to a desired end.)

The turbulent internal environment at BT Payphones brought with it a heightened degree of political activity. In the downsizing, technical level employees attempted, through their union representatives, to influence the degree of change and ensure that no involuntary redundancies were introduced. Though this rhetoric was touted by top managers as proof of the integrity of the process, in reality managerial and technical staff saw this as a sign that the union was without power and the firm was able to do much as it pleased:

> We were fearful. Management had carte blanche to do whatever it liked. It was only because it used to be a public company that I think the government persuaded them to hold back on sackings. (*Manager*)

At the managerial level, the downsizing brought problems to those managers who wanted to hold on to their best performers. Some managers tried to block their best talent from taking the severance packages:

> There were examples of managers saying to people, you are not eligible for this, or, wait until next year, the deal will be better. (*Manager*)

This distortion of the initiative was also seen at the other end of the performance spectrum, where managers tried to 'ease out' underperforming staff:

> We weren't allowed to target individuals but we could put pressure on those who were pretty useless. We could persuade them to take a package, perhaps by saying that the terms would not always be as good as those on offer. (*Manager*)

Characteristics of the Context

Organization size

Organizational context can have a powerful influence on employee cognitions, particularly where the absorption of rhetoric is concerned (Spreitzer, 1996; Thomas and Velthouse, 1990). Large organizations have complex structures, differentiated units and a high degree of internal diversity (Thomas et al., 1994). Large organizations tend to create strong inertial forces which limit the degree to which new information or initiatives may be accepted. Size is usually accompanied by difficulties in communication. As Kimberley (1976: 547) states: 'As the number of members increases arithmetically, the number of possible communications networks increases exponentially.' With an increase in communication linkages, communication between levels becomes more difficult (Hull and Hage, 1982; Damanpour, 1991). Large organizations will also tend to have greater differentiation in terms of organizational structure and hierarchy. Organizational initiatives will, in this type of environment, pass through various levels of the corporate hierarchy and across the variegated structure. Differences of interpretation and implementation from managers at different levels will affect how the initiative is actually manifested to employees. As Snell (1992: 14) argues: 'Structural differentiation associated with largeness – information tends to become filtered and distorted before it reaches executives.' The problem was acute at Lloyds Bank. One manager said: 'The sheer scale of trying to achieve change in an organization this size is bewildering. It's like turning a supertanker. You have to take everyone with you but you can't hope to reach everyone.' At BT, the setting up of the Payphones business helped to alleviate some of these problems. Its smaller size, flattened structure and clear branding to bring greater identity to the business, were factors in getting organizational initiatives across. The improvement of procedural and communication channels, encouraging greater openness and feedback, also brought the three levels of hierarchy into greater alignment.

Process discipline

The likely success of organizational initiatives being implemented in the intended fashion will be influenced by the nature of the processes and practices within the organization, which will serve to embed the information. Part of this will involve the nature of the communication channels, their efficiency and their effectiveness. There have to be systems in place to ensure that the plans and policies of the organization are being implemented, and to indicate problem areas that could be revised and improved. Clear standards for the new plan/value, consistent incentives and sanctions to reinforce the initiatives, and formal opportunities to provide feedback characterize a good discipline environment (Ghoshal and Bartlett, 1994). The procedural justice of the decision-making process can affect the relationship between top management and lower level employees and so influence the receptiveness to organizational initiatives. Process fairness (or procedural justice) has been shown to affect outcome satisfaction (Kim and Mauborgne, 1993), commitment (Tyler, 1984), trust (Folger and Konovsky, 1989) and social harmony (Alexander and Ruderman, 1987). It can be argued that greater attention to procedural justice would be reflected in employees' greater willingness to absorb organizational initiatives. At Glaxo, the merger with Wellcome prompted top management to take a 'ground zero' approach to integration, and managers at all levels were asked to design structures for the new organization. At BT, the legacy of paternalism and absence of competition has left a company which was relatively inexperienced in monitoring and paying for performance, and a history of top-down implementation which meant that the explanation of decisions and processes to employees was often not forthcoming. The new competitive environment, and the intention to give employees responsibility and greater discretion has ensured that these former characteristics of poor supporting processes and poor process justice are being remedied.

Rules of the game

The rules of the game are 'a set of assumptions, norms, values and incentives – usually implicit – about how to interpret organizational reality, what constitutes appropriate behaviour, how to succeed' (Ocasio, 1997: 196). These rules are products of the firm's history and culture and they determine to a large extent the boundaries of strategic decision making and organizational responses to competitor moves. They are strongly bound up with the concept of organizational identity and, to this extent, they represent a constraining force to large-scale change and the initiative which accompanies it. The concept also has affinities to the concept of the psychological contract. In those terms, the former 'deal' at BT, WH Smith and Lloyds Bank was one of job security and career advancement based on tenure. Rules of the game were to be deferential to one's boss and deliver one's (short-term) targets. These rules are currently changing, as the old deal no longer holds. The new deal is job security for high performers and the promise of employability for those who have the capacity to manage their own careers. Such a break with the past has proved very difficult for some, whose absorptive capacity is reduced by the expectancies and experiences they have built up over the years at these companies.

Multiple strategies and values

The Leading Edge organizations have diverse and changing strategic aims and wide product market variations. Such diversity led the organizations to follow multiple strategies and, at times, induced conflicting values. The Unwritten Rules of the Game data revealed this fact clearly, for example, in the case of Kraft Jacobs Suchard, where the demands of delivering short-term financial targets were combined with the goals of being innovative, while at BT Payphones, increasing the level of teamwork was combined with a reliance on an individualistic payment system. Such examples represented contradictory assessments of the needs of the organization and obviously undermined the power of the initiatives.

Discussion and Conclusions

The research findings confirmed the importance of interpretation in showing how information that is transmitted within the firm either detracts from or enhances integration. Against the dominant trend of a plethora of literature on organizational initiatives which highlights failure of implementation as the major cause of lack of integration, I find that a cognitivist approach is necessary for a full understanding of the factors leading to the integration of organizational initiatives. I identified six factors which influenced the acceptance of organizational initiatives and described an emergent model based on the findings from the extensive interview data. My findings support those of Szulanski (1996) who concluded his study of barriers to best practice transfer by arguing that knowledge-based barriers were more important than motivational factors in blocking transfer activity. My findings in terms of the influence of cognitive factors are consistent with prior empirical work in the area of issue interpretation (Thomas et al., 1994), strategic change initiatives (Isabella, 1990) and organizational learning (Dutton, 1991).

Undoubtedly, failures of implementation play a significant part in determining the integration of organizational strategy. In terms of the context of the implementation, lack of supporting structure and processes to reinforce the initiative will hamper its integration. Providing appropriate incentive schemes and organizational structures, according high priority to the implementation and a clearly articulated need will influence the degree of acceptance organizational strategy will receive. Concerning the content of the change initiative the poor framing of the message, leading either to ambiguity or to a lack of saliency for particular groups, will affect its absorption. Ambiguity produces equivocality in employees – information is equivocal when 'multiple and conflicting interpretations exist' (Daft and Lengel, 1986: 556). As Kanter (1989: 5) argues, organizations should ensure that they 'make more information available to more people through more devices'. But it is not just quantity of information that is required, but quality and appropriateness. In cognitive terms, if the initiative exceeds the conventional organizational norms, or disrupts the dominant logic by extending organizational identity too far (Reger et al., 1994), this represents poor framing and will adversely affect the integration of the initiative. In a number of firms, senior managers now largely avoid information cascades and give messages to employees directly if possible. Better framing of initiatives so that employees can understand and interpret information to suit their own environment is an important process. The initiative must be specific, accessible and desirable if employees are to be motivated by it. A directive which is not seen as useful or as somehow adding value will be by-passed. Greater attention to procedural justice in the implementation of initiatives may also gain employee-buy-in to new directives and is a positive step towards increasing the potential for aligning employers and employees (Kim and Mauborgne, 1993).

Better framing may help to mitigate against such factors, but there are the more hard-wired issues. At the contextual level, organizational size increases the number of employees, number of hierarchical levels and internal differentiation. The number of filters through which initiatives have to permeate may distort the message. Large organizations tend to pursue multiple strategies, which also increase the potential for mixed messages. In terms of content, new organizational content will usher in a new organizational context, and there will be an element of uncertainty surrounding the content and how it may fit into this new context (Szulanski, 1996). In cognitive terms, framing is an inescapable feature of employees' sense making activity, which entail multiple interpretations and simplifying meanings to fit individual cognitive schemas. Political activity is also said to be inherent in organizations (Cyert and March, 1992) and this, too, increases the potential for distortion of message and resistance to initiatives.

As the number of employees increases, along with hierarchical levels and the scope of the firm and internal differentiation, greater attention to choice of communication media becomes crucial. Increased use of feedback loops will help to reduce the impact of hierarchical level filters and will also reduce the distance between the cognitive schemata of top management and lower level employees. The degree of change can be a source of much anxiety for employees. A clear end point for change, wide consultation and sensitive handling of former power configurations will increase the receptivity of the organizational initiatives (Jick, 1990). The problem of multiple strategies is difficult, but accepting trade-offs will be important and the use of the balanced scorecard, as used in several of the Leading Edge companies, may be one way to institutionalize this process.

Because the implementation of the change process depends on the relationship between the giver and the receiver, this relationship should be as harmonious and as close as possible. The source of the change should be perceived as credible and legitimate and should have the trust and confidence of employees. Increased top management visibility and interaction with lower level employees, perhaps using informal as well as formal communication channels, may help to increase understanding of the organization and its aims and may also increase the level of trust between senior management and employees.

To reduce the impact of the effects of sense making and its potential to dilute or distort the interpretation of organizational change initiatives, greater attention should be paid to the differentiation among employee groups when designing change initiatives. There is clear evidence that departmentalization, or segregating organizational attention on discrete units, can enhance learning (Levinthal and March, 1993), because decomposing the initiatives will make it simplified and relevant. Further, increased use of socialization may reduce the gap between the interpretations of employees and the interpretations of senior management concerning organizational issues. Greater use of feedback in performance and the use of two-way communication processes will also serve the same end.

An important step is to realize that, in large organizations, commitment tends to have different foci and bases. If commitment is sought between employee and supervisor, or employee and business unit, rather than to the organization as a whole, this may produce better performance and increase the receptivity of organizational initiatives.

References

Adler, P.S. and Borys, B. 1996: Two types of bureaucracy: enabling and coercive. *Administrative Science Quarterly*, 41, 61–89.

Alexander, S. and Ruderman, M. 1987: The role of procedural and distributive justice in organisational behaviour. *Social Justice Research*, 1, 177–98.

Bacharach, S.B., Bamberger, P. and Sonnenstuhl, W.J. 1996: The organisational transformational process: the micropolitics of dissonance reduction and the alignment of logics of action. *Administrative Science Quarterly*, 41, 477–506.

Comstock, D.E. and Scott, W.R. 1977: Technology and the structure of sub-units: distinguishing individual and workgroup effects. *Administrative Science Quarterly*, 22, 177–202.

Cyert, R. and March, J. 1992: A behavioural theory of the firm. Cambridge: Blackwell.

Daft, R.L. and Lengel, R.M. Organisational information requirements, media richness and structural design. *Management Science*, 32(15), 554–71.

Damanpour, F. 1991: Organisational innovation: a meta-analysis of effects of determinants and moderators. *Academy of Management Journal*, 34, 555–89.

Dearborn, D.C. and Simon, H.A. 1958: Selective perception: the identification of executives. *Sociometry*, 21, 140–4.

Dutton, J.E. and Duckerich, J.M. 1991: Keeping an eye on the mirror: image and identity in organisational adaptation. *Academy of Management Journal*, 34, 517–54.

Eisenhardt, K.M. 1989: Building theories from case study research. *Academy of Management Review*, 14, 532–50.

Folger, R. and Konovsky, M.A. 1989: Effects of procedural and distributive justice on reactions to pay raise decisions. *Academy of Management Journal*, 32, 115–30.

Ghoshal, S. and Bartlett, C.A. 1994: Linking organisational context and managerial action: the dimensions of quality of management. *Strategic Management Journal*, 15 (Special Issue: Summer), 91–112.

Hull, F. and Hage, J. 1982: Organising for innovation: beyond Burns and Stalker's organising type. *Sociology*, 16, 564–77.

Isabella, L.A. 1990: Evolving interpretations as a change unfolds: how managers construe key organisational events. *Academy of Management Journal*, 33, 7–41.

Jermier, J., Knights, D. and Nord, W. 1994: Introduction. In J. Jermier, D. Knights and W. Nord (eds) *Resistance and power in organisation*. London: Routledge, pp. 1–24.

Jick, T.D. 1990: Implementing change. In T.D. Jick (ed.) *Managing change: cases and concepts*. Homewood, IL: Irwin, pp. 192–201.

Kanter, R.M. 1989: *When giants learn to dance: mastering the challenge of strategy and careers in the 1990s*. New York: Simon & Schuster.

Kim, W.C. and Mauborgne, R. 1993: Procedural justice theory and the multinational corporation. In S. Ghoshal and D.E. Westney (eds) *Organisation theory and the multinational corporation*. New York: St Martin's Press, pp. 237–55.

Kimberly, J.R. 1976: Organisational size and the structuralist perspective: a review, critique and proposal. *Administrative Science Quarterly*, 21, 471–597.

Levinthal, D.A. and March, J.G. 1993: The myopia of learning. *Strategic Management Journal*, 14 (Special Issue: Winter), 95–111.

McGovern, P. 1995: Learning from the gurus: an analysis of the unwritten rules of the game. *Business Strategy Review*, 6, 13–25.

Maurer, J.G. 1971: *Readings in organisation theory. Open systems approaches*. New York: Random House.

Mintzberg, H. 1979: *The structure of organisations*. Englewood Cliffs, NJ: Prentice-Hall.

Ocasio, W. 1997: Towards an attention-based view of the firm. *Strategic Management Journal* (Special Issue: Summer), 18, 187–205.

Reger, R.K., Gustafson, L.T., Demarie, S.M. and Mullane, J.V. 1994: Reframing the organisation: why implementing total quality is easier said than done. *Academy of Management Review*, 19, 565–84.

Snell, S.A. 1992: Control theory in strategic human resource management: the mediating effect of administrative information. *Academy of Management Journal*, 35, 292–327.

Spreitzer, G.M. 1995: Individual empowerment in the workplace: dimensions, measurement and validation. *Academy of Management Journal*, 38, 1442–65.

Spreitzer, G.M. 1996: Social structural characteristics of psychological empowerment. *Academy of Management Journal*, 39, 483–503.

Staw, B.M., Sandelands, L.E. and Dutton, J.E. 1981: Threat-rigidity effects in organisational behaviour: a multi-level analysis. *Administrative Science Quarterly*, 26, 501–24.

Szulanski, G. 1995: Unpicking stickiness: an empirical investigation of the barriers to transfer best practice in the firm. *Academy of Management Journal* (Best Papers Proceedings), 437–41.

Szulanski, G. 1996: Exploring internal stickiness: impediments to the transfer of best practice within the firm. *Strategic Management Journal*, 17 (Special Issue: Winter), 27–43.

Thomas, J.B., Shankster, L.J. and Mathieu, J.E. 1994: Antecedents to organisational issue interpretation: the roles of single- level, cross-level and content cues. *Academy of Management Journal*, 37, 1252–84.

Thomas, K.W. and Velthouse, B.A. 1990: Cognitive elements of empowerment: an interpretive model of intrinsic task motivation. *Academy of Management Review*, 15, 666–81.

Tyler, T.R. 1984: The role of perceived injustice in defendants' evaluations of their courtroom experience. *Law Society Review*, 18, 101–24.

Walsh, J.P. 1988: Selectivity and selective perception: an investigation of managers' belief structures and information processing. *Academy of Management Journal*, 31, 873–96.

Westley, F.R. 1990: Middle managers and the microdynamics of inclusion. *Strategic Management Journal*, 11, 337–51.

Part 4

Barriers and Enablers to Strategy Implementation

13. The Primacy of Imagination
    Charles Carroll

14. Developing and Implementing Strategy through Learning Networks
    Tony Dromgoole and Liam Gorman

15. Implementing Turnaround Strategies in Strongly Unionized Environments
    Niall Saul

16. Teams and Strategy Implementation: Some Case Examples
    Ken Smith and Henry Sims

13

The Primacy of Imagination

Charles Carroll

Introduction and Approach

Strategy leaders strive to shape markets, resources and competitive postures to secure a company's competitive strength and profitable growth. Experience shows that particular strategies can become *locked into* set patterns of investments, people and structures. Over time such patterns inevitably suffer diminishing returns. Strategic renewal means reshaping or even totally uprooting those patterns. That is inherently difficult for managers to do. This chapter argues that strategic leadership is a type of public art, in which creative imagination plays a primary role. 'New things' must first be *imagined*. Likewise, imaginative failure entails certain consequences.

Mainstream strategy literature has not perhaps dwelt on this theme in a way that relates it to the material content of strategy and the practical dilemmas facing managers. The data of imagination are not easily described or scientifically scrutinized. Yet as Hans-Georg Gadamer (1975) puts it, restrictions of method should not determine questions of truth. The study of the imaginative lies beyond 'scientific method'; the mode of inquiry should be appropriate to the object. This chapter makes no claim, therefore, to be a 'scientific' elaboration of its theme. Its more modest scope is to bring together some previously disparate experiences, observations and thoughts into a more-or-less coherent meditation. The goal is understanding and insight.

To an extent also, it reflects the author's preoccupation with significant twentieth-century thinkers in fields of thought such as political science and philosophies of symbolic form (Voegelin, 1952, 1968, 1987, 1990; Cassirer, 1970), the philosophy and sociology of knowledge (Scheler, 1994; Berger and Luckmann, 1966), the study of situations as 'text' (Gadamer, 1975; Ricoeur, 1975) and studies of imagination and creativity (Morgan, 1988, 1997a, 1997b; Koestler, 1969). While this entails a more 'philosophic' approach than is usual in strategy studies, it complements many existing insights from cognitive and social psychology. Taken together with concrete case illustrations from the experiences of a traditional jobbing printer in Dublin, Ireland, it seeks to bring the importance of imagination into sharper focus. It also offers some pragmatic insights into how to resolve many dilemmas of strategy implementation.

Strategy and Implementation: the Challenge

The special challenge of strategy implementation arises from the very nature of strategy. We must distinguish those decisions that are truly strategic from those that are not. The following elucidation is not exhaustive and concentrates on a 'consciousness of principles'. Later, the case history (Smurfit Print, Dublin) will exemplify a specific context.

Every enterprise addresses various market *sectors* and deploys *resources* (that is, capital investment and people), in whatever configuration is necessary to succeed. Success also requires a *competitive posture* of some kind, for instance, cost-price leadership or some form of distinctiveness through differentiation or superior quality (see, for example, Porter, 1980; Carroll and Clayton, 1994).

For the purposes of delineating the subject, it matters little how a particular strategy came to be. Management may have *intended* the strategy or it may have simply 'emerged' from some obscure process, two of the modes of strategy-making which Mintzberg (1985) and others identify. Suffice to say that the questions *Which market sectors?*, *What resources?* and *Which competitive postures?* are the material content of strategy. Different modes are variations on the theme of addressing these questions.

Economic performance is a central goal of business strategy. As Peter Drucker memorably puts it, the strategic leader must 'outfox' the inexorable law of diminishing productivity on capital. A key to successful strategy making is to 'work smarter' rather than 'work harder' (Micklethwait and Wooldridge, 1996).

Typically, strategy making takes a medium- to long-term view. It is also integrative, involving a whole business or business unit. By definition, any decision that lies within the complete discretion of a specialist function, such as marketing or financial control, is not truly strategic. Such functional fiefdoms often are a serious barrier to strategic change. Hence the recent emphasis on cross-functional teams as vehicles of strategy making.

The questions we have posed above are fundamental. They imply setting a pattern for investment, people and structures to express a strategy. Changing *set patterns* is inherently difficult; *that* is the essence of the implementation challenge. Strategic renewal implies new commitments to new patterns. Naturally, they are difficult to make, but once made, they are 'relatively irreversible', and that is precisely why strategy making is different from tactical or operating actions which lie within the limits of some existing set pattern.

Some strategy writers (Pascale et al., 1997) argue that strategies should avoid too much commitment or set patterning. Change is too fast. Agility and rapid learning are the critical characteristics. It is difficult to argue with this contention, particularly for sectors such as electronics or new Internet businesses where knowledge is changing at great speed. But this perspective is simply another way of addressing the same questions. The principles are the same. The *speed* of a specific context alone is different. In these cases the 'relatively irreversible' commitment attaches itself to core competences rather than to specific products or business units (Prahalad and Hamel, 1990).

Finally, strategy making happens under conditions of uncertainty. I must emphasize that uncertainty is of the essence. It is not an accidental affliction that unfortunately happens to us every now and then. It is amazing how widespread is the management mentality that hankers after some perfect strategy which, in time, will deliver some *nirvana* of certainty and repose. This is 'the myth of the manager', who through the eventual perfection of knowledge and technique will bring all social and economic phenomena under control. Perhaps this is a residue from the Enlightenment with its encyclopaedic dream of mapping all knowledge and accomplishing social perfection. This 'end of history' myth lurks deep in the unconscious of Modernity. Uncertainty is a more usual and normal state of affairs (see Jean Hartley in chapter 8). As Voegelin (1987) has argued, a desire for order in the sense of *faithful search* is normal and healthy; a desire for some final fixed certainty about destiny is subtly pathological – and dangerous when it becomes a social force (I return to this issue below).

Accepting that uncertainty is normal has some crucial implications. The human side of uncertainty is the sense of adventure. Strategy can be thought of as an adventure story – an enchanted quest. It skirts danger in a symbolic universe with whatever equipment and foresight it can muster. This is very different to the notion that strategy is merely reacting to or adapting to a changing environment as certain evolutionary-ecological schools of strategy would have us believe (Hannan and Freeman, 1977). Strategy is about creation. It is an assertive and creative enactment of new patterns, and since it deals with people – and their need for solidarity and purpose – strategic leadership can be thought of as a public art. Politics and architecture spring to mind as appropriate metaphors. Reasoning and technical skills remain crucially important, but more as 'policing' and enactment functions.

Approaches to Change

Arguably, managers have more limited power to change things than they fondly like to believe. Quantum results are more likely if they focus upon a few high-leverage starting points. It is not a matter of breaking the problem into manageable parts and then tackling each, in parallel or one at a time; it is rather a question of deciding which 15 per cent of items are most likely to leaven change throughout the other 85 per cent. The work of Gareth Morgan (1988, 1997a, 1997b), particularly his work on 'imaginization', was invaluable in treating this and the creative aspects of our case story. The idea of reframing by looking at the same phenomena by reference to different contexts or new or startling metaphors forms the core of his approach. Likewise, Arthur Koestler's (1969) concept of 'the creative act' provides valuable insights.

It is now something of a commonplace that changes do not happen solely or necessarily by changing the physical, systemic or structural artefacts of an organization; nor do they emanate from quantitative analysis or linear analytic thinking alone. Intangible factors such as stories, rituals, symbols, rhetoric and everyday conversation – those mundane 'realities of everyday life' – can be much more powerful focal points for change initiatives. As Berger and Luckmann (1966) put it, these are the filters through which people construe reality. This is not to forget that physical and structural artefacts also possess powerful symbolic content. The work of Gerry Johnson (1990) was important in highlighting the particular importance of symbols.

The writings of the twentieth-century philosopher and political scientist Eric Voegelin (1987, 1990) provided rich insights into the nature of symbolism. His extensive historical work invites us to use the metaphor of the theatre in searching for reality in any human milieu. In Voegelin's view, people are not passive spectators of their socio-political situations. They are drawn willy-nilly into active participation like actors in a drama. The plot is often obscure but never entirely so. Groups move among symbols that evoke a communal and intelligible existence. The symbols are not important in themselves; it is the 'equivalencies in experience' that are important. Thus, no change initiative ever confronts a blank sheet. People and groups already possess an articulated self-interpretation, which defines their identity and character. Symbols are representative; they 'render present' the substance of those experiences, and according to Voegelin (this is his central thesis) they signify a *search for order*. The emphasis is on the restless tension of search rather than on arrival at any final state (which constantly recedes beyond our grasp).

A signal for change occurs when symbols lose their luminous power and cease to represent an intelligible existence. This might happen, for instance, as a result of competitive deterioration, organizational decay or leadership failure. Such events, which often emerge only after some period of strategic drift, precipitate a renewed search for order.

A 'sense of disorder' presumes some idea of order, albeit that we can only approach but never fully reach it. Doctors can only define ill health against some idea of what constitutes a 'healthy person'. A doctor knows, for instance, that a person should only have two legs, even though he may have to amputate one to preserve overall health. If, in a fit of creative evolution, some doctor sent a person home with *three* legs, public opinion would spontaneously decide that there was a mad doctor in the house! The social sciences are not so clear. Mad sociologists can surround us on all sides without our realizing it. The medical analogy is not perfect, of course. None the less, it conveys a partial insight. A search for order is drawn towards 'ideal forms' even if these are no more than a renewed consciousness of first principles. It also assumes that 'action' is ordered towards some such conception.

The foregoing ideas provide some interpretive schemas (or 'productive prejudices' as Hans-Georg Gadamer calls them), for understanding a particular case history of strategy implementation, which is described in the next sections. The goal is understanding and insight and the focus is upon those actions only that illuminate the theme.

Smurfit Print, Dublin: Implementing a Business Strategy

In 1988, Smurfit Print, Dublin, was a traditional jobbing printer, that, to quote the general manager, 'was beset by all the worst characteristics of that sector in the late 1980s'. A new strategy radically changed that situation. The basic facts are set out below on a 'before' and 'after' basis.

	Before	*After*
Raw materials:	3 weeks	1 day
Work-in-progress:	3.5 weeks	1 day
Finished goods:	4 weeks	2 weeks
Working capital:	15% of sales	Nil
Quality system:	None	ISO 9000/Qmark
Factory:	1930s	Same factory
Production:	Batch	Continuous flow
Volume:		+500%
Employees:		+50%

The following details a few selected characteristics of the 'before' situation. The plant was dirty and unattractive and the workforce was thoroughly demoralized. There was a problem of office–shop floor 'distance' – symbolized by a windowless wall separating the shop floor from the offices and the story that no one from the 'offices' had ever spoken to anyone on the shop floor. Plant 'silos' produced another problem – operatives at one stage of production could not stray into another part; another symbol of these territorial fiefdoms was the wearing of different coloured overalls. Production stages were misaligned and workstations were utterly disorganized (nothing was ever 'to hand'). In addition, operatives had a bad habit of coming to work poorly dressed.

A telling symptom of disorder was the number of occasions a production run had to be repeated because the original run 'could not be found'. Another symptom was the 'forty yard' problem: between one stage of production and another there was, at any one time, 'forty yards' of work-in-progress sitting on the floor using valuable space and tying up working capital.

Since the 'product' of a print jobbing plant is the plant itself, it is not hard to imagine how this state of affairs inhibited the marketing and sales effort. In the general manager's words: 'It was not the kind of place you would feel comfortable bringing customers.'

This was the business that he needed to change. How to do it? Where to begin?

In this case, an ideal of order was found in the *principles* of World Class Manufacturing (WCM). It is worth while probing how this learning found its way into this company. The plant was part of the Smurfit Group. Multinational customers in Ireland had already pressed a number of its sister plants to upgrade. The general manager cites a seminar by Schonberger at the Irish Management Institute as another influence, together with visits to model plants in the USA – in this case plants not connected with the print sector. For instance, one such plant made aluminium ladders – and lessons from this and other sectors were transferred to the print operation in highly imaginative ways.

This is not the place to elaborate on the principles of WCM. Interestingly, in this case, the general manager did not work through a detailed 'list' of items. Instead he distilled WCM to its core themes, such as 'waste elimination' and 'simplicity'. Such words became part of his daily conversation with the employees. The rhetoric was not about 'working capital reduction'. Rather, it was:

> 'Working capital is **Waste** and the worst part is inventories – I **Hate** inventories and all inventories are **Waste**.'

No one knew better than the employees where the 'waste' was or how things could be done with greater 'simplicity' – and they could devise far more meaningful 'lists' than the general manager.

To resume the narrative, the general manager began the change process in small incremental steps in a highly original way. To tackle the dirty plant problem, he selected one square yard of floor and had it thoroughly sanded and beautifully painted.

And just left it there. ... And said nothing ... Silence!

It then became a talking point. It evinced a stark contrast with the surrounding dirt. Some operatives began asking (these conversations are dramatic reconstructions):

> 'Are you going to do any more – are you going to "do" the rest of the plant like that?'
> 'What do *you* think?' was his reply.
> 'Sure, why not!' they ventured.

He needed no further invitation. Start with one workstation! Volunteers. But, was it not pointless to have a nice new clean floor under a workstation that was itself disordered? Why not evolve a new model workstation as well?

> 'When are you going to do the same for us?' the others began to ask.

And it hardly made sense to work that programme through the whole plant without also suggesting some more rational realignment of the entire production flow.

At what point in the conversation did the questions of 'whether' become questions of 'when'? No one could really tell.

There was a subtle form of symbolization embedded in the physical structure and plant layout. 'Reading' the plant as a 'text', almost everything about the old order symbolized *fixity*. Printing machines are heavy and immobile. Conceivably, a change initiative might uproot the existing plant layout and refreeze it in a new and different pattern of fixity. Instead, putting plant and equipment on wheels symbolized a shift from a climate of fixity to a climate of *flux*. Why did certain operations *have to* be in a certain place? Because that was where the electrical points were! A liberal scattering of electrical power points around the plant soon fixed that. Together with putting everything possible on wheels, few symbols did so much to imaginize the company's commitment to a new philosophy of continuous improvement.

The 'forty yard' problem? Mobile plant made it possible to work gradually to eliminate the waste in work-in-progress – even at the rate of an 'inch a day'. McDonalds Fast Food was a favoured analogical model; everyone was familiar with it. The general manager would say:

> 'What does the counter assistant at McDonalds do when you ask for a Big Mac? He turns around and sees if there is one in the chute! That is where we want to get to – when you want your next job you turn around and there it is – in the chute.'

Furthermore, if it is there 'in the chute', there is no need for any intervening agencies, such as supervisors and schedulers. The process simultaneously created both cost and capital efficiency.

He demolished the 'windowless wall' between office and factory, thus removing the 'symbol'. But the 'equivalencies in experience' had also to change, and that was done in a two-pronged attack. Managers and other office staff joined shop floor continuous improvement teams, and the teams were empowered to requisition any manager's office for their meetings. Needless to say, not every manager or the original plant supervisors could live with this new way and many did leave. Other changes to the traditional symbols of 'managerialism' may have induced this action. Managers had to 'clock in' (highly symbolic) and had to wear the same clothing as operatives (suits disappeared). Managers also gave up their separate executive dining suite along with reserved car parking spaces and other aspects of status that symbolized the old era. This last action, incidentally, led to the discovery that visiting customers had never been able to find parking spaces!

Other changes were more delicate. Many operatives came to work rather poorly dressed. Could he change that? His solution was a stroke of genius. He installed a large wall mirror in the entrance foyer of the plant and others in both the male and female toilets. The problem gradually faded.

Some of these examples and actions may seem small and even trite, but they are the 'realities of everyday life' – the stuff from which ordinary people, as Berger and Luckmann (1966) tell us, 'construct their perceptions of reality'. In Voegelin's metaphor of the theatre, these factors expressed the plot, constituted the scene of the play and were the stage props. These actions engendered real change.

Discussion and Insights

We should remember first that business results are a core issue in strategic management. Even when we approach business organizations as social or political entities we should never lose sight of this fact. Tough economic and financial analysis is crucial. It is important not to allow vacuous notions about process to deflect attention from the content of this arduous task – particularly when even a cursory perusal of cash flow patterns reveals a company already bleeding to death.

In our example, consciousness of a definite competitive goal drove the organizational change. Management intended and achieved a very high reduction in working capital and hence the capital intensiveness of the business. A batch system rapidly assumed the aspect of a continuous flow. Layers of cost vanished. Labour productivity climbed steadily, while the number of jobs in the plant actually grew. Reorganization was intentionally aimed at quality and cost-effectiveness – the two sides of the coin of customer value that drives market share. (The Smurfit Group, as a matter of corporate policy, aimed to achieve commanding relative market shares.) Mintzberg (1991) speaks of strategy as 'seeing'. In this story, it was possible to detect the presence of an imaginative 'vision of the whole' in the way that management acted.

How exactly did these change initiatives exemplify the themes of creative imagination and symbolization? Changing the symbols of the old order which have lost their meaning will not, of itself, engender desirable change. That is analogous to those programmatic change initiatives that formally change structures and systems, but little else. Managers must excavate and engender change in *the underlying equivalencies in experience*. Re-symbolization is a creative re-enactment of a new plot, complete with new scenery and new props. The importance of symbols lies in the fact that meanings and sense making are not so much conveyed by formal 'communication programmes', and contrived 'interactive skills', 'empathy', 'contracting' and the like. Meanings are 'caught'. Symbols are communal and sympathetic and strike a deeper chord. Symbols do not inform; they evoke. They 'catch people's imagination'. It should not surprise us that, in the history of social, political and religious struggles, the protagonists strive to gain control of the symbols of representation.

Creative imagination is not imprisoned within existing patterns of 'facts'. It is open to differentiating experiences and drawn towards ideas from 'other' worlds (Morgan's 'other contexts' and 'startling metaphors'). These other worlds may be outside our experience, the sector, the business, or even our social and cultural milieu. Imaginatively resourceful managers take ideas and the lessons of best practice from diverse sources. Several aspects of this case illustrate this creative action. For instance, a valuable source of inspiration was an internal video made by Hewlett Packard entitled *Stockless Production*. Virtually every theory expounded in the video was put into practice at Smurfit Print, but in a completely different way to suit a printing plant. Management also drew inspiration for improving production flow, process efficiency and customer orientation from experiences as diverse as McDonalds Fast Food, an aluminium ladder plant in the USA and even playing golf. The challenge was to take good ideas from another industry or activity and have the imagination to 'carry over' their application to a different type of operation.

The idea of the full-length mirror in the entrance foyer came from the story of an American Hotel (that is, far away and in a different context). The hotel lift was notoriously slow and was the subject of unending customer complaints (this case was referred to at an Irish Management Institute programme attended by the general manager). Replacement would have been too expensive. So the hotel management panelled the sides of the lift with mirrors. The complaints stopped. As the lift attendant explained: 'People just love looking at themselves.' From a hotel 'far away' came a solution to an unusual, albeit different, problem in a small plant in north Dublin.

The idea of painting one square yard of floor occurred to the general manager while shopping in a home improvement store with his wife. They were shopping for new flooring. Now, these stores merchandise new flooring by laying it out in attractive displays of square yard pieces. Eureka! Why not 'merchandise' the idea of a clean floor to the plant operatives in the same way? The symbol of the clean floor was also an authentic example of Morgan's notion of the 'vital 15 per cent'. The clean floor was pivotal to precipitating change in virtually everything else.

Arthur Koestler's (1969) concept of the 'act of creation' is another valuable insight into this type of consciousness. To Koestler, creativity was not some uniquely personal and generative faculty or a solipsistic form of self-expression. The nineteenth-century Romanticist cult of genius has skewed modern perceptions on this issue. New ideas reveal themselves through an individual's openness to the unusual or unexpected juxtaposition of existing and sometimes paradoxical elements and experiences in everyday life (what Koestler calls the 'bi-association' of ideas). To the distinguished German phenomenologist, Max Scheler (1994), the creative individual is less a 'creator' than a *receiver of gifts*. Creative insights are 'revelatory' events. He argues persuasively for this notion as a valid form of knowledge. Likewise, Eric Voegelin speaks of a type of consciousness that is 'luminous to reality' and uses the expressions *to apperceive* and *refusal to apperceive* to denote the presence or absence of this disposition.

There is much confusion about these issues within contemporary strategic thinking. It seems indeed that the rhythm of organizational life is shot through with the paradoxical. Apparent contraries attract, contend and succeed one another in ways that generate creative tension. We should therefore learn to live with contraries without trying to resolve them. It never is a question of chosing 'either/or'. Maintaining the tension of 'both/and' contains the promise of new syntheses (Pascale, 1990; Hamel and Prahalad, 1994).

This way of thinking misses a crucial distinction. It is not contraries, but *opposite poles* that attract and succeed one another and which we should never seek to 'resolve'. Opposite poles *complement* and mutually sustain one another. Contraries are antagonistic, and negate one another. Summer does not contradict spring, the masculine does not contradict the feminine in the same way that, for instance, yes is the negation of no, or evil is the negation of good. When contraries attract and succeed one another in human conduct it is because *they conceal a deeper affinity*; in other words, they are not true opposites. A 'friendship' that turns easily to betrayal is already latently imbued with infidelity. The 'flat organization' only appears to be the contrary of authoritarian bureaucracy; both express a similar mechanistic type of operating culture. The real contrary of bureaucracy is a *living* hierarchy. Hierarchy and empowerment are true polar opposites; they mutually sustain one another.

Toleration of contradiction is destructive. It is the reason why many efforts at strategic renewal alter *the shadow* but not *the substance* of what went before; very often they intensify its worst aspects, concealing the underlying affinity beneath a new guise. Worse, to appear successful, they squander whatever goodness remains. Examples are those process re-engineering programmes that engender spectacular short-term profitability but silently erode any remaining innovative capability.

Such confusions are admittedly fed by currents of thought that assume that creativity is purely *immanent*; that is to say, new things 'emerge' from some obscure systemic, dialectical, historical or sociobiological process. Complexity and chaos theory (Waldrop, 1992), genetics (Dawkins, 1976) and sociobiology (Wilson, 1998) are examples of such influences on contemporary strategic thinking. Managers should discern the emergent waves of change at the edge of the future and learn to 'surf' them expertly. Yet, not unlike so much overworked psychologizing of our time, such theories confound the *foundational* role of vital instinct, energy and history with the *formative* function of intellect. As Cassirer (1970) has observed, the uniquely human capacity for symbolic expression belies such partial and one-sided explanations. Formative acts of intelligence are not merely 'epiphenomenal' – any more than we can say that architectural forms 'emerge' from stone or musical compositions 'emerge' from noise. Immanent events may *condition* the presence, but do not necessarily *determine* the formal content of creative acts. Strategic leadership can be thought of as an assertion of imaginative freedom; the opposite is strategic drift.

Finally, Voegelin's explanation of the *refusal to apperceive* is an important insight into the subtle ways in which genuine renewal can be confused and subverted. He sees it as flight from the quiet dread of existence in-between order and uncertainty. At its core is the imaginative inability to resolve contradictions or live with polar tensions. According to Voegelin, such situations are vulnerable to the construction of 'second realities', dogmatically sealed illusions, deformed by denial of significant parts of reality. While evincing optimism and energetic activism, these 'second realities' almost unfailingly reflect frames of mind that are brutally reductionist. Typically, they construe unrelenting self-interest, destructive conflict and endemic distrust as normal 'states of nature'. Coercion, in word and deed, becomes the main ordering force. Typically, such cultural milieux are drawn to the cult of 'the strong leader'.

The situation becomes organizationally dangerous when a group elevates this restrictive type of consciousness to the status of an exclusive insight with themselves as the 'New Elect' and heralds of a 'New Beginning'. A highly selective 'climate of opinion' is enforced. Debate becomes a game with a loaded dice, impermeable to rational discourse. Real questions are forbidden, thus destroying the social function of persuasion. Those who ask them are socially boycotted and, if possible, politically defamed. While this syndrome is intrinsically destructive and precipitates long-term decline, it presents the appearances of progress. It derails real change by enacting a counterfeit in its stead. Management instruments, including *words*, are abused and corrupted; for instance, consent is 'manufactured' through propaganda, not sought through free persuasion. Voegelin describes this complex mental state as 'pneumopathological', that is to say, individuals and groups engage in a resentful 'quarrel with the world'. The psychology of the situation – what individuals and groups hope to gain – is a possessive and ironclad sense of certainty.

To *apperceive* on the other hand, is the imaginative disposition to 'see through and beyond' the *facticity* of events. Like a vaccine it assures an essentially naïve sense of wonder and adventure, what Paul Ricoeur (1975) has called a posture of 'second naïveté' or 'willed naïveté'. It is important to see this imaginative competence as *integral* to the consciousness of the strategic leader.

Conclusions

The primary importance of imagination has ramifications for how I conceive strategic leadership. The imaginative disposition to apperceive new patterns of order can be thought of as 'gifted' in the sense used by Scheler. Imagination can be thought of as the site in which a leader articulates, attracts and secures group solidarity around new patterns. Cultures that are characterized by resentful *antipathy to gifts* will be wracked by crises of leadership (Scheler, 1994).

There is a crucial point to make here. Lack of imagination is a serious and crippling defect – like the loss of a limb or a sense, even worse. One has to think of the unimaginative leader ('hasn't an original thought in his head') as needing crutches or a wheelchair. Imagination is the site of that crucial ability to dream and fantasize (not to be mistaken for illusion, which is a different matter entirely). Everything new begins as a 'castle in the air'. The fantasist and the dreamer are gifted with greater acuity thanks to their 'artistic' insights. They *see through* events and things and uncover and sense the deeper causalities and reasons that elude the mere technician. Paradoxically, it is the ability to see more deeply that makes the fantasist a true realist as well. The unimaginative person gropes in the dark. For the imaginative, the sun always shines.

A shrinkage or crippling of imagination is also the source of *mimesis*, which, according to French scholar René Girard (1987) has such a malign influence on individuals and groups. This is the *imitative* urge that characterizes poor and unimaginative thinking. We see this characteristic in benchmarking practices whereby companies seek to mimic best practice within their sectors. Yet merely imitating competitors leads only to sameness, conformity or 'accomplished mediocrity'. Taking ideas and best practice from *outside* one's sector and from other diverse sources and imaginatively carrying them over into a new context creates patterns that are genuinely new. The idea is to be different. The story of Smurfit Print, Dublin, exemplified this truth.

[handwritten margin note: Benchmarking (can be bad.)]

Finally, the cultivation of imagination and, hence, the sense of adventure is an important priority for management development, particularly for the nurturing of senior managers capable of strategic leadership. This would require a move away from the present emphasis on the vocationalizing of management programmes (designed to make them action oriented or 'relevant' to current problem solving) towards the cultivation of imaginative resourcefulness (Chia, 1996). Without imagination, other vocational competencies operate in a vacuum of true insight – producing the phenomenon of the technical *homunculus*, the pedantic bureaucrat or, at best the competent administrator. But given the model of positivistic science that predominantly underpins the intellectual priorities and pedagogical approaches of present day business schools, the implications for management educators are large.

Acknowledgements

I am indebted to Mr John Coghlan, Managing Director, Smurfit Print and Packaging, UK, for access to the examples from Smurfit Print Dublin and his suggestions in the writing of this chapter. Senior colleagues at the Irish Management Institute also gave generously of their time to help me to structure my thoughts. I am grateful to senior specialists Mike Fiszer, Michael Keogh, Lynda Byron, Stephen McCormick and Frank Byrne; also, Patrick Flood, Professor of Organization Behaviour at the University of Limerick and George O'Connor, former Assistant Chief Executive, Organization Development at Aer Rianta. I must also thank Gareth Morgan, Distinguished Research Professor, Sculich School of Business at York University in Toronto, for both his personal encouragement in pursuing my line of thought and his insightful suggestions for improving the text.

References

Berger, P. and Luckmann, T. 1966: *The social construction of reality*. Garden City, New York: Doubleday.

Carroll, C. and Clayton, T. 1994: *Building business for Europe: evidence from Europe and North America on the 'intangibles' behind growth, competitiveness and jobs*. Final Report to the European Commission. Irish Management Institute, Dublin and PIMS Associates, London.

Cassirer, E. 1970: *Essay on man: an introduction to the philosophy of human culture*. Toronto, New York and London: Bantam Books. (Note: This is an updated and abbreviated version of Cassirer's original classic *The philosophy of symbolic forms* (3 vols), trans. R. Manheim, Yale University Press, New Haven, 1957.)

Chia, R. 1996: Teaching paradigm shifting in management education: university business schools and the entrepreneurial spirit. *Journal of Management Studies*, 33(4), 409–30.

Dawkins, R. 1976: *The selfish gene*. Oxford: Oxford University Press.

Gadamer, H.-G. 1975: *Truth and method*. New York: Seabury.

Girard, R. 1987: *Things hidden since the beginning of the world*. Stanford, CA: Stanford University Press.

Hamel, A. and Prahalad, C. K. 1994: *Competing for the future*. Boston: Harvard Business School Press.

Hannan, M. and Freeman, J. 1977: The population ecology of organizations. *American Journal of Sociology*, 82, 929–64.

Johnson, G. 1990: Managing strategic change: the role of symbolic action. *British Journal of Management*, 1, 183–200.

Koestler, A. 1969: *The act of creation*. London: Hutchinson.

Micklethwait, J. and Wooldridge, A. 1996: *The witchdoctors*. London: Heinemann.

Mintzberg, H. 1985: Of strategies, deliberate and emergent. *Strategic Management Journal*, 257–72.

Mintzberg, H. 1991: Strategy as 'seeing'. In Juha Nasi (ed.) *Areas of strategic thinking*. Liikesivistysrahasto, Helsinki, Finland: Foundation of Economic Education, pp. 21–5.

Morgan, G. 1988: *Riding the waves of change: developing management competencies for a turbulent world*. San Francisco: Jossey-Bass.

Morgan, G. 1997a: *Imaginization, new mindsets for seeing, organizing and managing*. Thousand Oaks, CA: Sage.

Morgan, G. 1997b: *Images of organization*. London: Sage.

Pascale, R., Millemann, M. and Gioja, L. 1997: Changing the way we change. *Harvard Business Review*, November–December, 127–39.

Pascale, R. 1990: *Managing on the edge*. London: Viking.

Porter, M. 1980: *Competitive strategy*. New York: Free Press.

Prahalad, C.K. and Hamel, G. 1990: The core competence of the corporation. *Harvard Business Review*, May/June, 79–91.

Ricoeur, P. 1975: *The conflict of interpretations: essays in hermeneutics*. Evanston, IL: Northwestern University.

Scheler, M. 1994: *Ressentiment* (trans. L.B. Coser and W.W. Holdheim). Milwaukee, WI: Marquette University Press.

Voegelin, E. 1952/1987: *The new science of politics*. Chicago: University of Chicago Press.

Voegelin, E. 1968/1997: *Science, politics and gnosticism*. Washington: Gateway Editions, Regnery Publishing, Inc.

Voegelin, E. 1987: *In search of order*, vol. 5 of *Order and history*. Baton Rouge: Louisiana State University Press.

Voegelin, E. 1990: 'Equivalences of experience and symbolization in history', pp. 115–33; 'Reason: the classic experience', pp. 265–91; 'Remembrance of things past', pp. 304–14; and 'Wisdom and the magic of the extreme', pp. 316–75. In Ellis Sandoz (ed.) *Published essays 1966–1985*. Baton Rouge: Louisiana State University Press.

Waldrop, M.M. 1992: *Complexity: the emerging science at the edge of order and chaos*. Harmondsworth: Penguin.

Wilson, E.O. 1998: *Consilience: the unity of knowledge*. New York: Alfred A. Knopf.

14

Developing and Implementing Strategy through Learning Networks

Tony dromgoole and Liam Gorman

The literature on strategy implementation and on change management emphasizes recognition of the need to change as a prerequisite to effective implementation (Beckhard and Harris, 1987; Hunt, 1992). However, in the late 1990s, waiting for the external driver of an actual or looming problem will most likely be too late for most situations. Timescales for making the change will have been severely truncated, the risk of reaching for panic measures will be high, and there is the distinct possibility that the degree of choice around a course of action will be limited the later the need for change is recognized. It is very difficult to change in the absence of a felt need for change, yet by the time this need is realized it may be too late. There is a real need, therefore, among the management community to identify ways around this dilemma.

The literature on the learning organization (Garratt, 1990; Senge 1990) is built on the need for organizations and managers to develop mechanisms to help them work their way around this dilemma. The concept of the learning organization is fashionable but it is not new. The need for organizations as well as individuals to acquire a capacity for continuous learning in the face of exponential rates of change has fuelled the popularity of the (as yet unseen) full-blown learning organization.

Recognizing this, the Irish Management Institute put a proposal to the European Commission in 1996 for funding an initiative at the heart of which was the development of a model which would help managers and organizations to develop the capabilities of the learning organization, enabling them to transform themselves continuously through learning to the benefit of their stakeholders.

The objective was to develop such a model, which would most likely be of a contingency nature. It would be standardized in so far as is possible, and would be replicable both in Ireland and in Europe generally. The European Commission

accepted our proposal and funded the project, the National Action Learning Programme (NALP), in 1997.

The initial model envisaged a range of management development techniques and
technologies applied to inter-organizational networks over the course of the programme. It would use a mix of approaches – programmed learning, action learning,
learning networks, coaching, facilitation, consulting, benchmarking and self-assessment – in real time with the participating organizations. Establishing optimal para-
meters for that mix in particular settings would then become the core of the initiative
with a view to replication on a wider scale. The pilot phase of the programme was
completed by the end of 1998.

In this chapter there are four major sections. First we provide a discussion of the
core ideas which influenced the design of the programme. Then we move on to
describe the structure of the programme. Later a review of the programme's progress
and the findings of that review are described. Finally ideas from learning and change
theories which influenced the programme structure are outlined.

Core Ideas Influencing Programme Design

A core idea influencing our work is that of action learning. The idea of action
learning is not new. Indeed at IMI we have been running action learning based
programmes for almost twenty-five years (Mulcahy, 1981; MacKechnie and Dromgoole, 1996). In action learning-based programmes, managers are asked to focus
primarily on their own live experiences rather than dissecting 'dead bodies', such as
case studies of how other managers behaved in other situations (Mumford, 1995).
Mumford encapsulates the key features of action learning as follows:

- First, learning for managers and leaders should mean learning to take effective
  action, not just learning to diagnose a problem.
- Second, it involves actually taking action, and the risks which go with it.
- Third, the action must involve taking action in relation to an issue which is
  important or significant to the manager.
- Fourth, the manager learns best with and from others in similar situations.
- And finally, in keeping with this, the managers must meet regularly and probe
  each other's progress.

All these conditions were met in the design and conduct of the NALP.

Another set of ideas that had a strong influence on the structure of the programme
is taken from the work of Argyris and Schon (1978). These writers make a distinction between 'single-loop' and 'double-loop' learning. In single-loop learning
performance levels are compared to a standard and if there is a shortcoming the
'error' is corrected. The standard itself is not questioned. Such learning may have
been adequate in more stable environments than organizations now confront but in
rapidly changing and competitive environments there is a need for 'double-loop'
learning. In double-loop learning the standards for performance are questioned and

the dimensions along which standards are set are questioned, perhaps amended or discarded. In addition, new dimensions of performance are often identified and new standards set. Double-loop learning, therefore, involves more than taking corrective action; it involves questioning fundamental beliefs and assumptions. This may be necessary if strategy making is to be thorough and geared towards future needs and not a mere extension of past strategic responses. Double-loop learning is at the heart of the learning organization. Considerable effort has gone into simulating real-life situations in order to allow executives to practise and double-loop learning.

There is, however, a vital ingredient of action learning on which simulation misses out – the risk of living with one's decisions. This risk has not been removed in the intervention described here, as our participating organizations simply do not have time to 'play games'. We have worked with them in their real world in real time with a view to assisting them to move towards becoming true learning organizations.

A third major orientation influencing the approach to the programme is the way we see the need for change arising in organizations. We have noted earlier that many change models emphasize the need for a crisis and recognition of a crisis. The project described here takes a more optimistic view and emphasizes the possibility of business and organizations undertaking change through processes other than responding to crisis, for instance, through strategic leadership, by creating change needs through benchmarking, and through 'mimetic isomorphism' (Di Maggio and Powell, 1983) where firms copy each other's worthwhile practices.

Related to this point, a fourth major influence on the design of the programme is the value of creating learning networks of firms that face similar strategy implementation problems. These learning networks are relatively long-term purposeful arrangements among distinct but related organizations that allow companies in the networks to gain or sustain competitive advantage *vis-à-vis* competitors not in the network (Jarillo, 1988). During the phase of the programme described here, the objective was to facilitate through a networking process a firm-based improvement process which went through four major stages: a self-assessment process, a consequent development of a plan of action, the taking of action and reflection on the action initiated. How the learning networks used in the programme contributed to the change process in the participating firms are described later.

Kanter and Eccles (1992) contend that a gulf remains in bringing to bear, on practice, what is already known by the academic community about networks. This gulf, they contend, is based fundamentally on differences in perspective between academics and managers. The former typically refer to 'networks' or 'networking organizations', while the latter more commonly refer to 'networking'. Academics are interested in *understanding* the noun and adjective whereas managers are interested in *using* the verb. We attempt to cater for both perspectives in this chapter. For managers, we recount the operations over a period of time and the perceived value of the strategic learning networks which were put in place. For academics, we additionally attempt to understand both the behaviour within and the dynamics of the 'networks in action'.

Structure of the Programme

The first phase of the programme described here involved initially twenty companies based in Ireland. These companies were chosen because they had expressed a strong interest in one of four themes which faculty members of IMI had suggested as being of high contemporary relevance to companies based in Ireland. The four themes chosen were:

- Securing and expanding the mandate of the multinational subsidiary.
- Rejuvenating the mature organization.
- Developing and managing the high growth SME.
- Adopting world-class practices in the well-established organization.

Participating companies were also required to commit to three other conditions before taking part in the programme. First, each company agreed to be open in discussion with the other companies in their theme group, and to give and receive feedback from other team members; secondly, each company undertook to maintain confidentiality; and, thirdly, each company agreed to put the required resources (mainly managerial time) into the programme.

The programme began with five companies in each of four learning networks (called development teams) grouped around one of the four themes described earlier. Development teams had two senior representatives (usually including the chief executive) from each of the five participating organizations.

Teams were facilitated by two IMI faculty members. When required, teams were supplemented by consultants with particular knowledge of the themes of the groups, by academics or international speakers who had carried out relevant research and by managers from companies with strong track records in relation to the relevant themes.

In the second phase of the programme a considerably larger sample of companies in Ireland (eighty in all) will be involved. Later still, it is planned to extend the programme to other European Union countries and the programme will be amended in the light of what was learned in phases 1 and 2. After the programme had run for approximately a year, as phase 1 drew to an end, a review of the programme was carried out by the second author of this chapter and the outcome of this review is described later.

NALP was designed to use a variety of change mechanisms, approaches which are typically used separately but used together here with a view to creating a greater impact on the individuals and companies involved. Seven approaches in all were utilized on the programme.

First, a detailed self-assessment instrument was completed in relation to the relevant theme by each company. A second approach entailed the monthly present-ation by each company of the progress (or lack of it) against the agenda on which it was working. Considerable pressure was experienced by each company's represent-atives in order to show that they were achieving something in relation to their stated goals. A third part of the process was the feedback from peer companies and team leaders. This process was described by one participant as 'sympathetic confrontation'. A fourth approach involved lectures by speakers which included business managers, consultants and academics. However, since this was an action learning programme, inputs from speakers were always chosen to be relevant to issues that development teams were actually confronting. A fifth approach was to provide reading material tailored to the needs of the companies in each development team. A sixth approach involved one-to-one coaching by the team leaders with the company representatives. In this part of the process, company representatives could get some personal coaching on their roles in their company's development and could raise issues that were more personal in nature than business oriented and which might be seen as not sufficiently related to business issues to raise in the plenary sessions of the development teams. The final approach used in the programme was company visits and business consulting by the team leaders. Here, as distinct from the coaching, the focus was on the business.

What is distinctive about the programme?

All of the approaches listed will have been used frequently to change individuals or businesses. What, then, is distinctive about the present programme? Four features that we think worth mentioning in this regard are:

1. It is the *combined* use of this range of approaches in one programme that contributes to its distinctiveness. Most programmes use one or several of the above approaches but few set out to combine all seven approaches in bringing about change in individual managers or in businesses.
2. Peer networking is not new. Many network type organizations exist but the difference between the use of company networking here and in many other situations was pointed out most succinctly by one of the programme participants. He said that he was a member of many networks but in other networks there is typically a looser structure and some exchange of ideas with a large number of other companies with whom loose relationships are made. In the NALP there was a high degree of structure to the process and one interacted with a small number of similar companies with which there was a close, trusting relationship.
3. A third distinctive element of this programme is its 'action learning' emphasis. All of the approaches used are firmly rooted in the real concerns of the businesses. The input of speakers or the content of the reading materials are not focused on general development. On the contrary, they are anchored in the concerns of the companies and actions and decisions that are being taken by the companies in real time. Clearly this is also true of the self-assessment process, the presentations on progress, peer feedback and the coaching and consulting. If we go back to what we said earlier about action learning, we can see that all the essential elements of action learning are present:
    *   the managers *are* taking effective action and learning from it, not just recommending action or helping solve someone else's problem;

- the change initiatives in their companies *are significant changes* and there is *real risk*;
- they are learning *with and from each other* in the network.

4. Finally, the degree of control participants have over the content and pace of the programme is distinctive. Participants opted for the general theme they would work on, were consulted on inputs to be made on the programme and on learning methods to be used and could spend more or less time, according to their needs, on the issues that were being dealt with.

Review of the Programme (Phase 1)

The review involved visits to the seventeen companies that remained in the project (three companies having discontinued their participation in the programme) and an interview with thirty-two of the thirty-four managers who had participated. The reviewer also attended one day-long meeting of each of the four development groups to familiarize himself with the approach being used. The interviews took place a year after the commencement of the programme and concentrated on the following four areas:

- perceived benefits to the participating companies from the programme;
- perceived personal benefits for managers participating;
- perceived strengths of the learning process;
- participants' suggestions for strengthening the process.

We can divide the perceived benefits to the participating companies into two categories. First, benefits at a general level, which almost all participating companies experienced and, secondly, specific benefits to particular companies. The perceived general benefits are summarized in table 14.1.

We can now give examples of some specific issues on which companies made advances during the period they were participating in the NALP. It is not proposed to give an exhaustive list of these initiatives, rather it is intended to give some sense

Table 14.1 Perceived benefits to the participating companies

Benefit	Proportion of companies claiming this benefit
1. The company having a more strategic outlook	95%
2. A changed perception of their problems being unique	95%
3. Greater objectivity in relation to strategic decisions	90%
4. Increased awareness of measurement and its importance especially from the use of self-assessment instruments	85%
5. Programme helped develop the managers participating in it.	80%
6. Heightened awareness of the importance of the change management process	80%

Sources: Interviews with executives in participating organizations ($N = 17$).

of their variety. It should also be stated that while progress has been made on all of these initiatives many of them are still in progress.

- A fast growth, acquisition-oriented company in a rapidly developing industry which had recently floated on the stock exchange has created a new organizational structure more appropriate to its strategic recent and future developments. It has also tackled the problem of communicating a more precisely focused vision to all its employees. Thus, it is in better shape to pursue further acquisitions which are planned.

- An engineering business, until recently 100 per cent family owned but now with an investment company participation with 30 per cent involvement, has gone through a rationalization programme and is now on the acquisition trail. Senior people in the company feel they avoided possible mistaken acquisitions through their participation in the programme but will continue seeking appropriate acquisitions. Meantime the organization is being strengthened in its marketing and information technology capacities.

- A 100-year-old company embarks on a path towards world-class manufacturing. Senior people feel the company is now clear on what world-class manufacturing means, and is more realistic about what needs to be done to reach that standard. Against a background of very traditional ways of managing, managers now feel more confident, have a more systematic approach to problem solving and have taken initiatives to create a more team-based approach in the organization.

- A high growth health care company was successfully turned around a few years ago. It has recently made a substantial acquisition in the United States. During the programme it has substantially improved the effectiveness and efficiency of the acquired company.

Among other helpful factors on the programme, the peer feedback process has been very useful in this regard. Some of the written material demonstrated that the company's problems were not unique and gave indications of where solutions could be sought.

- A manufacturing company altered the relations and ways of working together between accounts, despatch, operations and sales departments with strong benign effects on customer relations and cost savings. It became clear that some high cost people were doing low value-adding jobs. From peer critique and some of the case studies supplied it became obvious that stocks could be considerably reduced.

- A well-established multinational subsidiary with a strong record of performance and technical excellence is developing its mandate into logistics (hub), manufacturing technology, customer services and research and development. Peer multinational subsidiary managers offer support and counselling on the handling of the transition process. The subsidiary also acquired a new parent in this period, a transition which some of the other members of the development team had earlier experienced so they were in a position to offer valuable comment.

- A successful company in the software field got help in making an important strategic move from selling software packages to customizing its software packages to its clients' specific needs. This company also got far more clarity and focus regarding its strategy during the course of the programme. Common membership of a group with companies which had made successful acquisitions allowed this company see that acquisition was another way of expanding its business effectively and proposed to undertake expansion in that way: 'To expand our company I thought you had to sell more; from the other companies I learned how to expand by buying (companies) as well.'

- An organization in the public sector is working on redesigning its operations and production flow. It benefited from exposure on how companies in the private sector were doing things. It is now doing pilot work on major changes in its operational processes. The changes made in the pilot will be extended to other areas as experience is gathered. The organization may end up with a radically different structure based on teams and with very different mindsets among employees.

So much for the companies. What about the managers directly participating in the programme? What did they get out of the process at a personal level? In table 14.2 there is a summary of their perceptions of the personal benefits of the programme.

In addition, participants on the programme were asked about the aspects of the programme they felt were a particular strength of the programme. Their views are summarized in table 14.3.

Table 14.2 Perceived personal benefits to those participating on the programme

Benefit	Proportion of group claiming this benefit
1. Improved acceptance of feedback on performance, actions and ideas	95%
2. Acquired a more strategic outlook on business	95%
3. Greater awareness of need for continuous learning	80%
4. Established a valuable network	80%
5. Increased sense of personal confidence	75%

Sources: Interviews with participating executives ($N = 32$).

Table 14.3 Perceived strengths of the NALP learning process

Perceived strength	Proportion of Group referring to this strength
1. Participants capacity to influence the learning process	95%
2. Basing the programme on real concerns of the group	95%
3. Value of open and trusting atmosphere	90%
4. The opportunity to learn from the other companies' experiences	90%
5. The self assessment instruments	85%
6. The reading material	80%
7. Speakers from business and academia	80%

Sources: Interviews with participating executives ($N = 32$).

While there was general satisfaction with the basic dynamics of the process, participants had some suggestions for improving it. Briefly, these dealt with the need for the facilitators to be alert for periods at which energy became low and to create some new element in the process that would help towards creating new energy, always making sure that the facilitators did not weaken the group's ownership of the process.

Why does the Programme Work?

It is clear from the perceived outcomes of the review described above that in many cases considerable changes were perceived by the participants in their own behaviour and attitudes and in the performance of their organizations. Let us consider why the programme, as we described it, is effective in bringing such changes. In other words, we shall examine the theory underpinning the success of the NALP initiative.

We aim here to give some description of the concepts from the individual and organizational change literature which influenced the design of the programme. The student of individual and organizational change interested in designing a change process has a wide range of literature and research findings to draw upon. Here we try to give illustrations of some of the literature we found useful and, in particular, try to illustrate the wide variety of this literature.

The change process began with a self-assessment exercise which, as the counselling and change management literature recommends, leads to *ownership of the diagnosis* (see Nelson-Jones, 1997; Bennis et al., 1976). This ownership was reinforced by the control the participants exerted over the agenda and pace of the programme (Sadler, 1996).

The literature on andragogy, which is the science of adult learning (Knowles and Associates, 1985), emphasizes the importance for adult learners to perceive the relevance of learning experiences to their personal, career or business needs. This condition was met by the action learning emphasis of the programme.

Another condition for learning and change, stressed particularly in the social learning literature (Bandura, 1977), emphasizes the importance of credible and prestigious models in advancing change. The peer companies in the groups were typically acceptable and often prestigious models because of media reports of their track records and successes, and this accounted for considerable openness to learning from each other and to the feedback given by peer companies.

The monthly presentations that team members were required to carry out were effective for several reasons. The effort that team members put into these presentations increased their commitment to the group and the change process. We know from cognitive dissonance theory that work voluntarily entered into for a particular purpose increases commitment to that purpose (Aronson, 1995).

A process of escalating commitment was then built into the monthly presentations for those companies that carried out this task thoroughly. Being required to make regular public commitments before peers (especially admired peers) to certain actions added an additional push to the desire to see these actions through in order not to appear inconsistent: 'Saying is believing.'

In addition, the monthly presentation process relied on the power of goal setting to advance change. Locke and his associates (Latham and Locke, 1979) have made an extensive study of the power of goal setting to motivate people to reach new levels of achievement (see also Stephen Carroll in chapter 2). Participants were encouraged to be specific in their presentations; as one participant put it: 'There was no room for waffle and self-delusion.' We know from work such as that of Locke, that specific goals are more effective in motivating performance than goals of a general nature.

From the fields of counselling and learning (see Nelson-Jones, 1997) we know that situations that are psychologically safe – that is, free from ridicule, arbitrary evaluation and with a strong emphasis on reward and the creation of a positive climate – are those which lead individuals to review their behaviour and to create new visions of alternative ways of behaving. Such a climate is good for 'unfreezing' (Lewin, 1951) individuals' and companies' present behaviour and enables alternative actions to be considered, planned for and hopefully executed. After some months, high trust levels with high degrees of psychological safety were created in the groups. This process was expedited in some groups by the openness modelled by individual team members who encouraged others to feel that it was safe to be open.

Thus a high degree of openness and trust was created in each group which led members to voice aspirations, fears and doubts which would not have surfaced in a lower trust group. If these ambitions and anxieties had not surfaced the group would have been interacting and discussing many more superficial issues than those that it was really necessary to discuss – that is the real issues of many of the businesses.

A feature associated with stories on failure is the tendency for individuals after the event to increase their sense of security and reduce felt anxiety by using 'prevention learning' as a way of enhancing their illusion of future control (Langer, 1983). Argyris (1990, 1992) argues that threatening events trigger patterns of defensive reasoning which may appear as reasoning, but in fact tend to limit it. Research on learning from failure reports that people who work as performing artists and athletes often become obsessed with their performance failures, constantly reviewing video playbacks of the events in order to isolate faults. In contrast, the research shows that business people appear to practice avoidance. They say they keep themselves too busy to spend time reflecting on negative outcomes. In their haste to move out of the emotional discomfort zone generated by an embarrassing failure, business decision makers may opt for a quick-fix plan that does not address the root problem. Senge (1990) attributes this, in part at least, to the prevalence of single-loop learning in organizations where one might expect to see evidence of double-loop learning. Single-loop solutions deliver 'a feel good factor' more rapidly than double-loop analyses, giving managers the comforting illusion that something is being done to solve the problem, when what is usually required is double-loop learning and a questioning of fundamental beliefs and assumptions.

While the climate of the development teams was supportive and psychologically safe, it was not a 'pollyanna-ish', 'love in' type atmosphere. Mutual feedback and 'sympathetic confrontation' were sought and given by members, and in this respect the atmosphere was more 'tough love' than 'love in'. As another participant put it: 'There was no place to hide.'

Coaching by team leaders was characterized by the same approach. While the coaching style adopted was supportive it was not a collusive joining of the participants in a self-delusionary process. It is our contention that the conduct of NALP, the conditions pertaining and the atmosphere of 'tough love' reduced the chances of single-loop learning dominating the process.

This latter point brings us to another framework that influenced the programme design. This framework is derived from Gestalt therapy (Beisser, 1970). Beisser calls this framework the paradoxical theory of change. The basic idea here is that individuals and systems change when they confront and know their own behaviour and its impact. The job of the therapist, facilitator or change agent is to use all the means at her or his disposal to create greater awareness of the present in the individual or system. The focus, therefore, is not on the past or on the future; it is on the *present*.

The paradoxical element is that change will occur if the realities of the present are fully confronted. An example of this point of view in action is the power of CCTV (close circuit television) to change individual behaviour. When one sees oneself on CCTV, it does not tell us how we *ought* to behave it shows us how we *do* behave. This revelation typically leads to a powerful desire to change our behaviour because we see what that behaviour is and we judge what its impact is. Thus a full confrontation with reality often leads to a diagnosis of how we need to change if our impact is to be more satisfactory; satisfactory from our own point of view and in relation to our own goals.

Examples of the use of this approach by a company change agent would be the creation of benchmark data, the provision of customer feedback, employees' climate survey data and the creation of mechanisms that lead to self-diagnoses by the system of its strengths and shortcomings. All of these are designed to create a fuller acceptance of reality and of the present activities which usually reveal that, in relation to the company's aspirations, present activity is not wholly satisfactory.

In phase 1 of the NALP, increasing knowledge of their present situation for the companies was created by using nearly all of the approaches described earlier. The self-assessment work was consciously designed for this exact purpose. The presentations leading to peer feedback led to more realism about where they were. The written case studies showed where they lagged behind the standards to which they aspired. The coaching used a non-directive approach to induce self-diagnosis, and the consulting was designed to provide means for a wide range of people in the companies to give input to a diagnosis of their present situations.

General Conclusions

Our review of the first phase of the NALP programme confirms that the programme is perceived by participating managers and firms to be yielding considerable benefits to the companies participating. These benefits include: a more strategic outlook; a changed perception of their problems as being unique; greater objectivity in strategic decision making; greater sensitivity to measurement benefits; management development spin-offs; and heightened awareness of the importance of the change management process.

We have also given examples of specific benefits accruing to the actual companies participating, and some of the real-world examples are:

- sorting out the communication problems of the fast-growing acquisitive plc;
- screening out unsuitable acquisitions in the case of the family business;
- bringing a more systematic approach to operations management in the traditionally managed business;
- helping the multinational subsidiary to handle the transition process when its parent was acquired.

The managers participating in the process confirm our belief that the programme has yielded strong personal benefits to them as managers as well as benefits to their companies. These personal benefits have included:

- an improved acceptance of feedback;
- acquisition of a more strategic outlook on business;
- greater awareness of the need for continuous learning;
- the establishment of a valuable network into the future; and
- an increased sense of personal confidence.

In examining what was distinctive about the programme, we concluded that the four features which differentiate it are:

- the combined use of a range of approaches;
- the structure of the process and of the network;
- the fact that the programme was firmly rooted in the reality of the managers' world, that the managers took effective action and learned from it, that the changes they attempted were significant and involved real risk to them, and that they learned with and from each other in the network;
- the degree of control participating managers had over the content and pace of the programme.

While we fully realize that the data supporting our contention that the first phase of this programme was successful is mainly perceptual in nature, we nevertheless strongly believe that it is a new departure and that it is pioneering in nature. Change certainly has happened in the companies and in the thinking of the managers involved. We are satisfied that NALP is a powerful approach in the quest for the learning organization.

Earlier in the chapter reference was made to the gulf which remains in bringing what is already known by the academic community about networks to bear on practice (Kanter and Eccles, 1992). We set about writing this chapter with two audiences in mind: managers and academics. Managers we believed would be interested in the account of the operation of the networks over a period of time and the perceived value derived by participating companies. We believed that academics would be interested in the contribution we could make to understanding behaviour within networks and the dynamics of the networks in action.

We believe we have added a valuable weapon to the armoury of those managers who see relevant and effective organization and management development as the way forward towards the learning organization. We also believe that we have made a valuable contribution to the body of knowledge of how learning occurs in networks.

References

Argyris, C. 1990: *Overcoming organisational defenses: facilitating organisation learning.* Needham, MA: Simon & Schuster.

Argyris, C. 1992: *On organisational learning.* Cambridge, MA: Blackwell.

Argyris, C. and Schon, D.A. 1978: *Organisational learning: a theory of action perspective.* New York: Addison-Wesley.

Aronson, E. 1995: *The social animal* (6th edn). New York: Freeman.

Bandura, A. 1977: *Social learning theory.* Englewood Cliffs, NJ: Prentice-Hall.

Beckhard, R. and Harris, R.T. 1987: *Organisational transitions.* Reading, MA: Addison-Wesley.

Beisser, A. 1970: The paradoxical theory of change. In J. Fagan and I.L. Shepherd (eds) *Gestalt therapy now.* Palo Alto: Science and Behaviour Books Inc.

Bennis, W.G., Benne, K.D., Chin, R., and Corey, K.E. 1976: *The planning of change* (3rd edn). London: Holt, Rinehart & Winston.

Coughlan, P., Dromgoole, T., Duff, D. and Harbison, A. 1998: Continuous improvement through collaborative action learning in five Irish firms. Paper presented to Second EurCINET Conference, University of Twente, the Netherlands, September 1998.

Di Maggio, P.J. and Powell, W.W. 1983: The Iron Age revisited: institutional isomorphism and collective rationality in organisational fields. *American Sociological Review*, 48 (April), 147–60.

Garratt, B. 1990: *Creating a learning organisation.* Cambridge: Simon & Schuster.

Hunt, J. 1992: *Managing people at work.* London: McGraw-Hill.

Jarillo, J.C. 1988: On strategic networks. *Strategic Management Journal*, 9, 31–41.

Kanter, R.M. and Eccles, R.G. 1992: Making network research relevant to practice. In N. Nohria and R.G. Eccles (eds) *Networks and organisations; structure, form and actions*, Boston, MA: HBS Press, pp. 521–7.

Knowles, M.S. and Associates 1985: *Andragogy in action.* London: Jossey-Bass.

Kotter, J.P. 1995: Leading change: why transformation efforts fail. *Harvard Business Review*, March–April.

Langer, E.J. 1983: *The psychology of control.* Beverly Hills, CA: Sage.

Latham, G.P. and Locke, E. 1979: Goalsetting – a motivational technique that works. *Organisational Dynamics*, Autumn, 69–80.

Lewin, K. 1951: *Field theory in social science.* New York: Harper & Row.

MacKechnie, G. and Dromgoole, T. 1996: An action learning programme for senior managers. Paper presented to the Mid Career University Education Workshop, Copenhagen Business School, 8–12 September.

Mulcahy, N. 1981: Action learning – the link between theory and practice: a progress paper. Paper presented to the International Federation of Training & Development Officers, Annual World Conference, Dublin.

Mumford, A. 1995: Learning in action. *Industrial and commercial training*, 27(8), 36–40.

Nelson-Jones, R. 1997: *Practical counselling and helping skills*. London: Cassell.

Nohria, N. and Eccles, R.G. (eds) 1992: *Networks and organisations; structure, form and actions*. Boston, MA: HBS Press.

Sadler, P. 1996: *Managing change*. London: Kogan Page.

Senge, P.M. 1990: *The fifth discipline: the art and practice of the learning organisation*. New York: Doubleday.

Tichy, N.M. and Devanna, M.A. 1986: *The transformational leader*. New York: Wiley.

15

Implementing Turnaround Strategies in Strongly Unionized Environments

Niall Saul

Introduction

Turnaround situations tend to be crisis driven. Processes of change management in such turnaround situations tend by their very nature to be more fraught, tense and stressful for all concerned, than change processes which can be implemented in a more measured manner over a protracted timeframe. Of benefit in approaching the issue of 'turnaround' is, to define what is meant by effective turnaround in the context of this chapter. Successful turnarounds involve that critical piece of learning for the organization which builds in the capability for managing the change necessary to sustain competitiveness, agility and business growth, rather than limping from one crisis-driven change initiative to another. This is the litmus test of effective change management.

Some authors (notably Kotter, 1995; Beckhard and Harris, 1987), have developed models of the elements involved, but the difficulty is in executing the detail. The challenge is in understanding the context within which the turnaround process is taking place and in testing the applicability of the various models and adapting and refining them to meet the situation facing the particular organization. The aim of this chapter is to give some insight into the key issues involved in designing and implementing turnaround strategies from a practitioner's point of view.

This chapter will seek to identify the key elements of successful turnaround strategy, referring to models of change espoused by Kotter (1995), Beckhard and Harris (1987), Handy (1994), Waterman et al. (1980), and using a composite model which the author has found effective in managing a number of turnaround situations in highly unionized entities across a number of service and manufacturing industries. It also seeks to illustrate these elements by reference to the turnaround of Waterford Crystal, in the mid-1990s.

The chapter is therefore approached from the standpoint of the practitioner and draws heavily on the author's own practical experiences in a number of major change initiatives, including the Waterford turnaround.

Market/Competitiveness/Change Framework

During the last twenty years or so there have been huge changes within the whole business environment. More and more, companies have been forced to recognize that the market is the final arbiter of business success. Organizations which ignore the market, or install or hide behind artificial protections or barriers against the market, are forced at some point to face the reality that success in business is directly dependent on the organization's capacity to meet the market's requirements, not just today, but on a consistent and long-term basis – even if that market changes from that in which the organization originally thought it was a participant.

Those organizations who innately lead or stay very close to the market, as it changes, appear to have within themselves a capability for change, which facilitates their ability to stay close to the market and which places them in a more competitive position than others over the longer term. This capability for agility is a valued core competence.

Many organizations, however, lose this connection with the market from time to time, and depending on the extent to which that connection is lost or the duration for which it is lost, the need for major transformational or turnaround change may arise, to enable the organization to reposition itself as a competitive player.

The market, therefore, is the fundamental driver of business change, but it does not of itself achieve change. Only people, through leadership and involvement, can achieve change.

The competitive imperative

In recent years we have seen the globalization of competition, reflected as it is in trade agreements and market developments on a scale not experienced before. The days of localized competition, protected from competitors by geographical location, or artificial barriers (taxation and so on) are gone, or are in serious decline.

The issues of business have become much more complex, with the emergence of competitors with skills and capabilities, which can give them real competitive advantage in markets which we thought were ours. These new competitors can be those with lower labour cost (the Far East, the former Eastern Bloc countries, South America, China), those with high technology (more efficient producers in Western Europe, USA), or those with greater marketing muscle, whose brand strength can give them a presence and in some cases a premium, which others cannot command.

There is another aspect to the global competitiveness equation, and this is the emergence of outsourcing and internal benchmarking within organizations as a major tool in competitiveness, and the now common phenomenon of global organization with manufacturing facilities in many countries around the world. Manufacturing has virtually become a commodity item, and added value is located in other areas, such as supply chain and logistics management.

Add to these the changes occurring as the business you are in changes or becomes fudged across lines you never thought you would see, or the emergence in your market of competitors from other sectors, who see the business differently or change the way your customer wants to do business. An example of this is in financial services, where banks and insurance companies thought they would become competitors to each other (but they broadly work to the same rules and norms). How will such organizations handle the emergence of powerful retailers (Tesco, J Sainsbury, Marks & Spencer, Boots, Virgin) as providers of financial services, given the skills that these retailers have in managing customer information, the frequency of customer/supplier contact, the intimacy of their connection with the customer and their lower cost bases?

As so many of these factors are in play, companies with quite successful track records can often be lulled into a false sense of security about their market. In such situations organizations can move quickly from relative success to serious crisis.

Overlay the emergence of e-commerce and an increasingly better informed and more demanding customer community, and we can start to get a flavour of the dilemmas facing many organizations in strategy formulation on the one hand, and in the critical area of strategy implementation on the other.

Change – the real leadership challenge

The challenge for most business leaders is twofold: selection of suitable/correct strategies, and delivery of these strategies in an effective and timely way. For those in heavily unionized industries there is a third challenge; to structure and negotiate agreements that pave the way for delivery of the necessary strategies within the required timeframe.

Where radical turnaround is involved, with collapse of the business the likely outcome if a change initiative fails, there may not be sufficient time or opportunity to revisit the change process before the business succumbs. Selection of the correct change process assumes a fundamental importance.

Ensuring successful implementation of strategic business plans is the greatest leadership challenge in today's business environment. The capability of leaders to contextualize the need for change for organizations in such a way as to harness support for the change at every level of the organization to ensure timely and effective delivery is, in my view, the key differentiator between top-class managers and the others.

'Timely' implementation of change has been mentioned twice in the last two paragraphs, and with good reason. I say this because at the current rate of change, delays in implementing required changes can be as damaging as no change.

A critical aspect of the need for change is that, in a competitive setting, it is unceasing – a journey, not a destination. So for leaders, a key element of successful turnaround or transformational change, is to get this established as a clear value in the organization. Also, for some organizations, particularly those competing internationally, it may be necessary to face up to four or five waves of change in a single decade, which is greatly disconcerting for their employees.

The difficulty in heavily unionized environments has been a tendency to solve today's problems and deal with tomorrow's problem as a separate issue. This creates the effect of lurching from crisis to crisis, rather than seeking to tackle the underlying issue of competitiveness in a more holistic and long-term manner. To do this requires both management and unions to resolve the problems in current norms of practice and move to a new format.

The problem is that some drivers of change (technology, cost restructuring, business re-engineering) are associated in people's minds with loss for employees, rank, status, overtime, jobs and so on, and there appears to be a preference to avoid such loss, notwithstanding the fact that the ultimate loss caused by failure to tackle such issues could be much greater, i.e. total collapse of the business and loss of all jobs.

There is some evidence to show that true success in turnaround events should be measured not just by the short-term agreement on installation of new work practices, cost restructuring proposals, technology or outsourcing. A key measurement may be the extent to which the relationship between the management and staff in the organization (whether unionized or not) is fundamentally changed, and switched to a genuinely participative approach to securing and retaining the organization's long-term commercial competitiveness, maximizing the organization's potential to provide and retain employment, in terms of both quality and quantity.

In my experience, organizations, where such a 'mindset' change is achieved at all levels, emerge from turnaround situations with a capability to expand and deal more effectively with the changes in the business and with much higher levels of mutual trust across the organization. My concern is that many organizations who come through turnaround situations without such a mindset shift – or without supporting and nurturing it (with appropriate processes and procedures) are at serious risk of entering a cycle of such turnaround crisis-based situations with increased levels of bitterness, acrimony and distrust.

Where turnarounds are necessary in highly unionized environments, this adds additional complexity, as it is often necessary to structure and negotiate formal agreements before the change process can take place. The capacity to 'force' or impose change is more limited, and a wider range of skills is required to persuade people that the change process must be embraced.

It is this added complexity which seems to place a higher level of importance on some steps in Kotter's (1995) eight-step model for transformation. These steps centre around contextualizing the need for change, preparing a concrete road map for the future, creating a robust plan for negotiation of an agreement on change, and establishing a strong consensus for effective management and delivery of that agreement.

The key elements

The model outlined here is one that I have found effective in a number of turnaround situations, in various industries, over the past twenty years. Although different in its emphasis, because of the unionized environments involved, it has elements that echo Kotter's (1995) eight-step model for organizational transformation.

Within the application of the model – particularly in working with people on visioning, planning, communication, searching for quick wins, and converting achieved changes into a platform for new change – I have drawn on the work of Beckhard and Harris (1987), Waterman et al. (1980, '7S' model) and Kotter (1995). The model covers five main elements:

1. Analysis of the issues and contextualization of the need for change within a competitiveness framework.
2. Preparation of a plan to restore the organization's competitive position and creating/developing the political will to implement it.
3. Gaining agreement on that plan across the whole organization.
4. The effective and timely implementation of the change programme – achieving quick wins and recognizing them as important steps in the process.
5. Through the change process, the creation of a competitively focused entity, incorporating the processes and procedures, which support a culture of commitment to ongoing change.

It is this last area which has the capacity to underpin the long-term viability of the organization.

Within non-unionized environments, the gap between the second and fourth steps can be narrow, because to a large degree the management has all the levers of control at its disposal and is free to use them in a more or less unfettered way. The main sources of failure in such organizations can often be found in the quality of the plan and its capacity to create awareness of the need for early change or, more critically, in the implementation phase.

In unionized environments the effective management of the model's third step potentially adds huge levels of complexity to the process, but also has the potential to add considerably to the quality of the final outcome.

This third step opens the management's plan and vision to critical examination and challenge. In doing so, it places a much higher level of importance on the analysis step, and the planning phase. The management's plan in the highly unionized environment must be robust and capable of standing up to scrutiny and challenge, not just from the union negotiators and employees, but also from third party agencies who perform mediation or arbitration functions in such disputes and to whom such plans can be referred frequently within a country's industrial relations system.

The biggest issues in achieving agreement are generally the time taken to finalize agreement by negotiation, and the fact that the industrial relations (IR) system in some countries does not offer a guaranteed 'step of final resort', at which the outstanding differences can be resolved by independent binding arbitration. This fault in IR systems in some countries creates a potentially vicious circle of confrontation, as one of the parties, normally the top management, seek to get closure on this step in the process, and to move into the implementation phase.

In heavily unionized environments the standard of work required in each of the steps (analysis, plan preparation, negotiation and implementation to ensure success) is more demanding than similar change in non-unionized environments. While it can have its negatives, it is arguable that the standards demanded by the heavily unionized environment, if properly managed, can deliver very effective outcomes.

In highly unionized environments, a different emphasis is required than in other circumstances. For example, in creating a vision of the future some turnaround plans focus heavily on labour cost issues, often to the exclusion of other key areas which could contribute to recovery. It is critical that, where major changes on the labour side are required (such as downsizing, changes in work practices, reward structures and so on), these can be clearly shown to be for some longer term gain (such as stability of employment, opportunity for business growth, profit sharing) so that any sacrifices required will be seen by the majority as worth while to make.

In creating the vision, techniques such as the McKinsey '7S' model (1980) and a version of the 'standing in the future' model, can be used to help people understand the gap between the desired state and the current state, and the action steps required to bridge that gap. These models also help the workforce to understand the integrated and entwined nature of the steps required, by framing the change process in an understandable format. Where 'two-stage' change processes are necessary – (a) stemming losses, stabilizing situation, and (b) developing the business from a more secure platform – models for showing transition stages of the organization (Beckhard and Harris, 1987) are useful tools in enhancing understanding.

Many companies have limited the communication of 'The Vision' to the trade union representatives, relying on them to convey the message to the membership. This abrogation of a primary managerial responsibility is one of the main sources of failure of such change initiatives. It is critical that in turnaround situations or cases of major change in highly unionized environments, that management takes a leadership role in communicating the business analysis, vision, plans and sacrifices, directly to the workforce and allows critical evaluation and direct questioning of these in an open way. This is not always easy to do, because often in times of turnaround, people are angry, concerned and fearful, but the willingness by management to deal directly with them, as adults, is often greatly appreciated, and can help build trust.

Such extensive communication does not cut across the role of elected union representatives, but instead involves differentiating the two processes of communication and negotiation. The latter can continue within the normal collective bargaining framework.

Indeed, as part of an overall desire to create an informed environment within which critical decisions may be made by the individuals concerned, a policy of direct 'organization-wide' communication creates a situation in which everyone has received a common or shared message about the problems involved, the seriousness of the situation and the vision of the recovered entity. In unionized environments, the employer's capacity to force or impose change is limited. The real change skill is that of persuasion – leadership by contextualizing both the need for change and the change itself in a way that makes the changes proposed the preferred option of the bulk of the employees. It is this issue of persuasion that Steve Carroll refers to in chapter 2 as a critical aspect of successful change management.

Case Study: Waterford Crystal

This case involves Waterford Crystal, which in the period from 1986 to 1992 plunged from high profitability to virtual bankruptcy, despite several restructuring plans. In 1992/1993, the company underwent a major turnaround process which, by 1994, had restored profitability. Between 1994 and 1997 it had generated dramatic growth in sales and profitability, built on a shared commitment between management and workforce to developing and maintaining long-term competitiveness.

Background

The company is a subsidiary of the Waterford Wedgwood Group. Until 1991, the company manufactured and distributed premium crystal from four plants in County Waterford, Ireland. The USA was its main market; over 70 per cent of its product was sold in the USA, rising to 85 per cent when one counted sales to US tourists to Ireland. Up to the mid-1980s a strong US dollar ($1.05 to IR£1 in 1985) ensured that the company enjoyed high profits.

Between 1985 and 1992, the US dollar dropped in value from $1.05 to $1.89 to the Irish pound. Waterford, over-exposed to the US dollar, with sales in US dollars, costs in Irish pounds, spiralled into crisis. The collapsing US dollar exposed critical strategic weaknesses in the business (outdated technology, poor industrial relations, unsustainable manufacturing costs), to the extent that by 1992, despite a number of cost-saving plans, Waterford was virtually bankrupt. In addition, by using price increases to offset the fall of the US dollar it had priced itself out of the sector of the market in which it had been successful and customer resistance to its pricing policy was growing rapidly. In 1990, it experienced a 14-week strike, which almost caused the collapse of the business. After the strike, the industrial relations climate was extremely fractious and every effort at introducing operational changes was strongly resisted by the workforce. Trust between management and workforce had virtually collapsed.

The crisis in 1992 was further exacerbated by a range of other factors such as the recession in the US market, which hit the luxury branded goods market quite heavily as consumers moved from conspicuous spending evident up to that, to a search for value rather than brands. The emergence of new competitors (Gorham and Mikasa – marketing companies who outsourced manufacturing), and the pressures on large retail department stores in the USA (in 1992, 25 per cent of Waterford's US retail base was endeavouring to avoid bankruptcy) increased the complexity of the problem.

The Somers/Patterson plan

In 1992, the board appointed Bernard Somers, well known for his work as a receiver, and Brian Patterson, then chief operating officer, to examine the viability of the Irish manufacturing operations.

In 1991, the company had launched a sub-brand of Waterford, called 'Marquis by Waterford'. This product range was more contemporary in nature than traditional Waterford, and occupied price points vacated by Waterford products due to the US dollar decline in the late 1980s. The most important element of the 'Marquis' story, however, was that it was not made in Waterford, but outsourced and manufactured to defined quality standards in the Czech Republic, Slovenia and Germany.

In early/mid-1992, having identified that the Irish-based manufacturing entities could survive if certain dramatic steps were taken, the Somers/Patterson plan was developed, in conjunction with the company's top team, a small group of senior, middle, managers and two external consultants.

In mid/late 1992, Waterford recruited the author, as HR director, and subsequently recruited Michael Wilcock of Semperit, as manufacturing director. These last two recruits meant that, of the top team, only two people had had more than seven years' service in Waterford. The strategy followed by the chief executive, Paddy Galvin, was to ensure that he had a top team with the skillset and experience to bring the plan to fruition. This strategy links closely with Kotter's (1995) identification of the need for formation of a powerful guiding coalition. A majority of the top team were managers with extensive experience in change management internationally in a range of industries spread across automotive products, electronics, pharmaceuticals, food industry and cosmetics. The turnaround plan consisted of two key stages.

STAGE 1   Get the cost base right, stem the losses, return to profitability. This involved reducing labour costs by £5.2m per annum. It required pay reductions across the company of between 7 and 25 per cent and the introduction of internationally recognized industrial engineering based standards. A realignment of plants to maximize efficiency of product flow and designation of plants to certain product types was also deemed necessary.

In order to ensure true competitiveness, the plan provided for the establishment of a benchmarked system of 'make or buy' for all new products. Central to the plan was a requirement to stabilize the heretofore unstable industrial relations environment. The route chosen was an industrial peace clause, which provided for all issues which could not be settled by direct negotiations, to go through a set of procedures culminating in an arbitration stage, where the third party decision was binding on all parties.

The aim of this stage of the overall plan was to build a platform for competitiveness and a high level of commitment to the changes that would be required to deliver it, for rebuilding the business.

STAGE 2   If stage 1 was satisfactorily completed, the plan was to put in place a strategy based on developing a technocraft-based industry, linking existing craft skills with state of the art technology (in melting, forming, cutting, design and so on). This involved the creation of a culture and performance level to entice shareholders to make the required investment (circa £10m) to deliver this.

It was believed that successful implementation of this plan would effectively move Waterford from being production driven to market led, build true and sustainable competitiveness and, in turn, genuinely profitable business growth.

In heading into the plan, morale in the company was at an all-time low:

- Extensive short time had left deep scars and there was almost total mistrust between management and the workforce.
- The workforce was cynical about the plan – having seen the 1987, 1989 and 1990 plans all come to nought.
- The share price was 14p – only the 'brand name' itself supported that value.

Communication/negotiation/implementation

The project team charged with delivering the plan tackled the issue on two major platforms. First, they sought to contextualize the plan for the workforce, within the overall business framework. They did this by a process of relentless communication and education, on a face-to-face basis, with the workforce. Secondly, they relied on the common sense of the vast majority of the workforce as the company's major strength. From August 1992 to January 1993, there followed an extensive series of collective bargaining negotiations, culminating in a Labour Court Recommendation, which though broadly supporting the company's position, built in some provisions to protect the interests of the workforce, notably an alteration to proposed 'make or buy' rules, and a capping of any potential loss at a maximum of 25 per cent for any one individual.

Simultaneously, the company management engaged in an extensive series of direct communication meetings with the workforce in groups varying in size from 200 to 100 to 50, followed up by direct information about the impact of the plan on each individual. The intention of this process (each employee would have attended six such sessions in the six-month period) was to ensure that everyone, irrespective of rank or status, understood the issues, and had the same information as everyone else. It sought to convince people that the creation of genuinely competitive manufacturing operation at Waterford was the best way to eliminate short-time, and expand the business for the future. This commitment to communication of the new entity echoes Kotter's (1995) step for extensive communication of the vision.

The process involved extensive negotiation with the union on the general picture and with each of its seven sections on the detailed changes for each section. Owing to problems with one section, delays at the end of the process – which the company had sought to complete by 31 December 1992 – forced the company to issue protective notice to the whole workforce. Finally, the package was accepted with 97 per cent of the workforce voting in favour of the arrangements.

Taking the next step: 1993 and 1994

As the company moved to implement the agreement through 1993 it got an unexpected break; the US dollar moved up in value for the first time since 1987. This generated a profit in 1993. While not in itself substantial, it did, unlike other plans in 1989 and 1990, lend great credibility to the new agreement.

During 1993, at the behest of the Amalgamated Transport & General Workers' Union (ATGWU), a debate took place on the way forward. The company proposed greater involvement of the union representatives in the whole area of competitiveness, and established a joint management/union task group to review all matters of competitiveness, make or buy decisions, technological innovation, budgetary issues, product pricing, and new product development. This group met weekly under the chairmanship of the manufacturing director and began to crystallize the issues of change to ensure future viability.

On the industrial relations front, most issues were settled by direct negotiation. A number of issues were referred to binding arbitration by the Labour Court with the company winning some, and the union winning some.

By the end of 1993, the company was back in profit and paid out a small amount in profit share, in line with arrangements in the 1993 agreement. Throughout 1993, the company communicated with the workforce and the union representatives on performance and future plans, reinforcing commitment to the plan.

Before the end of 1993, the company and union representatives had agreed on a consultative approach to the future on the basis of a shared agenda.

The creation of a competitive, market led operation, capable of sustaining 1,200 +/– 70 jobs in Ireland, consistent with sustaining long term competitiveness.

The initiatives taken in 1993 tie in closely with other elements of Kotter's (1995) model for transformation, particularly empowering others to act on the vision, and planning for and implementing short-term wins.

This vision fed into events of 1994, when the company moved to the next stage of the plan, the investment in development of a leading edge technocraft manufacturing environment, which would reduce employment from 1,400 to about 1,200. This, if successful, would deliver on another element of Kotter's (1995) model; consolidating improvement and creating still more change.

Negotiations and communications on this proposal took place in early 1994. The key issue was an examination of a matrix of competitors (such as other manufacturing sources who either competed against Waterford Crystal in the marketplace or were potential outsourcers for its product). There were four categories: those with high labour cost/high technology (companies in western Germany, France, Scandinavia); low labour cost/high technology (companies in France, Austria, Italy); low labour cost/low technology (companies in Eastern Europe, South America); and high labour cost/low technology (traditional UK manufacturers, Ireland – Waterford being an extreme case – Val St Lambert, Belgium).

The message was clear. Each category had certain competitive advantages – except the high-labour/low-technology category as it was not possible to compete from this category in the medium to long term. The choice was to go to low-labour-cost/low-technology, which would mean going to labour costs between half and one-tenth of Waterford's own pay rates, or go up the technological ladder into a technocraft environment.

This information and the choices were fully presented to the unions and the workforce as part of the now well-established policy of creating an 'informed and questioning workforce'. The result was a comprehensive agreement, negotiated directly, incorporating a pay agreement, 1994 to 1998 inclusive, at national norms (National Agreement terms), continuation of the industrial peace/binding arbitration clause and, most significantly, an undertaking from the shareholders to invest IR£10m in new technology.

The agreement included a framework for effective management of all redundancy, redeployment and retraining issues arising from the technology step, and a voluntary severance/early retirement package. The agreement included the establishment of a joint monitoring committee to oversee and review the process of radical restructuring, including such major issues as redeployment, redundancy/early retirement, operational change and technology initiatives, to ensure smooth and timely implementation of those changes. The level of mutual trust between management, workforce, and Union negotiators had grown dramatically and topics that could not be raised in earlier years were now openly debated.

A shared commitment to growth and competitiveness

Waterford Crystal had doubled its business between 1993 and 1996, and by the end of 1998 under its new CEO, Redmond O'Donoghue, has doubled its business again. In the USA it has grown at 17 per cent compound per annum. Profitability has dramatically improved. The company introduced a wide range of new products in the crystal area, under the Waterford and Marquis brands, and latterly the John Rocha sub-brand. It is interesting to note that the John Rocha designed product could not have been made in Waterford if the technology change had not taken place in 1994.

In terms of benefits to employees, the company's Irish operations have increased employment to 1,600 (against the 1993 vision of 1,200 – reducing from 1,400 after the introduction of technology) and dramatically increased the profit share to employees, to the extent that pay sacrifices made by most categories in 1993 had been overtaken by profit share by 1997. In this period the company had maintained a strike-free environment.

Its strategy since 1995 has been built around four key values, relentlessly espoused by its current CEO:

1. It will never become uncompetitive again.
2. It will never again fall behind on technology.
3. It will never compromise on quality.
4. It will always keep its workforce fully informed.

On the marketing front, the company has successfully leveraged the brand out into other product areas: linens, writing instruments, china and others. It has invested heavily in education and retraining, encouraging employees to focus on personal 'employability' and self-improvement, as keys to the future. Waterford is now the leading edge technocraft premium crystal company in the world.

Significantly, through these processes and agreements the company has built a sustained change-oriented culture, driven by sharing plans and information with the total workforce, and investing in its people. By any measure, this is an impressive transformation. Dr A.J.F. O'Reilly refers to it as the most dramatic turnaround he has ever seen. In his comments on the turnaround the current CEO, Redmond O'Donoghue, has praised the leadership shown at both managerial level, and by trade union representatives, but in particular he has paid special tribute to Waterford's workforce, who have demonstrated extraordinary levels of courage, personal sacrifice, creativity and willingness to make the changes necessary to rebuild and transform the business. He readily acknowledged the unique partnership that has been forged across all levels and operational arms of the business to help to deliver long-term sustained competitiveness.

Issues for Trade Unions

For many trade unions, union officials and members, the issues around radical organization change brought about by global competition and technology can prove traumatic. In their own way the trade unions are struggling with the new market scenario in which they must play.

At a recent conference sponsored by the Irish Congress of Trade Unions (ICTU) the dilemmas facing trade unions were discussed. Among the issues identified were skillsets of union officials and union procedures and structures. Advances in business processes, communication, technology and in legislation, have changed the skill requirements for trade union officials and have thrown up huge educational and retraining needs. For the official to provide a professional service, it is argued that he or she must be familiar with such concepts as world-class manufacturing (WCM), just-in-time (JIT), business process re-engineering (BPR) and others, and be capable of guiding members through the web of issues that emerge in the change process. One difficulty is that the change process often reverses the traditional roles of unions and management, with management having an agenda of 'claims' on union members for operational change or elimination of restrictive practices, often with no scope for entering the payment for change arena of previous times. There is a pressure on unions to balance protection of existing rights and benefits against future employment of the members.

The 'uniformity' of treatment for people in terms of pay and bonus issues and structure of work (the emergence of atypical employment models) that were evident in traditional heavily unionized organizations, are now under direct threat. This has tested the willingness and capability of unions to move away from a 'uniformity' philosophy of traditional models into areas like flexible pay, flexible hours, performance pay (individual or team based), share option schemes, profit share arrangements and so on.

In recent times we have heard much of partnership and collaboration on managing the change agenda. In this the unions face two major difficulties. The first is: What is partnership for and whose agenda does it serve? In this regard unions have tended to view partnership in a narrow sense focusing on representative structures and bureaucratic arrangements, which can undermine the level of agility needed to ensure organizational change. The second problem is that elected union committee representatives often have difficulty in wearing the 'collaborative hat' of participation and involvement, and the 'conflictual hat' of collective bargaining. Equipping such representatives to cope with the requirements of this dual role is critical to the successful management of change. Failure to address this issue effectively can leave elected representatives, who operate in a political environment, open to criticism from their members and to replacement at the next election.

It does appear from the Waterford Crystal case and other experiences, that the establishment of a genuine social contract type agreement or framework – that is, balancing competitiveness with investment in both technology and people, and underpinned by some commitments on communication, employment, and profit sharing – can form the basis of a management/union relationship that can assist in the successful management of both turnaround and major change situations. The commitment and personal leadership of the Amalgamated Transport & General Workers' Union (ATGWU) representatives at Waterford has shown how this delicate balance can be managed.

Issues for Management

Apart from the critical issue of leadership and relentless communication of the need for change, it appears that change at Waterford has been successfully achieved, and turnaround situations sustained and developed upon, by managements who have moved their perceived 'control' role within the organization to that of economic navigators, identifying the opportunities and risks facing the organization in the short, medium and long terms and interpreting the implications of those risks and opportunities for the business and its people.

The experience over recent decades has effectively established that imposed change is not only very difficult to achieve, but is virtually impossible to sustain over the medium to long term, whereas creation of a change framework based on a sensible balance between addressing the competitive challenges and the genuine concerns of the workforce, can often lead to much more effective and long-lasting change.

Investment in training and education is, in my view, a critical issue. The old adage 'if you think education is expensive – try looking at the cost of ignorance' has never been more valid. Fear of the future, or the consequences of radical change, can paralyse people and can lead to quite extreme forms of resistance.

In the Waterford case, one key element that developed and sustained the commitment to change was extensive investment in training and education. By helping people to become confident of their ability to remain relevant in the changing environment in the company, or by enabling them to acquire skills more generally marketable within and outside the organization, the company helped to eliminate fear from the workforce and from the change process.

Review of the Critical Issues

On reviewing my experiences over the past twenty years, successful change management in highly unionized environments seems to depend on broadly the same factors as change in any organization, but with added complexity in terms of the communication process and negotiating requirements.

At the centre of successful turnaround situations is effective leadership – incorporating sound business analysis, vision formulation, planning, effective communication and contextualization of the need for change, coupled with a relentless focus on the key deliverables to ensure achievement of true long-term competitiveness.

In turnaround situations there is a risk, particularly in heavily unionized environments, that the turnaround is viewed as the achievement of a fixed state. As demonstrated by the Waterford case, the real value is in the development and implementation of processes and trust-building initiatives, which ensure organization-wide understanding of the change process as a journey – not a destination. True value also lies in the development of a genuine capacity in the business for managing ongoing continuous change to sustain long-term competitiveness in a constructive and ordered manner.

References

Beckhard, R. and Harris, R. 1987: *Organisational transitions: managing complex change* (2nd edn). Reading, MA: Addison-Wesley.

Handy, C. 1994: *The empty raincoat*. London: Hutchinson.

Kotter, J.P. 1995: Leading change: why transformation efforts fail. *Harvard Business Review*, March–April, 59–67.

Waterman, R.H., Peters, T.J. and Phillips, J.R. 1980: Structure is not organisation. *Business Horizons*, June, 1–13 (McKinsey & Co.).

16

Teams in Strategy Implementation: Some Case Examples

KEN SMITH AND HENRY SIMS JR

In recent years, a great deal of emphasis has been placed on the use of teams in organizations. Teams have been identified and fostered at every level from the shop floor to the corporate office. In this chapter, we examine how teams have been and might be used in the implementation of strategy. We explore the matter from three different perspectives. In the first, we examine the role of the top management team. Given that senior managers are uniquely responsible for the formulation and implementation of strategy, it is crucial to assess the unique requirements of top managers as a team. In the second perspective, strategy has been formulated and teams are used as the mechanism to put that strategy into action, – that is, strategy is implemented *through* teams. From the third perspective, teams and team structures are seen as critical *components* of the strategy itself. No longer simply means to an end, teams are an end in themselves, with the result that the formulation and implementation of strategy begin to merge. In short teams *are* the strategy. We conclude by summarizing the opportunities for the use of teams in strategy implementation along with organizational preconditions if teams are to prove beneficial.

Teams: some issues of definition

Some scholars, such as Ilgen (1999), use the terms 'group' and 'team' interchangeably, while others believe that a group is not necessarily a team. For example, Katzenbach and Smith (1993) defined teams as 'a small number of people with complementary skills who are committed to a common purpose, performance goals, and approach for which they hold themselves mutually accountable'. Building on this idea, Smith and Sims (1995) assert that the essence of teams is synergy. For synergy to be achieved, a combination of specialization, interchangeability and trust is required. Individual team members often contribute to the team effort through their unique skills, but performance is enhanced if members understand and have some degree of skill in all the functions of the team. This allows members to rapidly and continuously switch between specialization and generalization as the context requires. Finally, trust allows members to extend themselves, knowing that they can count on other members for support.

Associating 'teamness' with synergy suggests that not all identifiable groups of people are really teams. For instance, Hambrick (1994) has challenged strategy scholars to rethink whether 'top management teams' are, in fact, teams. Thus, we accept Katzenbach's (1998) three litmus tests of a true team regardless of organizational level:

- mutual accountability for group results;
- collective or joint work products of clear performance value;
- a sharing and/or shifting of leadership role among the members.

Top Management as a Team: Some Implementation Imperatives

At the top of most sizeable contemporary organizations, there exists a group of senior executives including the president or CEO. This group is often called a 'top management team', whether they function as a team or not. Over the last two decades, a great deal of research has been focused on top management teams (see Finkelstein and Hambrick, 1996). Although the majority of this research has focused on senior management's role in strategy formulation (Smith and Kofron, 1996), the role of top management in implementation has been recognized.

> [TMTs] are responsible for formulating adaptive responses to the environment, *as well as implementing those responses*. As such, the group sometimes is involved in discrete problems or choices...however, the group also engages in on-going, day-in/day-out administrative actions which collectively shape the organization's form and greatly affect the types of problems and alternatives that are even brought to its attention. (Hambrick, 1994: 175; italics added)

Key implementation roles of top management include the following:

- Clarify and communicate the organization's mission, values, and strategies.
- Create an appropriate structure to support the implementation of strategy.
- Acquire and allocate resources to those who do the work of the organization.
- Create and manage the control system of the organization, and play a co-ordinating role as part of that control system.

All of these are the responsibilities of top management regardless of whether or not top managers value teams as a way of doing business, or whether top management itself functions as a team. However, we believe that team effort on the part of top management, particularly with regard to these implementation responsibilities, enhances the likelihood of improved performance.

The main hypothesis underlying top management team research has been that a team effort at the top is required to effectively manage a complex organization. This idea has roots far back in organization theory – indeed Barnard's *The Functions of the Executive* (1938) refers more to the executive structure than to the single chief executive. Similarly, the notion of a 'dominant coalition' (Cyert and March, 1963) suggests a collective effort to lead large organizations. But does this effort truly constitute team work? Are top management teams really *teams*?

In his 1998 book, *Teams at the Top*, Jon Katzenbach suggests that the reality is that top management teams both are, and are not, teams in the strict sense, and makes the following observations:

1. The best senior leadership groups are rarely true teams, although they can and do function as real teams when major, unexpected events prompt that behaviour.
2. Most of them can optimize their performance as a group by consciously working to obtain a better balance between their team and non-team efforts rather than by trying to become an ongoing single team.
3. The secret to a better balance lies in learning to integrate the discipline required for team performance with the discipline of single-leader behaviour – not in replacing one with the other.

Summarizing Katzenbach's arguments, there is an inherent conflict between real team efforts at the top and the strong single-leader approach that is typical of most organizations. Note also that the typical planning model presumes a dominant CEO. It is very difficult to break the pattern of strong single-leaders because the single-leader mode works most of the time. Also, it is difficult to identify real collective work products at the top of the organization – that is, there is a lack of true technical interdependence at the top. Moreover, the fixation of the popular business media such as *Forbes*, *Business Week* and *Fortune* creates a strong legitimization of the single leader model. Nevertheless, integrating these two distinct approaches that are normally in direct conflict – teams and executive leadership – rather than compromising one for the other, is the key to enhanced leadership capacity.

Proactively identifying collective work products can provide important catalysts for senior leadership groups that seek a better balance of team performance. Examples of such work products include resolving a key strategic issue, redesigning a faulty management process, changing the organizational structure, or deciding to enter a new market. Indeed, classical re-engineering sometimes uncovers functional relationships, even at the top. Such work products can relate to strategy formulation or implementation. Katzenbach, however, notes that such tasks can be formulated either as collective work products or as the individual responsibility of a single executive. Care must be taken in how the task is structured if the result is truly to be a team effort.

Despite the strong current interest in top management teams, individual leadership remains important and often effective – and not all senior management tasks require a team effort. Thus, the key to increasing team performance at the top is to develop the ability to shift into and out of different modes of behaviour and membership configurations as appropriate. According to Katzenbach, chief executives who can play multiple roles are more likely to achieve an optimal balance between team and non-team performance within their executive teams. A balanced leadership approach at the top must be able to combine the essential individual leadership activities with the substantive collective work required for team performance.

The Champion International Case

Katzenbach cites the 'Gang of 8' at Champion International Corporation as an example of a management team that has worked hard to find this balance. Using the event of the CEO's planned resignation as the catalyst, top management set out to shape a new structure for itself more consistent with Champion's commitment to teams at the plant level. The transition process entailed training eighteen senior managers to build their strategic understanding of the company and to strengthen their ability to work together in a number of team configurations. Following the appointment of CEO Richard Olson, the top management group was finalized at eight, in accordance with the transition plan. This group, however, had had numerous experiences working in team structures leading up to the transition, and was now prepared to act as a team when necessary.

An early exercise for the team was to shape and staff the management structure below the top level, again, to bring management more in line with Champion's commitment to teams at the plant. Considering this structure a natural team product, Olson did not come to the table with preconceived notions. Rather, all eight top managers presented options and opinions, and worked together to solve problems regarding the best way to shape and staff the organization. It took several weeks and many working sessions before the structure was finalized, but the result was truly a team product, owned by all the players.

Katzenbach is quick to point out that Champion's 'Gang of 8' functions in a team mode some of the time, but not always. The sessions in which they function as a team are spent working on significant strategic and performance issues. As many of these meetings focus on operations, the team is regularly engaged in the implementation of strategy.

Implementing Strategy *Through* Teams

Assuming management's commitment to teams, how might teams be used in strategy implementation? One approach is to implement strategy *through* teams. In this approach, organizations continue to practise formalized strategic planning driven by top-down processes of rationalizing objectives in support of the firm's mission and strategic targets. Once the strategy is developed, the organization relies on team structures in and across units to put the strategy into action.

There have been several important historical drivers behind the introduction of teams into large organizations, chief among these being the intensifying global competition of the 1980s. In particular, many Japanese and other Asian companies ascended to prominence through the use of team-based structures in support of total quality management (TQM). Such firms as Toyota, Sharp, Komatsu, Honda and Kao capitalized on Asian collectivist culture to coalesce around the quality principles of Demming. The strategies that these firms pursued through the 1980s were developed at the corporate level in almost paternalistic fashion. However, they were implemented by highly committed employees who were organized in a variety of team structures.

The Case of Sharp Corporation

Collis and Noda (1993) have documented the implementation of Sharp Corporation's technology strategy through the 1980s. During the period from 1970 to 1990, Sharp transformed itself from a second-tier assembler of TV sets and home appliances to a premier, comprehensive electronics company with expertise in electronic device technologies which it used to develop and market innovative end products. Sharp's overall strategy has been to differentiate itself through its products, which are technology intensive and difficult to imitate. Its strategy has been measurably successful in terms of growth, profitability and reputation.

Importantly, Sharp's strategy is formulated in a top-down fashion by senior executives who make all key strategic decisions. Sharp engages in a formalized strategic planning process that includes the development of a ten-year vision, a three-year medium-term plan, and six-month operating plans. Plan targets are established for each business in terms of sales, profitability and market share. The planning staff then disaggregates the targets and allocates them to individual divisions and products. After the plans are set up, they are extensively communicated to all levels in the organization.

Neither the formality nor the comprehensiveness and content of Sharp's strategy is unique. Such formal processes (and strategic approaches) are replicated the world over. Rather, it is what happens to the strategy once it is articulated that is noteworthy. Sharp is successful not because it develops comprehensive strategies but rather because it effectively implements them. A key component of how Sharp does this is the use of teams.

Numerous teams and team structures may be observed at Sharp. At the top of the organization is the Executive Committee composed of twenty senior executives who meet twice monthly to discuss the company's future and ratify all critical decisions. Closely related to the Executive Committee is the Management Planning Board, composed of members of key executives plus a planning staff. This group is responsible for Sharp's strategic planning. However, the meetings of the Executive Committee support integration of the company's strategy as well as providing opportunity for review of current strategy and implementation progress on a regular basis.

Many of Sharp's implementation-related team structures take the form of regularly scheduled meetings among key personnel. Among these are the Corporate

Technical Strategy Meeting and the Laboratory Directors Meeting. The former is a monthly meeting chaired by the general manager of the Corporate R&D Group and attended by the five senior executive vice presidents, the general managers of Sharp's manufacturing groups, and the directors of the research laboratories. The latter is a meeting of the laboratory directors held immediately prior to the Corporate Technical Strategy Meeting. These meetings are designed to review, operationalize, integrate and monitor Sharp's technical strategy.

More formal teams include the Creative Lifestyle Planning Group, the Gold Badge Project teams, and the Production Technology Development Group. The Creative Lifestyle Planning Group is responsible for market research into new product ideas. Promising ideas may then be assigned to a Gold Badge Project team. These new product teams are led by a manager at the rank of general manager or higher – who serves as the project's champion – and a mid-level researcher chosen as project leader. This leader may freely choose twenty to forty staff members from the company as a whole to fill out the project team. All members wear the same gold badge, report directly to the president, and speak with his authority.

The Production Technology Development Group is another team structure that is responsible for co-ordinating production and process technology across Sharp's many manufacturing groups. Sharp also has many Quality Groups scattered throughout the organization. These are traditional quality circles at the manufacturing level that, among other things, share their findings with the Production Technology Development Group.

These are but examples of the many teams and team structures in place at Sharp. Their purpose is to implement and co-ordinate Sharp's strategy. The team structure allows for sharing of detailed information throughout the implementation process, ensuring that everyone is still 'on the same page' as well as contributing to flexibility when challenges are confronted, and rapidly diffusing lessons learned to where they can be most useful.

Under Sharp's model, planning remains quite formal and top-down in nature; but teams provide the mechanisms by which the strategy is implemented. Nevertheless, numerous benefits derive from this approach, many of which ameliorate specific problems that have been identified with traditional strategic planning.

Some Benefits of Teams as Strategy Implementation Devices

Key benefits of using teams to implement strategy include the following key points.

Clarity of purpose

Implementing strategy through teams enhances clear objectives. Top management team involvement facilitates a clear and shared definition of the business at the top of the organization. This, in turn, allows for the establishment of clear strategic objectives. Once established, team structures facilitate the disaggregation of high-order objectives into clear objectives at the business and operational unit level.

Teams at these lower levels can then do a better job of translating these objectives into operational tasks through action detailing. As a consequence, much more guidance is provided than simple statements of quantitative performance objectives.

Commitment to the strategy

The high level of involvement of senior executives in the planning process prevents the process from being co-opted by staff planners. It also keeps management commitment to the strategy very high. The elaborated team structure used to disaggregate and communicate overall strategy gives managers throughout the company a hand in operationalizing the strategy at their respective levels, creating a sense of participation in the process and subsequent commitment to the objectives and strategies. The net effect is improved commitment to the strategy throughout the organization.

Effective integration

Interlocking and interfunctional teams provide critical mechanisms for integrating the overall strategy during implementation. The high level of communication that accompanies effective teams ensures that the whole of the strategy moves forward. Further, such communication provides opportunities for broad-based organizational learning as implementation problems confronted and overcome in one part of the organization are shared across the organization. To some extent, such integration and communication also enhances the organization's flexibility.

Teams *as* Strategy

Clearly there is great promise for improving the implementation of strategy through the effective use of teams. However, a more elaborate approach to the use of teams in implementation is the adoption of teams and team structures as central components of the firm's strategy. Teams are considered valuable in themselves and not simply as means to ends. Under this approach teams provide mechanisms for widespread involvement in the strategy process with the result that the traditional distinction between strategy formulation and implementation begins to blur.

Key drivers behind the emergence of this approach include the models of hypercompetition, resource-based theory, and strategic human resource management. Hypercompetition posits a situation of rapid and intense competitive interaction that makes traditional planning problematic. Under these conditions, successful firms emphasize the development of capabilities that help the firm create and capitalize on disruptions in the competitive environment (D'Aveni, 1994). Resource-based theory (Barney, 1997) argues that competitive advantage derives from the development and exploitation of valuable, rare and inimitable resources and capabilities rather than from formal strategic planning. Strategic human resource management, in turn, recognizes the centrality of the human resource in the process of developing and implementing such capabilities.

In short, the approach of teams as strategy is based on the notion that teams provide a mechanism to develop the competitive value of the human resource. Most managers today recognize the people within their company as second only to their customers in importance to the organization. The approach of teams as strategy assumes that people have similar needs and desires regardless of their position in the company, that they want to take responsibility for their own actions, and wish to be rewarded as the organization thrives. Thus, teams provide the structure within which people can participate and develop along with the organization.

The Case of AES Corporation

Smith and Sims (1995) have documented AES Corporation's experience with teams and team structures as a central part of the strategy process. AES was founded in 1981 as an independent power producer to develop, own and operate electric power plants and sell electricity to public utility companies. Its stated mission is to help meet the need for electricity by offering a supply of clean, safe and reliable power. AES has grown to include over 100 power plants totalling nearly 31,000 megawatts and six electricity distribution companies serving millions of people in seventeen countries. Revenues for 1997 were $1.4 billion on total assets of $8.9 billion, making AES the largest independent power company in the world.

Since its inception, AES has emphasized the centrality of four core values in how it pursues its mission: to act with integrity, to be fair, to have fun, and to be socially responsible. These values drive AES's overall strategy and how it treats its people, with the result that every AES employee is viewed as an important member of the AES team. General team membership is operationalized through a network of teams such that every employee is a member of one or more identifiable teams at any point in time. Teams at AES include the top management team, the core vision team, the strategic planning group, the new-venture teams, teams at the plant level, and the Operating Committee.

AES's top management team is composed of the company officers. They carry out important policy and operating roles, many of which have shifted over the years. A primary responsibility of the top management team, however, is the management of AES's strategy process. At the core of the top management team is the core vision team, made up of the three founders of the firm. Although part of the top management team, this group provided the initial guiding vision for the company and is still most actively involved in the extension, enhancement and communication of that vision.

AES's strategic planning group is an identifiable team tasked with supporting AES's strategy process. Importantly, the role of the planning group is not to plan; rather, it is to provide relevant information to the planners and implementers, which, at AES, are as broad-based a group as possible. The planning group scans the environment and develops reports and white papers on a variety of topics that are circulated throughout the organization. The intent is to allow the company to act as 'informed opportunists' when opportunities arise.

The new-venture teams are tasked with developing new projects for the company, typically entailing the establishment of new plants. Key to the implementation of AES's growth strategy, these teams are composed of highly skilled and motivated individuals who shift roles and responsibilities in a dynamic fashion as the tasks involved demand. These teams have been labelled 'virtual teams' by Kristof et al. (1995), who documented their highly dynamic nature and role in the implementation of AES's strategy.

Virtually every one of AES's plants operates under some form of team structure. The company engaged in a major operation entitled Operation Honeycomb to encourage team-based structures to emerge at the plant level. Importantly, no single team structure was imposed by top management. Rather, top management outlined several elementary principles to be followed, such as few levels and open communication, and to encourage plants to develop their own structures. The diversity of structures that resulted provided AES with tremendous experience with teams at the plant level, and has reaffirmed the company's commitment to teams as an important component of company strategy.

The Operating Committee serves to integrate AES's broader team structure. It is composed of the company officers, the new-venture team leaders, the plant managers, and key representatives of the strategic planning team. The committee engages in an annual strategic planning cycle that, in contrast to Sharp's process, is bottom-up in orientation. The Operating Committee also meets two days each month primarily to address implementation issues and to revisit strategic direction. As a result, strategy formulation is treated on an ongoing basis.

Under AES's model, planning is diffused and bottom-up in nature. Teams provide the structure through which strategy is implemented and also contribute to the formulation of strategy. Although all of AES's teams have specific roles to play, AES expects everyone to take ownership and responsibility for all aspects of the company. From the perspective of teams *as* strategy, all are expected to contribute beyond their primary role.

We believe that 'teams *as* strategy' contributes to clarity of purpose, commitment to the strategy, and effective integration in much the same way as implementing strategy through teams. However, we believe there are additional benefits as well, as articulated by the following points.

Effective control

Judson (1996) identified structural and control issues as key reasons for the failure of strategies. Teams *as* strategy, however, integrates organizational structure with strategy to the extent that the flow between strategy and structure is reciprocal. The high level of team involvement in the strategy process facilitates the creation of incentive and control systems that complement strategic objectives, as well as shaping objectives that are realistically within the capabilities of the firm and its resources. Finally, the high level of communication, where teams are used as strategy, facilitates the free flow of information with the result that implementation difficulties are quickly identified and addressed.

Environmental sensitivity

Teams as strategy also expands the firm's environmental scanning capability, enhancing the firm's ability to identify strategic opportunities very early. Teams throughout the organization are empowered to provide input to the strategy process as they sense changes in their competitive environment. Thus, in addition to formal scanning done by staff planners, teams in marketing functions can provide new market information and teams in operations can provide information about improved processes. Although personnel in many organizations may observe strategically relevant information, only within a structure that facilitates the sharing of this information is it considered as part of the strategy process.

Strategic flexibility

Teams as strategy also contribute to strategic flexibility – a critical asset for implementing strategies in hypercompetitive environments. Rapid communication within and between teams provides a process for revising strategies during implementation without having to undertake a new, formal planning cycle. In fact, the annual strategic planning cycle becomes more of a starting point for strategy formulation rather than its end. Where teams are the strategy, significant change can be undertaken with short notice.

Summary and Conclusions

The benefits of using teams in strategy implementation are numerous. They include clarity of purpose, commitment to the strategy, effective integration of the strategy, effective control, environmental sensitivity and strategic flexibility. We believe that these benefits are becoming more important under conditions of hypercompetition. Although the use of teams in strategy implementation holds great promise, it is not a panacea. We believe that successfully implementing a team-based approach to strategy implementation depends on at least three organizational prerequisites.

The first of these is the commitment of top management. Top management is uniquely responsible for the strategic management of the organization. For teams to be effective, top management must understand the value of the team-based approach, desire it, and work hard for its implementation. To implement a team-based approach successfully, top management must resist the tendency to view implementation as the integration of individual tasks and structure the work of the organization as collective tasks wherever possible. This includes decentralizing decision making and delegating or relinquishing elements of the strategy process to other appropriate teams.

A second prerequisite to team-based approaches to strategy implementation is a strong team culture. 'Doing things in teams' should be the accepted *modus operandum* of the organization. Again, the top management team plays a central role in building such a culture. One way is through modelling team work. Top management must, at least occasionally, function as a team – and it must be observed to behave as one. Another is by establishing appropriate organizational values. The very presence of commonly held core values contributes to a sense of 'teamness'. The careful selection of core values, however, will pay dividends beyond their mere presence. Care should be taken to establish values that foster teamwork rather than internal competition.

The third and final prerequisite is the creation of appropriate processes for integration *between* teams. Without processes designed to integrate the parts into a whole, the organization may find itself with high-performance teams that are unable to work together, or worse, actually work at cross purposes. For organizational synergy to be achieved, top management must ensure that integrating mechanisms exist – building them or allowing them to emerge as appropriate.

To summarize, there are many opportunities for teams to contribute to the implementation of strategy. First, top management may improve its own performance by functioning as a team when its implementation-related work products can be formulated as collective tasks. Secondly, teams may provide a basic structure through which a given strategy is implemented – the mechanism by which intended strategy is deliberately pursued. Finally, teams may become the strategy itself – teams become a way of life, contributing not only to the traditional implementation process but also to the emergence of new objectives and strategies.

References

Barnard, C. 1938: *The functions of the executive.* Cambridge, MA: Harvard University Press.

Barney, J.B. 1997: *Gaining and sustaining competitive advantage.* Reading, MA: Addison-Wesley.

Chandler, A.D. Jr 1962: *Strategy and structure: chapters in the history of the American industrial enterprise.* Cambridge, MA: MIT Press.

Collis, D.J. and Noda, T. 1993: *Sharp Corporation: technology strategy.* Harvard Business School case 793–064: Cambridge, MA: Harvard Business School Press.

Cyert, R.M. and March, J.G. 1963: *A behavioral theory of the firm.* Englewood Cliffs, NJ: Prentice-Hall.

D'Aveni, R.A. 1994: *Hypercompetition: managing the dynamics of strategic maneuvering.* New York: Free Press.

Finkelstein, S. and Hambrick, D.C. 1996: *Strategic leadership: Top executives and their effects on organizations.* St Paul, MN: West Publishing.

Gray, D.H. 1986: Uses and misuses of strategic planning. *Harvard Business Review*, January–February, 89–97.

Hambrick, D.C. 1994: Top management groups: a conceptual integration and reconsideration of the 'team' label. In B. Staw and L. Cummings (eds) *Research in organizational behavior*, vol. 16. Greenwich, CT: JAI Press, pp. 171–213.

Ilgen, D.R. 1999: Teams embedded in organizations. *American Psychologist*, February, 129–39.

Judson, A.S. 1996: *Making strategy happen* (2nd edn). Cambridge, MA: Blackwell.

Katzenbach, J.R. 1998: *Teams at the top: unleashing the potential of both teams and individual leaders.* Boston, MA: Harvard Business School Press.

Katzenbach, J.R. and Smith, D.K. 1993: *The wisdom of teams: creating the high-performance organization*. Boston, MA: Harvard Business School Press.

Kristof, A.L., Brown, K.G., Sims, H.P. Jr and Smith, K.A. 1995: The virtual team: a case study and inductive model. *Advances in interdisciplinary studies of work teams*. Greenwich, CT: JAI Press, 2, 229–53.

Mintzberg, H. 1994: *The rise and fall of strategic planning*. New York: Free Press.

Smith, K.A. and Kofron, E.A. 1996: Toward a research agenda on top management teams and strategy implementation. *IBAR – Irish Business and Administrative Research*, 17(1), 135–52.

Smith, K.A. and Sims, H.P. Jr 1995: Team-based strategy making. *Advances in Applied Business Strategy*, 4, 121–46.

_____ Editors' Conclusions _____

In a book of this nature, where a number of different perspectives on strategy implementation are advanced, it is necessary to attempt to pull together some common themes as well as points of difference among these perspectives. Some implications are relatively straightforward but others are less obvious and more implicit. In the sections which follow we attempt to draw some of the less obvious points from the chapter contributions but at the same time mention some obvious but continuously overlooked points which seem to provide a source of continued difficulty in strategy implementation. Clearly quite a number of ideas relating to the changes needed to improve effectiveness in strategy implementation were described or could be surmised from the various chapters. Virtually all of these ideas about the factors influencing the success of change implementation programmes have some research support although the quality of this research varies enormously. In addition, most of the chapters involved reviews of previous theoretical and empirical work on the various topics covered. The variety of research methods used was a positive factor, because it enabled our writers to discuss a wide variety of issues related to strategy implementation. We believe that only some theoretical and research questions can be addressed by the more sophisticated research methodologies. Also, we indicated at the beginning of this volume that organizations are complex adaptive systems. An examination of complex systems usually requires a whole complex of research methods.

Change Implementation

Changes in the strategic management process and implications for management practice

The distinction between top-down and emergent strategy formulation and implementation is by now well known. However, there continues to be a cleavage in the adoption of one or the other approach depending on the values, disposition and industry experience profile of the senior management team. Those managers who have had a long tenure in machine bureaucratic organizational environments often find it difficult to adjust to the need for a more emergent approach, even though the rational planning approach may be failing to deliver the changes necessary to move the organization forward. One issue of some importance on the topic of strategy implementation has deals with the approach used to create the strategic decisions in the first place. As Paul Sparrow, Sarah Moore, Stephen Carroll and others indicate, there has been a general shift away from an approach using only a highly sequential and rational analysis by top level specialized or general managers to approaches using higher levels of involvement with managers below the corporate or top levels. In addition, these writers point out that in terms of implementing the strategy, there has been a shift away from a top-down and autocratic implementation approach to an approach involving very intensive persuasion techniques as well as the use of decentralized teams to create and implement strategy.

On the basis of previous theory and research we would expect that higher levels of involvement by managers from various levels in the strategy creation process would result in quicker and more successful implementation of strategic decisions. However, this does not ensure that the strategies themselves will be more effective. Strategic insight and effective implementation, as we know from the experience of companies who miss strategic shifts in the market, are not necessarily one and the same phenomenon. In several of the case studies cited (such as Waterford Crystal, Agway and General Electric) we can see that some lower level involvement in the strategy creation process can be beneficial not only in terms of the acceptance of strategy but also in the quality and ultimate competitive success of the strategy. While middle management is sometimes portrayed as a classic source of resistance to change, a systems perspective such as that adopted by Mark Fenton-O'Creevy highlights the often systemic nature of that resistance. Where systems of reward and performance management encourage and reinforce other than desired behaviours, it is the organizational routines and procedures that need to be remedied rather than the individual managers. These managers may be displaying rational behaviours, albeit guided by an irrational set of normative guidelines created by the organization's policies and procedures. Further evidence on this was identified in the research carried out by Philip Stiles and his colleagues on a set of leading edge British companies.

Changes in communication approaches to create more effective strategy implementation

Communication initiatives are at the heart of the employee engagement process in strategic change initiatives. Several authors have highlighted the importance of creating systems to ensure that clear unifying messages about the changes to be implemented are communicated to employees particularly as uncertainty has so many pervasive effects on organizational functioning as Jean Hartley points out. One very important suggestion, it seems to us, that has already been acted on by many leading companies is to communicate through a persuasion approach rather than through an edict approach. However, there are many persuasion alternatives. Some of the chapters in effect advocated more of a dramaturgical approach using stories and attention-getting procedures. This echoes the new emphasis in scholarly studies of leadership that utilize a dramaturgical action framework. Another finding, and one of the more useful insights found in the case studies presented, is the value of providing data and other justifications to a workforce to support and create a readiness to accept organizational change. A prime example of this approach was Niall Saul's Report of the Waterford Crystal case which has been described by Tony O'Reilly (former CEO of the Heinz Corporation) as the most dramatic example of a successful turnaround he has ever witnessed. Here information was given to employees about all the crystal competitors around the world and how they compared to Waterford in terms of prices and costs, quality and technological sophistication. The comparative data presented plus the reform of many managerial and manufacturing systems gave employees not only a sense of the severity of the market situation they faced but also a new-found confidence in the management team which led the eventual turnaround. This rational persuasion approach allows organizational members to be persuaded by the facts of a situation rather than just by rhetoric alone.

There is some previous research validation of this approach as well as many case studies. For example, a study by Nutt (1987) of sixty-eight strategic planning projects implemented in different ways found that a system in which evidence was presented to show that old standards were no longer adequate and that new norms were justified, resulted in a higher degree of implementation success than several other approaches. Nutt has since provided further validation evidence of the efficacity of this approach.

Still another aspect of more effective communication in a persuasion sense mentioned in the chapters is one of building trust through the use of openness and transparency in the criteria under which organizations administer rewards systems. To some degree, this is the opposite of the type of secret power politics found in many organizations, including some particularly dysfunctional ones. There is a great deal of research on the development of trust in organizations to which one can refer to develop appropriate responses but authors such as Jean Hartley point out that the appropriate response is to harness uncertainty and the political process rather than decry it. In this regard managers can learn from politicians who minimize resistance to change by being deliberately ambiguous about the final content of the decision to be taken, thus maximizing their vote-catching potential. However, there are also lessons for politically oriented managers as lower level employees will feel enormous frustration at such tactical manoeuvring which may be seen as mere incompetent procrastination. Clearly maintaining a repertoire of political skills is useful, but utilizing such an obviously politically motivated approach over the long term can have serious demotivating consequences if used as a primary implementation strategy. Uncertainty and the dysfunctional stress syndrome described by Carol Borrill and Sharon Parker must also be taken into consideration when utilizing such approaches.

It was also mentioned that it is sometimes difficult to obtain the attention and understanding of members of the organization when implementing strategic change, especially when the pace of change is very high. Here selective perception is operating and people perceive that organization-wide initiatives have little to do with their own unit of responsibility. In the persuasive communications that should accompany new strategic directions, an effort must be made to relate the achievement of strategic goals to the interests of all units and individuals in the organization. This also illustrates the value of choosing long-term strategies that are fundamental or basic enough to be successful over a long period of time.

Changes in appreciation of the importance of culture in change acceptance

There is frequently a problem of strategy–culture fit in strategy implementation. This is a particular problem if the strategic initiative is contrary to some professional culture, as is frequently the case in medical and hospital reforms. McKevitt, for example, has documented the very common feeling in many professional groups that non-professionals have neither the right nor the competence to measure their performance, which makes it difficult to monitor strategic initiatives. He points out also that there are many levels of culture and documents the response variation attributable to differences in national cultures. Additionally, he advocates that professionals should be involved in the actual design of any performance management system to which they will be subjected in order to avoid the systematic undermining of such initiatives. Otherwise the proverbial lip service is all that is paid to the new monitoring systems themselves. The tension between medical professionals and patient satisfaction was well summed up in one doctor's comments that patients must be given a little of what they need as well as a little of what they want!

The strategy–culture fit issues were also mentioned by Steve Carroll where he described the need for the CEO of GE to change the culture of the company to fit with the new strategic direction that he and his top management team established and the considerable effort this required. In that discussion the use of narrative for effective implementation was highlighted by the frequent use of metaphors used by Jack Welch, CEO of General Electric.

Changes in structures required to systematize the new strategic directions

There can also be structural barriers to strategy implementation. If practices and behaviours are to be changed in disbursed and independent units of the organization, then it is important to allow such units to develop their own tactics to achieve changes. At Agway, cited by Gillen, performance increased when the organization was decentralized into many separate units and when managers in those units were given autonomy and the power to manage the strategic initiatives themselves at the lowest levels. Creating the small company within the large company is a powerful driver for change that keeps units in touch with the customer and allows rapid responses to occur to competitors' actions and reactions. In general, decentralization and the creation of many smaller businesses out of larger ones, in itself seems to eliminate some of the many factors which impede effective strategy implementation, although obviously this creates some new problems in integration.

With respect to structural problems, there can also be the problem of over-specialization in the strategy implementation process. When New Venture Gear was structured in a functional way with people divided into various functional silos, performance was not satisfactory. When they were put together in multi-functional groups they could bring much more knowledge to bear upon a problem and customer needs could be met more quickly. Concurrent engineering perspectives borrowed initially from the Japanese have been found to improve certain types of performance very significantly.

Changing to team structures was advocated as a means of improving strategy implementation. One type of team directly related to strategy implementation is the strategic change team identified by Smith and Sims. Such teams are chartered on a time basis to generate innovative solutions and implementation strategies for critical competitive issues (Ketterer and Spencer, 1998). There are some obvious advantages for allowing a selective and diverse group of younger, higher level managers to take time off from their usual operating responsibilities to work together on such strategic initiative projects. It also had the important spin-off educative benefit of developing managers to take on larger responsibilities.

The chapter on the management of stress during periods of rapid change has also highlighted the need to give as much input as possible into the changes, whether they be structural or related to the work system.

Changes in training, development programmes and people management practices

Some authors, such as Gillen (chapter 10) amd Dromgoole and Gorman (chapter 14), have pointed to the importance of training and development practices in helping to achieve more effective strategy implementation. Learning initiatives can involve changes in the actual focus of the training as well as the methods used to change attitudes, skills, behaviours, or competences in general. This was well illustrated in the case of the learning network concept developed at the Irish Management Institute which utilized a wide range of learning approaches which, taken together, had synergistic effects producing learning at the individual and organizational levels. With respect to such approaches as a change management tool, all change methods must be based on what basic research has indicated are necessary prerequisites of change. Experiential learning, social learning, and goal setting all play a significant role in the most effective contemporary training methodologies, and action learning is particularly suited to practising managers who have much to contribute based on experience but frequently lack a framework within which that experience can be understood.

With respect to learning and the intellectual capital formation process certain subjects need focused attention. For example, more creative employees are needed today who are capable of working in the uncertain world described by Jean Hartley.

Creativity itself has been very well studied and many training techniques using creativity-stimulating exercises and problems have been developed. Such creativity or imagination-enhancing techniques should be emphasized in the training of leaders in organizations needing performance improvement. As Charles Carroll points out, imagination itself can provide the key insights necessary to unblock 'stuckness' in organizational efforts to effect strategic change. Of course, the new approaches for achieving convergent learning which operate by exposing narrow functional specialists to other diverse perspectives and even contradictory mindsets can facilitate the creation of imaginative courses of action. If organizational learning is to be fostered, and if leaders are to do this, then this type of activity must be encouraged in various ways. As indicated previously, one definition of organizational learning is that it involves learning new ways of doing things and taking actions to do them. Many types of training are available which allow the training to focus on identified organizational and personal deficiencies and have, as outcomes, on-the-job behaviours or achievements which can be measured. It is clear from all of the writers that there is no substitute for swift action on the part of managers charged with leading strategic change and the elimination of bureaucratic structures which encourage politics, procrastination and prevent convergent knowledge being developed. This factor is consistently identified as a structural prerequisite to effective strategy implementation. In all walks of life there are so called leaders who proclaim a willingness to initiate change and utilize impression management to indicate this willingness but whose actions demonstrate their disinterest. These leaders are ill suited to respond to the competitive forces sweeping organizations today.

A number of the writers in this volume have pointed to the importance of various HRM systems such as the performance evaluation, reward and promotion systems in shaping the behaviour of organizational members with respect to reactions to strategic initiatives, including resistance to change. This is not a new thought and has been extensively discussed over the years in other volumes, but somehow organizations continue to overlook these problems as Mark Fenton-O'Creevy and Philip Stiles rightly point out. Obviously in any significant strategic initiative it is important to analyse each HRM system in terms of the behaviours that are being encouraged and discouraged and make changes to ensure that the intended or desired behaviours are evaluated and reinforced in some way. In spite of the simplicity of this idea it is surprising that this common reason for the success or failure of strategy implementation initiatives is so often overlooked and under-appreciated.

Changes in facing up to hidden organizational realities

Several of the authors – for example, David O'Donnell – have pointed out that management in the past has paid insufficient attention to various hidden organizational systems and have not recognized that organizations are emotional and political entities as well as rational decision systems. Sarah Moore points out that understanding the narrative of the strategic change process through a focus on organizational talk as a sense-making device, is emerging from the academic literature as an important new way of deciphering organizational realities. Politics and power are important in dealing with union–management relationships and the negotiation of interest conflicts are appropriate for handling such political differences. Power and politics are necessary forces to enable strategic change, and the manager who wishes to be an effective enabler of change must recognize their legitimacy and become adept in harnessing these processes. The possession of social capital based on reciprocal exchange over a period of time is still an important source of influence.

Yet recent writings on the development of the so-called horizontal organization and the virtual organization seem to indicate that the delayered organization will be much less politicized. Evolutionary psychologists, however, have some insights here. Nicholson (1997), for example, tells us that individuals have an innate primitive tendency to create status hierarchies and will do so even if the organization structure is flat. Similarly, he highlights that dominance will continue to be used in struggles concerning resource allocation echoing our ancestral origins where survival of the fittest was one of the early building blocks of the tribal system. Despite the hype about the development of the network and horizontal organizations with their emphasis on empowerment, the need for dominant leadership will continue to be at the heart of strategy implementation.

Changes in the new psychological contract required for effective implementation

Although not specifically described in any of the chapters, effective strategy implementation may be facilitated by having a workforce that is long term and committed in an emotional way to the company. As we know from writings on the psychological contract, exchange and met expectations is at the heart of the bond between the individual and the organization. Organizational commitment itself may be of an affective or emotional nature or may be more transactionally based or, indeed, may be continuance based where employees are locked into their organization though idiosyncratic factors such as non-portable pensions. Clearly anyone embarking on strategy implementation needs to work out appropriate strategies to deal with the multi-tiered commitment orientation of employees.

Some of the companies mentioned in this volume as being successful in achieving strategic goals had this type of emotionally committed workforce. Such employees not only tend to have high amounts of organizationally relevant knowledge and skill, which is valuable in change programmes, but would also be more inclined to accept long-term goals than more temporary employees. Of course, it is not necessary to have permanent employment relationships with an entire workforce provided there is a significant core of employees, especially managers and professionals, who have the deep knowledge, both tacit and explicit, that embodies the distinctive competences of the organization. These distinctive competences may refer to the very detailed specifics required in technological change as well as the tacit understanding of how to activate the commitment of employees in effecting strategic change.

It is also important also that organizations who experience frequent changes in direction because of competitive pressures should hire those employees who are not only intelligent but also have a high degree of flexibility which, we know from research, is closely related to learning ability. Previous research has established that individuals high in need for security or need for structure have more difficulty in adjusting to changing work assignments. We also know that lower level employees tend to have high needs for security, particularly if they do not have a portable skill set or work in an organization not committed to the development of its workforce. Commitment is a two-way street and we firmly believe that organizations that do not invest in the long-term employability of their employees are unlikely to enjoy high levels of emotional commitment to organizational objectives. As strategic flexibility is a premium-based competence for organizations operating in today's competitive markets it behoves organizations and senior managers to be cognisant of this ability as the willingness to embrace strategic change initiatives is intimately related to this issue.

Changes in mindsets and perspectives to effect strategy implementation

Strategy implementation, like any action-oriented human activity, needs theory based on research to identify the key factors to evaluate and the key levers to push to achieve desired results. Paul Sparrow gave an extensive review on recent literature on the importance of emotional intelligence in this regard. We are all well acquainted with the senior management team who push levers which are totally disengaged from the interests of the workforce and, as a result, are stymied in their strategic initiatives. Taking a systems perspective, as we do in this volume, we see that there are quite a number of interrelated factors associated with strategy implementation. As in previous work on the topic of organizational change, the importance of leadership, workforce attitudes including trust, HRM practices, existing system processes, methods of persuasion, and approaches to following up change, have been identified in the various chapters. However, this volume, as compared to previous writings, has especially identified the importance of developing entirely new mindsets and perspectives as a necessity for strategy creation and implementation. Without these new management mental paradigms it seems unlikely that successful strategy implementation will be achieved. These new mental perspectives include such factors as awareness of the saliency of the emotional world of the organization and the replacement of the older linear and excessively rational perspectives which limit thought with more holistic, intuitive, imaginative ways of thinking as identified by Charles Carroll. Also, as Dromgoole and Mullins point out, there is the need to change older problem-solving mindsets with approaches for managing polarities as well as achieving greatly improved understandings of organizational audience characteristics facilitating the use of new persuasion techniques. These new mental perspectives include a new appreciation of the importance of organizational and inter-organizational knowledge creation and transfer and the need for a new increased emphasis on continuous individual and organizational learning.

Several of the authors have commented on the importance of focusing on the future rather than just on the present reality in framing one's change efforts.

Otherwise the organization finds itself in a reactive mode lurching from one crisis to another. Solving problems before they occur obviously makes a lot of sense. Some of the authors have indicated that one approach to taking a long-range point of view is through the process of benchmarking, where one assesses oneself against the standards achieved by others in various operations and/or against factors found to be related to success or excellence through research. Of course, it may be more difficult to sell the necessity of change in the absence of any obvious present difficulties. Consultants may be useful in certain instances as Tim Morris points out, but only a select few have developed adequately sophisticated models to cope with the complexities of strategic change. Again, in systems thinking terms it is important to know where the key elements and leverage points in a system are located, and these are likely to be different from one organization to another. Identifying the 'critical fifteen per cent' (that is, the key leverage points where changes introduced have positive system-wide ramifications) has been recognized by authors such as Gareth Morgan (1986) as crucial in successful strategy implementation .

A number of the chapters have identified conflicting goals and criteria of performance as a problem in gaining acceptance of strategic initiatives. As one author points out, there is probably little chance of increasing attention to customer needs in a firm in which only cost control and efficiency are evaluated and rewarded under the various evaluation systems employed. Thus the organization often communicates an interest in one behaviour or outcome but rewards other behaviours or outcomes. Conflicting goals and reward and performance evaluation programmes are particularly difficult when an organization needs to maintain seemingly different strategy emphases within the same implementation effort, such as as a simultaneous emphasis on cost control and total customer service. Intelligence was once defined by F. Scott Fitzgerald as having the ability to maintain two contradictory ideas in your head at the same time. If this is an important asset, appropriate selection criteria should be used to help to identify individuals with such conceptual abilities. This, of course, is related to the modern idea that appreciation of the need to manage polarities is necessary. While at first glance the concept of polarities suggest inconsistencies in approach, it is at the heart of the managerial problems of today, which demand multiple concurrent interventions to effectively implement strategic change in competitive environments.

Throughout the development of this book an emergent strategy dominated as the editors worked with authors on their ideas in an iterative fashion. Additionally, some polarities are evident throughout the book in the research approaches used between the various chapters and, indeed, in the positions advanced as they relate to strategy implementation. All the typical issues that arise in strategy implementation surfaced as we worked with the author team, including issues such as: Was the vision behind the book the right one to adopt? What should the content of the strategy be for the book? How do we get buy-in for the project from the author team? How will we deal with resisters and overshot deadlines? How do we handle the need to adapt flexibly to new market requirements? ... and so on. Yet, the book has emerged. As editors we feel we have learned a lot about strategy implementation through the experience of working with this dedicated multicultural team and their many insightful contributions. We leave it to you, the reader, to judge whether this effort has been worth while.

References

Ketterer, R.F. and Spencer, J.L. 1998. In D.A. Nadler and J.L. Spencer & Associates (eds) *Executive teams*. San Francisco: Jossey-Bass, 211–39.

Morgan, G. 1986. *Images of organizations*. Beverly Hills, CA: Sage.

Nicholson, N. 1997: Evolutionary psychology: toward a new view of human nature and organizational society. *Human Relations*, 50, 9, 1053–78.

Nutt, P.C. 1987: Identifying and appraising how managers install strategy. *Strategic Management Journal*, 8, 1–14.

_____ Biographical Notes _____

Editors

Dr Patrick Flood (PhD, London School of Economics) is Professor of Organizational Behaviour and University Fellow, University of Limerick. Previous faculty appointments include London Business School and the University of Maryland at College Park. His previous five books include *Managing without Traditional Methods* (1996), *The EU and the Employment Relationship* (1997) and *Personnel Management in Ireland* (1990). He has published in such places as *Strategic Management Journal, Industrial Relations, International Journal of Human Resource Management, Journal of Organizational and Occupational Psychology, British Journal of Industrial Relations and Business Horizons*. He is on the editorial board of *Business Strategy Review* published by London Business School and co-edits *Irish Business and Administrative Research*.

Dr Stephen J. Carroll completed his BA at UCLA and his MA and PhD at the University of Minnesota. He has been a faculty member at the University of Maryland since receiving his PhD in 1964. He is the author or co-author of more than twelve books and monographs and over one hundred published papers. He has been a consultant to more than forty business and government organizations. He has been elected a Fellow of the Academy of Management, The American Psychological Association, and the American Psychological Society. His current research interests have focused on subjects such as the changing nature of international management systems, persuasive leadership approaches, and strategic human resource management.

Mr Tony Dromgoole (BE, MIE, MBA) is Director Public and Research Programmes at the Irish Management Institute. Following a number of years in management consulting with KPMG, Tony joined the IMI in 1984 as Director of the *MSc in Management Practice*, a joint programme with Trinity College Dublin. He also directs a range of programmes in operations/manufacturing management. He is also a lecturer in the School of Business Studies, Trinity College Dublin. Tony is currently editing (with Prof. P. Coughlan, TCD) a special edition of the *International Journal of Operations and Production Management*, featuring a selection of the best articles of the 1988 EurOMA Conference. He is director of the IMI's National Action Learning Programme, a major action research programme on learning networks, funded by the European Commission.

Dr Liam Gorman is a Programme Director at the Irish Management Institute and lecturer in Business Studies at Trinity College Dublin. He has held faculty appointments at Fordham University, Helsinki School of Economics, Monash University and the University of Auckland. He has published six books on management topics including one on *Management of Irish Business*. He has published articles in a wide range of management topics, in such journals as the *Journal of Management Studies* and *Management International Review*. He has been a consultant to OECD on the future of management development and has worked in twenty countries on executive education and consulting assignments. He is a Fellow of the Irish Management Institute and has been conferred with a Special Award of Merit by the Irish Psychological Society for his outstanding contributions.

Contributor Biographies

Dr Carol Borrill is an organizational psychologists with many years of research and consultancy experience in the National Health Service (NHS). She is based at the Aston Business School, Aston University. She has recently completed a large-scale research study on the prevalence and causes of stress among staff in the NHS (over 21,000 staff have been involved in the survey), and evaluated interventions designed to reduce stress. She is currently the Director of Aston Health Service Research Centre and is involved in various management and health care research projects in the NHS. Other work has included evaluating Corporate Governance and Openness in the NHS for the NHS Executive, and introducing team-based working into health care organizations.

Dr Charles Carroll has practised in marketing and general management in the UK and Ireland. He is currently Senior Specialist in Strategic Management at the Irish Management Institute (IMI) and has served a five-year term as Head of Faculty. He holds a primary degree from University College Cork and his masters from Trinity College Dublin, where he also completed his doctoral studies. He has a Certificate of Recognition in Business Analysis from the Strategic Planning Institute, Cambridge, Massachusetts. Charles has been involved in developing the Institute's programmes in marketing, strategic management and senior management; he currently directs the IMI's *Directors and Senior Managers Programme*. He has worked with many Irish and European companies in strategy development and managing strategic change. Charles is author of *Building Ireland's Business: Perspectives from PIMS*, (IMI, 1985). This was a study of Ireland's industrial and business potential using the insights from the PIMS studies. In 1994–95, at the request of the European Commission, he (with Tony Clayton of PIMS Associates, London) applied the same interpretative approach to the European Union as a whole, contrasting Europe's experience with that of the US. He has written numerous articles and book chapters on marketing, business strategy, strategic change, R&D and innovation, governance and shareholder value. Current research interests focus upon strategic leadership considered as a work of imagination and as a form of public art. In this approach he has sought to complement social science perspectives with insights from philosophical hermeneutics, narrative history, political science, philosophical anthropology and critical theory.

Dr David McKevitt is senior lecturer at the Department of Management and Marketing, University of Limerick, and Associate, Centre for Governance and Public Management. He has worked in both the private and public sector, including the Department of Finance, Open University and University College Cork. His publications include *Health Care Policy* *in Ireland* (1989), *Readings in Public Sector Management* (1994), *Managing Core Public Services* (1998). His research and consulting interests are in strategic control, comparative public management and health care management.

David Mullins heads up the change management unit at AIB Bank plc, the largest publicly quoted Irish company. Prior to joining AIB he held a number of positions in industry in both Operations and Human Resource Management roles, including Ericsson and Intel. He holds an MSc (Mgmt) in Management Practice from the joint IMI/Trinity College Dublin programme. His thesis provided the foundation for his chapter in this book with Tony Dromgoole.

David O'Donnell is IMI Research Fellow on the Irish Management Institute/University of Limerick/University of Maryland research programme on top management groups. He is a graduate of University College Dublin, University of Limerick and Leicester University. He has worked for over twenty years in technical training, education and consultancy in Africa, Europe and the Middle East. His key area of expertise/research relates to the interdisciplinary and multicultural field of skills/knowledge development. His doctoral research explores the dynamics of intellectual capital creation within top management and core worker groups.

Dr Dennis Gillen is an Associate Dean of Executive Education and Associate Professor of Strategic Management for the School of Management at Syracuse University. He obtained his PhD from the University of Maryland at College Park. His research and professional interests include strategic management, executive development and transformational leadership. Dr Gillen's research results and consulting insights have appeared in various journals and have been presented at conferences held by the Academy of Management and the Strategic Management Society. He has also consulted or conducted research concerning strategic management, organizational change and learning, management development, and organizational design for various organizations.

Dr Henry Sims Jr is Professor of Management and Organization at the Maryland Business School – College Park, and, former Director of the Business PhD programme. He was recently Fulbright Fellow and Visiting Professor at Hong Kong Baptist University. He was the founding Academic Director of the Strategic Human Resource Management Program at Penn State University. Dr Sims' special areas of research are managerial leadership and self-managed teams. He has published over one hundred articles on this subject, and has been author or co-author of various books. Dr Sims has consulted with many US and international organizations including General Motors Corporation, Ford Motor Company, NASA, Korea Development Institute, and the US Agency for International Development. He is a popular keynote and after-dinner speaker, and executive development facilitator.

Dr Jean Hartley (BA, Reading; PhD, Manchester) is currently Reader in Management, Local Government Centre, Warwick Business School. Previously she was senior lecturer in Organizational Psychology at the University of London. Jean has held previous appointments at the universities of Sheffield and Manchester. She was a co-author of *Job Insecurity: Coping with Jobs at Risk*, and author of other books on employment relations. Her research interests are concerned with the personal and organizational aspects of change and uncertainty, including unemployment, job insecurity and conflict at work. She is currently undertaking longitudinal research into the management of uncertainty and transformational change in the public sector, including organizational change, sustaining quality initiatives and the development of competencies for community leadership.

Dr Ken Smith is an Associate Professor of Strategy in the Strategy and Human Resources Department of the School of Management at Syracuse University. Dr Smith's current research interests focus on the dynamics and influence of top management teams and his work has appeared in numerous journals and book chapters. Prior to his academic career,

Dr Smith was an international management consultant specializing in improving planning and management systems in public sector organizations in developing countries. He currently provides process consulting in the area of strategic management. Dr Smith was elected to the Board of Trustees of Geneva College in 1994 and now serves as Chairman.

Dr Mark Fenton-O'Creevy is lecturer in Management at the Open University Business School and visiting Research Fellow at London Business School. He has a PhD and MBA from London Business School. Mark has carried out research in and acted as a consultant to a wide range of organizations. Much of his research and consulting activities have focused on uncovering and overcoming barriers to change. Prior to embarking on an academic career Mark worked variously as an outdoor pursuits instructor, a mathematics teacher and as a Member of the Therapeutic staff and a senior manager of an organization specializing in the treatment of emotionally disturbed adolescents.

Mr Niall Saul is currently Group Head of Human Resources and Organisation Development with the Irish Life and Permanent Group. In this role, he carries overall responsibility for Human Resources and Organizational Development Issues in the Group's operations in Ireland, the UK, the USA and Hungary. Niall has over twenty years' experience in the areas of Human Resource Management, Industrial Relations and Change Management and has held senior personnel management and consultancy positions in various industries. His particular areas of interest are the role of the Personnel/Human Resource function in turnaround/survival situations, the Management of Change, the creation of 'competitively focused' organizations, and the development of competence-based approaches to performance management. He is a Fellow of the Institute of Personnel and Development (IPD).

Dr Paul Sparrow is a Professor in International Human Resource Management at Sheffield University Management School. He graduated from the University of Manchester with a BSc (Hons) Psychology and the University of Aston with an MSc Applied Psychology and was then sponsored by Rank Xerox to study the impacts of ageing on the organization for his PhD at Aston University. From 1982 to 1984 he was a freelance consultant principally involved in projects relating to changing patterns of work. He then became a Research Fellow at Aston University and a Senior Research Fellow at Warwick Business School researching emerging human resource strategies in the computer and retail sectors. He has written a number of books including *European Human Resource Management in Transition, Designing and Achieving Competency* and *Human Resource Management: the New Agenda* and published articles concerning the future of work, human resource strategy, management competencies, the psychology of strategic management and international human resource management. He is Editor of the *Journal of Occupational and Organizational Psychology* and Review Board Member of the *Journal of World Business*.

Dr Philip Stiles is Senior Research Fellow at the Judge Institute of Management Studies University of Cambridge, researching into leadership and senior management behaviours. He was previously Research Fellow at the London Business School, working on the Leading Edge Forum, which examined the change processes in eight blue chip corporations in the UK project in which he remains closely involved. A book detailing this project, *Strategic Human Resource Management: Corporate Rhetoric and Human Reality*, was published in 1999 (coauthors L. Gratton, V. Hope Hailey and K. Truss). Before joining London Business School, Philip worked at Henley Management College on a major project on boards of directors, in association with the Institute of Directors, published in 1995.

Dr Sarah Moore is a lecturer, researcher and Dean of Teaching at the University of Limerick. She has published empirical and conceptual work in a variety of areas including the dynamics of strategic behaviour, diversity management, organizational communication, group development and top management teams. She received her PhD from Cranfield

School of Management in 1998 and is currently developing a methodology for analysing strategic activity based on her doctoral research. She holds a national award for academic contribution and a UL excellence in teaching award.

Dr Sharon Parker obtained a BSc with honours in Psychology at University of Western Australia, Perth. She also obtained a PhD in organizational psychology from the Institute of Work Psychology, Sheffield, where she has been working as a senior research fellow. Sharon is currently a senior lecturer at the Australian Graduate School of Management, the University of New South Wales, Sydney. Her research interests include job design, work organization, modern flexible initiatives, employee development and equal opportunities. Sharon has published in leading journals such as *Academy of Management Journal* and *Journal of Applied Psychology*. She is currently working on a book with Toby Wall provisionally titled *Job and Work Design: Organizing work to promote well-being and effectiveness*.

Dr Timothy Morris is an Associate Professor at London Business School. He has a BA from the University of Cambridge and an MSc and PhD from the London School of Economics. Prior to joining London Business School he taught at Henley Management College and worked for several years in industry. He has published books and numerous articles on the management of professional firms, performance pay for managers, employee commitment, technological and organizational change and the financial management of trade unions. He has acted as a consultant to organizations in the public and private sectors and is an adviser on research and development strategy in the UK Health Service.

Index

Abrahamson, E.   132
Adler, P.S. and Borys, B.   174
AES Corporation   231–2
Agway case study   149–50
Alexander, S. and Ruderman, M.   176
Alvesson, M.   131
Ansoff, I.   47
Appelbaum, and Batt   91
Argyris, C.   51, 71, 72, 73, 75, 78, 126,
    205
   and Schon, D.A.   197
Aronson, E.   204
Ashby, R.   112
Ashforth, B.E. and Humphrey, R.H.   71, 72,
    78

Bacharach, S.B.   169
Bahn, C.   28
Baier, V.   114
Baloff, N. and Doherty, E.M.   156
Bandura, A.   204
Banham, J.   81
Bann, S. and Bowlt, J.   50
Barnevik, P.   40
Barney, and Hansen   238
Barry, D. and Elmes, M.   44, 49–50
Beckhard, R. and Harris, R.T.   196, 210,
    214, 215
Beer, M. and Eisenstat, R.A.   71, 75
Beisser, A.   206

Benington, J.   115
   and Harvey, J.   114
   and Stoker, G.   115
Bennis, W.G. et al.   204
Berger, P. and Luckmann, T.   183, 186,
    189
Bernstin, B.   52
Borrill, C.S.
   et al.   81, 87, 90
   and Haynes, C.E.   90
Bowman, J.   126
Boyatzis   23
Bradley, K. and Hill, S.   158
Brennan, M.   158
Brockner   88
Brookfield, S.D.   77, 78
Brower, R.S. and Abolafia, M.Y.   159, 163
Brown, S. and Eisenhardt, K.   109, 110,
    111, 112, 119
Brunsson, N.   118, 119
Bryman, A.   114
Buchanan, D. and Preston, D.   156, 158
Buhl, L.C.   155
Burgelman, R.A.   154
Burns, T.
   and Bass,   23
   and Stalker, G.M.   110, 111, 112
Bushe, G.R.   158
Business Week   81
Butler, P. et al.   20, 22

Cabana, S. and Fiero, J.   37
Caberna, et al.   37
Calori, R. et al.   19
Campbell, A.   113
Campbell, D.J. and Furrer, D.M.   40
Carroll, C. and Clayton, T.   184
Carroll, S.J.   34, 35
    et al.   40
    and Gannon, M.J.   40
    and Tosi, H.L.   33, 35
Carroll, S.J. and Gillen, D.J.   140
Carter, N.   106
Cartwright, S. and Cooper, C.L.   82, 85
Cassell, C.   17
Cassirer, E.   183, 192
Champion International Corporation   227
change
    and ambiguity   172
    approaches to   185–6
    case study   58–61
    coping styles   84
    creating/maintaining healthy
        workplace   87–8
    and dealing with 'survivors'   88–9
    dictatorial transformation strategy   76–7
    and (dis)order   186, 187
    drivers of   213
    and effective communication   91
    efficacy of classic strategies   57
    and emotionality   73
    and handling of downsizing   173–4
    and human issues   91
    and identity schemas   173
    illustrative   85–6
    implementation of   178
    and importance of culture   239
    and inclusion of all stakeholders   91
    incremental/discontinuous overlap   57
    managing   86–92
    and mergers/acquisitions   85–6
    and messy situations   58
    and nature of symbolism   186, 188,
        190
    as necessary and appropriate   91–2
    need for   196, 198
    and persuasion   215, 238
    preparing for   92
    principles of   75–6
    psychological reactions to   83
    as real leadership challenge   212–13

    recommendations for managing   91–2
    resistance to see resistance
    routine/non-routine   172–3
    saliency   173
    situational specificity of   75
    speed of   184–5
    and stress   83–4, 90–1, 92
    as successful/unsuccessful   88–90
    and teamworking   89–90
    two-step processes   215
    typology of   76
    and uncertainty   57, 185
change management
    as consulting activity   127–8
    New Public Management model   128
    transformation model   128
    in unionized environments   213, 214–
        223
Chapman, R.A.   114
Charan, R. and Tichy, N.M.   142
Chia, R.   193
Child, J.   110, 111, 113
Church, A.H.   73
Clark, T. and Salaman, G.   130
Claxton, G.   24, 25
Cleveland, H.   142
Cockerill, A.P. and Schroder, H.M.   22–3
cognition   17
    and competencies for the future   22–3
    and competition   19
    and constructionist logic   18
    and creative imagination   25–6
    and downstream/upstream choice   18
    implicit/tacit   24
    and inertia   19
    and the intelligent unconscious   23–7
    and intuitive expertise   24–5
    knowledge as organized   18
    and knowledge structures   18–19
    meta-   27
    objective/subjective intelligence   26
    and pre-inventive structures   26
Collins, J. and Porras, J.I.   141
Collis, D.J. and Noda, T.   228
communication   218, 237–8
    effective   91
    and strategy implementation   178–9
    through persuasion   238
    and trust   238
competencies   16, 28, 243

for the future   22–3
    process, rational, intellectual   27
competitiveness/learning rate
        relationship   145–6, 150–1
Condrey, S.E.   41
Connors, J.L. and Romberg, T.A.   158
consulting firms   125–6, 244
    as advisers   129
    analytical   126
    and client risk   133–4, 135
    converging on strategy execution   126–9
    as deliverers of service   129–30
    internal dynamics of   132–4
    interventions   129–30
    and knowledge/knowledge
        transfer   130–2, 136
    and leading edge practice   131
    leverage in   133
    performance drivers in   133–4, 135
    and problem-solving   130–1, 135
    professional-client relationship   129
    and risks/effectiveness of strategy
        execution   134–6
    sources of knowledge   131–2
    staff utilization in   133
    and standardization   135, 136
    systems specialists   126–7, 128
    technical/functional specialists   127
Cooper, R.K.   26, 27
    and Sawaf, A.   26
Coopey, J. and Burgoyne, J.   119
creative action, examples of   190–1
creativity   25–6, 28, 185, 241
Crick, B.   114
Crown, D.F. and Rose, J.G.   40
Cyert, R.M. and March, J.G.   138, 174,
        178, 226

Daft, R.L.   19
    and Lengel, R.M.   177
    and Weick, K.E.   112
Damanpour, F.   175
Daniels, K.   17
    et al.   18
D'Aveni, R.A.   230
Davis, H.   115, 116
Dawkins, R.   192
Develin & Partners   156
Di Maggio, P.J. and Powell, W.W.   198
Dillon, F.   31

Donabedian, A.   103
Donnellon, A.   51
Dopson, S.
    et al.   158
    and Neumann, J.E.   110
    and Stewart, R.   153
Downey, K.H. et al.   113
Drucker, P.   184
Dulewicz, V. and Higgs, M.   26, 27
Dunsire, A.   105
Dutton, J.E. and Dukerich, J.M.   177

Economist   85
Eisenhardt, K.   111, 113, 170
    and Tabrizi, J.   111
Elderkin, K.W. and Bartlett, C.A.   36, 39
Emery, F.E. and Trist, E.L.   110
emotional intelligence (EI)   26–7, 243
emotionality   16, 17, 26–7, 71–2
    awareness of   73–4
    and change   73
    and dealing with unfinished business   74,
        78
    and defensive routines   72, 73, 78
    defined   72
    mapping   75–7
    power of   72–5
    and rationality   77–8
    strategies/tactics related to   76
    and strong/weak situations   74–5
    and 'The Triune Brain'   72–3
employees
    involvement of   161–4
    psychological contract   242–3
    resistance of   169–70
Empson, L. and Morris, T.   128
environmental uncertainty   111–12
    contingency effect   112
    effect   111
    information seeking   112
    politics/management of   114–18
    response   111, 116
    sense-making behaviours   112–13
    state   111
Extronics case study
    context   58–9
    drive for diversification   59
    framework for   61–3
    intervention revisited   61
    need to address complexity   60

Extronics case study (*cont'd.*)
   unintended consequences of
      change   59–60

Fenton-O'Creevy, M.   161, 163
Ferlie, E.
   et al.   115
   and Pettigrew, A.   153
Fineman, S.   17, 47, 71
Finke, R.A. et al.   28
Finkelstein, S. and Hambrick, D.C.   225
Floyd, S.W. and Wooldridge, B.   153–4
Flynn, N.   115, 118
Ford, J.D. and Ford, L.W.   51
'forty yard' problem   187, 189
Foulkes, F.K.   41
Freind, J., and Jessop, W.N.   112
French, W. and Bell, C.   129
Friedlander, F.   139, 145
Friend, J., and Hickling, A.   112
Fry, R. and Pasmore, W.   141, 144

Gadamer, H.-G.   183, 186
Galbraith, J.R.   111, 112
Garratt, B.   196
Geneen, H.   31
General Electric   37
Gersick, C.   119
Ghoshal, S. and Bartlett, C.A.   1, 73, 176
Giddens, A.   159
Giles, J.   72
Gill, J. and Foulder, J.   85
Gillen, D.
   et al.   36
   and Fitzgerald, E.   142, 148
Girard, R.   193
goal-setting   31–2, 244
   acceptance of   38–9
   competitive   189–90
   current approaches   36–7
   designing/implementing effective
      systems   37–8
   and effective performance
      management   40
   effectiveness of   33–4
   and individual/group integration   40
   new issues in   39–41
   and persuasion   39
   principles   40
   reasons for success of   34–5

traditional implementation systems   32–3
   and trust   40–1
   variance in MBO process
      characteristics   35–6
   and visioning   38–9
Goleman, D.   26, 73
Greenhaugh, L. and Sutton, R.I.   85
Grint, K.   109, 110
Grove, A.   39
Guth, W.D. and MacMillan, I.C.   156

Hales, C.   134
Hambrick, D.C.   225, 226
Hamel, G. and Prahalad, C.K.   145, 146, 191
Hammond, K.R. et al.   24
Handy, C.   210
Hargadon, A. and Sutton, R.   132
Hart, S.L.   46
Hartley, J.F.   83, 85, 113, 115, 116, 119
   and Benington, J.   113, 115, 116
   et al.   111, 114, 115, 119
Hayes, R. and Wheelwright, S.   60
health care, primary *see* strategic
      management initiative (SMI)
Hegel, G.W.F.   61
Heifetz, R.   114
   and Sinder, R.   118
Henkoff, R.   157
Hernstein, R.J. and Murray, C.   27
Hesselbeing, F. et al.   38
Hirschorn, L.   85
Hodgkinson, G.P.   19
   and Johnson, G.   19
Howard, G.   80
Huber, G.P. and Daft, R.L.   21
Huff, A.S.   19, 119
Hull, F. and Hage, J.   175
human resource management
      (HRM)   169–70
   and health of workplace   88
   research on   170
Hunger, J.D. and Wheelan, T.L.   141
Hunt, J.   196
Huselid, M.A.   82

Ilgen, D.R.   224
imagination   183–4, 190
   and contradiction   191
   creative   190–1, 192, 241
   cultivation of   193

and immanent events   191–2
   lack of   193
   and mimesis   193
   primary importance of   193
   and refusal to apperceive   192
imaginization   185
information overload   19–20
   dealing with problem of   21
   defined   20
   implications of   21
   interactions at heart of   21–2
intelligent unconscious
   emotionally attuned manager   26–7
   intuitive manager   23–6
Isabella, L.A.   177

Jackson, P.R. et al.   89
Jarillo, J.C.   198
Jermier, J. et al.   169
Jick, T.D.   85, 178
Johnson, B.   63–4, 65
Johnson, R. and Lawrence, P.   153
Johnson, T.J.   129
Judson, A.S.   232

Kanter, R.M.   157, 177
   and Eccles, R.G.   198, 207
   et al.   71, 72, 75, 84
Kaplan, and Norton,   131–2
Kaplan, R. and Murdoch, L.   60
Karasek, R.A.   87
Karmiloff-Smith, A.   25
Katz, D.   72
Katz, and Kahn   157
Katzenbach, J.R.   225, 226–7
   and Smith, D.K.   224
Kaufmann, S.   109
Kets de Vries, M.F.R. and Balazs, K.   74, 85,
   86, 91
Ketterer, R.F. and Spencer, J.L.   240
Kim, W.C. and Mauborgne, R.   176, 178
Kimberley, J.R.   175
Kirkpatrick, S.A.   38
knowledge
   academic   131–2
   application   130–1
   client   132
   explicit   142
   internal creation   132
   specialized/convergent   142–5

tacit/formal   133
Knowles, M.S. and Associates   204
Koestler, A.   183, 185, 191
Kotter, J.   130
Kotter, J.P.   210, 214, 217, 218, 219
Kozlowski, S.W.J.   88
Kristof, A.L. et al.   232

Langer, E.J.   205
Larwood, L. et al.   38
Latham, G.P. and Locke, E.   205
Lawler, E.E.   86
Lawrence, P. and Lorsch, J.   96, 111
Lawton, A. and McKevitt, D.   115
Leach, S.   115
   et al.   114
leadership, and uncertainty   113–14
leadership/learning relationship   138–9
   capabilities   139–40
   case studies   147–50
   and imagination   146–7
   and specialized/convergent
      knowledge   142–5
   and vision, mission, core values   140–1
Leading Edge Forum   170
learning see leadership/learning relationship
learning organizations   196
   model see National Action Learning
      Programme
learning/competitiveness model   145–6
Lemon, L. and Reis, M.   50
Levinthal, D.A. and March, J.G.   179
Lewicki, P. et al.   25
Lewin, K.   205
Lindblom, C.E.   46–7
Locke, E.A. and Latham, G.P.   34
Lucas, R.   119

McCaskey, M.B.   57–8, 61–2, 63
McClelland, C.E.   105
McGovern, P.   170
MacKechnie, G. and Dromgoole, T.   197
McKenna, C.   126, 131
McKevitt, D.   97, 99, 100, 101
   and Lawton, A.   106
Maister, D.   133
management
   assumptions   16
   bottom-up/top-down knowledge
      approach   18–19

management (*cont'd.*)
  cognitive limits of 17
  and competitive knowledge 19
  and emotional environment 16, 17, 26–7
  and future competencies 22–3, 28
  and information overload 19–22
  intuitive 23–6
  involvement of 237
  polarity 63–8
  problems/solutions 17
  and revenge effects 17
  senior 171, 172
  training/development
    programmes 240–1
  and turnaround strategies 222
  and uncertainty 113–14
  and understanding strategy 15–16
management by objectives (MBO) 32
  achievement of 35
  effectiveness of 33–4, 37
  research on 38–9
  traditional 32–3
  variance in process characteristics
    of 35–6
March, J. 111
  and Simon, H. 131
Marks, M.L. and Mervis, P.H. 85
Martell, K. and Carroll, S.J. 33
Matejka, L. and Pomorska, K. 50
Maurer, J.G. 171
mental health
  creating/maintaining healthy
    workplace 87–8
  and managing change 86–92
  and minimizing stress 90–1
  successful/unsuccessful management
    of 88–90
Micklethwait, J. and Wooldridge, A. 184
middle management 152–3
  changing role of 153
  characteristics of 173–5
  conflicting demands on 158
  and employee involvement 161–4
  as endangered breed 168–9
  and political activity 174–5
  reassessment of 169
  relationship with senior management
    172
  resistance/acceptance 155–6, 171
  role tension 155

and selective perception 173–4
  and strategy 153–5
  training/skills of 158
Millar, M. 102
Milliken, F.J. 111, 116, 117
Mintzberg, H. 32, 46, 47, 52, 96, **152**, **169**, 190
Mischel, W. 74
Mohrman, A. et al. 113
Morgan, G. 72, 112, 119, 146, 147, 183
Morris, T.
  and Empson, L. 132
  and Pinnington, A. 133
Mulcahy, N. 197
Mullarkey, S. et al. 86

Nahapiet, J. and Ghoshal, S. 144
Nanus, B. 38
Narayan, V.K. and Fahy, L. 52
narrative strategy 49–50, 241–2
  analysis of 51–4
  defined 50
  exploration of 53–4
  sources of 50
  specificity 52
  strategic orientation 51–2
  subject focus 52
  time orientation 52
  use of 54–5
  written/spoken comparison 50–1
Nathan, M.L. 38
National Action Learning
    Programme 196–7, 240
  and action learning 197, 198
  distinctiveness of 200–1, 207
  influences on design 197–8
  and learning networks 198, 207–8
  perception/benefits of 206–7
  in practice 204–6
  review of 201–4
  and single/double-loop learning **197–8**
  structure of 199–201
Nelson-Jones, R. 204, 205
New Venture Gear 240
New Venture Gear case study 147–9
Nicholson, N. 157, 242
Nilakant, V. 156
Nonaka, I. and Takeuchi, H. 142
Norman, D. 21
Nutt, P. 130

Nutt, P.C. 238

Ocasio, W. 176
O'Donnell, D. 26
organizational learning 138–9
organizations
  competitiveness/learning rate
    relationship 145–6
  and complexity 60
  and consequences of change 59–60
  core values 141
  and corporate memory 21
  diversification in 59
  dominant orientation in 58–9
  dualities in 15–16
  and 'fit' 15, 67
  hidden realities in 241–2
  and imagination 146–7
  institutional level 169
  and intra-organizational information
    market 21
  managerial level 169
  and messy situations 58, 61–3
  and organizational units 144
  and polarity management 63–8
  and process discipline 176
  and rules of the game 176–7
  and shared knowledge 144–5
  size of 175
  and stress 80–6
  structure 242
  technical level 169
  and uncertainty 109–10
  uncertainty/effectiveness
    relationship 111–12
Osborne, D. and Gaebler, T. 115
O'Shea, J. and Madigan, C. 125

Parker, S.K.
  et al. 86, 88, 90
  and Sprigg, C. 90
  and Wall, T.D. 86, 89
Pascale, R.T. 61, 191
  et al. 184
Patterson, M.G. et al. 82
Perls, F. et al. 71, 73
Peteraf, M. 135
Peters, T. 71, 144
Pettigrew, A.M. 71
  et al. 51

and Whipp, R. 96, 99, 106
Pfeffer, J. 113
polarity management 63–4, 67–8
  application of 65, 67
  components of 66
  and problem-solving 64
Porac, J.F. et al. 18
Porter, M. 139, 146, 184
Prahalad, C.K. and Hamel, G. 185
Prasad 54
public service sector
  politics/management of uncertainty
    in 114–18
  rationality and values 118–19
  see also Street Level Public Organizations
    (SPLO)

Quinn, J.B. 46, 47

Ramamoorthy, N. and Carroll, S.J. 40
Ranson, S. and Stewart, J. 115
rational planning 46–7
  language of 47
  psychological explanation of 47
  and self-reporting 47
Redman, T. et al. 154–5
Reger, R.K.
  et al 171, 173, 178
  and Palmer, T.B. 19
Remenyi, A. and Halford, K. 81
resistance
  avoidance of 165
  employee 169–70
  example of 160–1
  individual level explanations of 157
  meaning/provenance of 156–61
  middle management 155–6, 164–5
  radical/critical explanations of 158–61
  as structurally embedded 159, 164
  studies of 161–4
  systems explanations of 157–8
Ricoeur, P. 192
Ricouer, P. 183
Rodgers, R.C. and Hunter, J.E. 34, 36
Rouleau, L. and Seguin, F. 51
Rushman, and Romanelli 111
Ryback, D. 26

Sadler, P. 204
Salaman, G.S. 80

Schein, E.H.   114, 139, 140
Scheler, M.   183, 191, 193
Schoemaker, P.   52
Schuler, R.   113
Schwartz, P.   52
Scott   173
Scott, B.   96
Scott, W.R.   111
Senge, P.M.   138, 139, 140, **196**, 198, 205
senior management
  legitimacy of   171
  relationship with middle management   172
  as teams   225–7
Sewell, G. and Wilkinson, B.   86
Shalley, C.E.   35
Sharp Corporation   228–9
Shell   156
Slater, R.   141, 146
Smith, G.D.   138
Smith, K.A.
  and Kofron, E.A.   225
  and Sims, H.P. Jr   224, 231
Smith, K.S. et al.   40
Smurfit Print case study   187–9
Snell, S.A.   175
Sparrow, P.R.   15, 20
  and Daniels K.   21
Spender, J.-C.   24
Spreitzer, G.M.   173, 175
Sprigg, C.A. et al.   89
Stace, D. and Dunphy, D.   71, 75, 76
standard business units (SBUs)   144
Starbuck, W.   131
Stinchcombe, A.L.   112
strategic management initiative (SMI)   100–2
  and citizen-client/strategy implementation   102–3
  evaluation   106–7
  features of   101
  implications   106
  professional view of physicians   103–4
  public managers and 'hands-off' control   104–5
strategy
  acceptance of   38–9
  changes in thinking concerning   15
  common-sense principles for   77

and creative imagination   25–6
as creative vision   48–9
and culture   239
debate concerning   44–5
definitions of   46–9
and emotional issues   16, 17
failure of   232
and 'fit'   15
formulation   141, 142, 184–5
and information overload   21
as interactive narrative   49–55
and middle management   153–5
quality of   15–16
as rational planning   46–8
and strong/weak situations   74–5
top-down/bottom-up   71
and uncertainty   16, 17
understanding of   16
upward/downward implementation   153–4
and vision   16
strategy implementation
case study   187–9
challenge of   184–5
and changes in mindsets/perspectives   243–4
changes in process of   236–7
characteristics of content   172–3, 175–7
and commitment   179
and communication   178–9
and consulting firms   126–9
contemporary system for   39–41
as critical to planning   31
effective   75, 134–6
failures of   177
giver/receiver relationship   178
and information overload   21
and information transmission   177–8
and middle management   153–5
models   57
and persuasion   237
and procedural justice   178
and psychological contract   242–3
and senior managers/board directors   149–50
and SLPOs   106
structural barriers to   239–40
through teams   227–8
and transference of organizational intent   171

Street Level Public Organizations
     (SLPO)   96–7
  control model   99
  environment   97
  evaluation   106–7
  and government influence   99–100
  model of   97–100
  and rules of the game   98–9, 100
  and strategic management initiative
     100–6
  strategy implementation/implications
     106
  tensions in   98
stress   238
  causes of   82–3
  and consequences of change   83–4
  costs of   81–2
  creation of   80–6
  defined   81
  illustrative changes that cause   85–6
  job   90
  and mergers/acquisitions   85–6
  minimizing   90–2
  prevention of   92
  and reduction in mental health risk
     86–92
Sugarman, L.   83–4
SWOT approach   32
Szulanski, G.   177, 178

Taylor, M.S. et al.   40
teams   240
  benefits   229–30
  benefits of   233
  case studies   227, 228–9, 231–2
  and clarity of purpose   229–30
  commitment of   233
  and commitment to strategy   230
  and effective control   232
  and effective integration   230
  and environmental sensitivity   233
  implementing strategy through   227–8
  importance of strong culture   233–4
  integration between   234
  issues of definition   224–5
  and strategic flexibility   233
  as strategy   230–1, 234
  and strategy implementation   224
  top management as   225–7
  virtual   232

Teasdale, E.L. and McKeown, S.   90–1
Terpstra, D. and Rozell, E.J.   34
Thomas, J.B. et al.   174, 177
Thomas, K.W. and Velthouse, B.A.   175
Thompson, J.D.   111, 112
Thompson, P. and McHugh, D.   111, 113
Thune, S. and House, R.J.   47
Thurley, K. and Pecci, R.   153
Tosi, H.L.   32
  and Carroll, S.J.   35
  et al.   34
trade unions, and turnaround
     strategies   213, 214–15, 221–2, 223
training   240–1
turnaround strategies   210–11
  case study   216–21
  and change   212–13
  competitive imperative   211–12
  key elements   213–15
  management issues   222
  and the market   211
  success of   213
  in unionized environments   213, 214–15,
     223
Turnbull, P.J.   86
Tushman, M.L. and Romanelli, E.   119
Tyler, T.R.   176

uncertainty   109–10, 238
  and ambiguity   110
  and change   185
  consequences of   115–18
  definitions of   110–11
  environmental   110–13
  and leadership/strategy implementation
     113–14
  managing   119
  and organizational effectiveness   111–12
  organizational response to   112–13
  politics/management of   114–15
  in public service sector   114–18

Van de Vliert, A.   21
Verespej, M.A.   156
visioning   140–1, 142
  developing   48–9
  long-term nature of   48
  outcomes of   48
  as process oriented   53
  and turnaround strategies   215

Voegelin, E.   183, 185, 186, 189, 192
Vuori, H.   103

Waldersee, R. and Sheather, S.   74
Waldrop, M.M.   109, 119, 192
Wall, et al.   87
Wally, S. et al.   33
Walsh, J.   18, 19
Walsh, J.P.   173
Waterford Crystal
   background   216
   communications/negotiation/
      implementation   218
   later years (1993/1994)   218–20
   shared commitment to growth/
      competitiveness in   220–1
   Somers/Patterson plan   216–18
Waterman, R.H. et al.   210, 214
Waterson, et al.   89
Watson, G.   157

Weick, K.E.   18, 20, 47, 67, 110, 111, 113
Welch, J.   141, 146
Westley, F.R.   169
Wheatley, M.   109
Wheelwright, S.C.   58
Whetten, D.   85
Whittington, R.   159
Wiersema, M. and Bantel, K.   111
Wilkinson, A. et al.   156
Wilson, D.O.   48
   and Game, C.   114
Wilson, E.O.   192
Wolpin, I. and Burke, R.J.   85
Wood, R.E. and Locke, E.A.   35
Wood, S.   86
Woodman, R.W. et al.   52
World Class Manufacturing (WCM)   187–8
Wurman, R.S.   22

Yukl, G.   114